Localizing Knowledge in a Globalizing World

Localizing Knowledge in a Globalizing World

Recasting the Area Studies Debate

Edited by ALI MIRSEPASSI, AMRITA BASU,
and FREDERICK WEAVER

SYRACUSE UNIVERSITY PRESS

#50859274

Library of Congress Cataloging-in-Publication Data

Localizing knowledge in a globalizing world : recasting the area studies
debate / edited by Ali Mirsepassi, Amrita Basu, and Frederick Weaver.—
1st ed.
p. cm.
Includes bibliographical references and index.
ISBN 0–8156–2963-X (alk. paper)—ISBN 0–8156–2982–6 (pbk. : alk.
paper)
1. Globalization. I. Mirsepassi, Ali. II. Basu, Amrita, 1953–.
III. Weaver, Frederick Stirton, 1939–
JZ1318 .L63 2003
303.48'2—dc21
2002151021

Manufactured in the United States of America

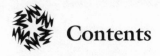 Contents

Acknowledgments   vii

Contributors   ix

1. Introduction: *Knowledge, Power, and Culture*
    ALI MIRSEPASSI, AMRITA BASU,
    AND FREDERICK WEAVER   1

        PART ONE: *Rethinking Local-Global Connections*

2. American Baroque
    DORIS SOMMER   25

3. Place, Nature, and Culture in Discourses of Globalization
    ARTURO ESCOBAR   37

4. The Disappearing Local
    Rethinking Global-Local Connections
    ANGELIQUE HAUGERUD   60

5. Globalizing Local Women's Movements
    AMRITA BASU   82

6. Asserting the Local as National in the Face of the Global
    The Ambivalence of Authenticity in Egyptian Soap Opera
    LILA ABU-LUGHOD   101

    PART TWO: *In a World of Uncertain Places, Where Are Area Studies?*

7. Why Area Studies?
    DAVID LUDDEN   131

8. The Multiple Worlds of African Studies
    SANDRA E. GREENE   137

9. Deterritorialization and the Crisis of Social Science
    TIMOTHY MITCHELL   148

10. The Middle East as an Area in an Era of Globalization
   RASHID I. KHALIDI   171

   PART THREE: *Globalization and the Area Studies Debate*

11. Culture Against History? The Politics of East Asian Identity
   ARIF DIRLIK   193

12. Knowledge, Place, and Power
   A Critique of Globalization
   EQBAL AHMAD   216

   Works Cited   233

   Index   255

Acknowledgments

A Ford Foundation grant supported a yearlong Five Colleges seminar entitled "Crossing Borders," and the idea of a symposium grew out of the seminar. Another Ford Foundation grant made the Five Colleges symposium possible, and "Global-Local: Revisioning the Area Studies Debate" was held at Hampshire College, Amherst, Massachusetts, on 16–18 October 1998. Most chapters in this volume were presented originally at the symposium. We are grateful for the opportunities that the generous grants afforded us.

The entire enterprise would have been much more difficult, if not impossible, without Five Colleges, Inc.—a consortium of Amherst, Hampshire, Mt. Holyoke, and Smith Colleges and the University of Massachusetts at Amherst. Although many people at Five Colleges were very accommodating, Lorna Peterson, the consortium's director, was outstanding in her encouragement and commitment.

At Hampshire College, we are grateful especially to Chris Carey, assistant dean of international education, and to a range of helpful individuals in the president's office and in the dean of faculty's office.

We were fortunate to be able to work with Professor Mehrzad Boroujerdi, series editor, and the capable (and patient) people of Syracuse University Press. Annie Barva did an excellent job of copyediting a difficult manuscript.

Finally, we wish to thank the authors. Despite occasional differences about schedules and page numbers, it was a delight to work with them.

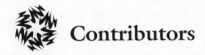 Contributors

Lila Abu-Lughod is professor of anthropology at Columbia University. She serves on several editorial boards for journals such as *Middle East Report, Ethos,* and the *Journal of Contemporary Ethnography.* Some of her recent publications include *Veiled Sentiments: Honor and Poetry in a Bedouin Society* (1986), *Writing Women's Worlds: Bedouin Stories* (1994), and the collected volume *Remaking Women: Feminism and Modernity in the Middle East* (1998). She has published numerous articles in journals such as *Middle East Report, Women's Studies Quarterly, Representations,* and *Social Text.* Her works in progress include *Melodramas of Nationhood: The Cultural Politics of Egyptian Television* and *The Social Practice of Media: Anthropology in the Age of Electronic Reproduction,* edited with Faye Ginsburg and Brian Larkin.

Eqbal Ahmad (1932–1999) was professor emeritus of international relations and Middle Eastern studies at Hampshire College, Amherst, Massachusetts. He was a managing editor of the quarterly *Race and Class* (London); contributing editor of *The Middle East Report* (Washington, D.C.); editorial board member of *Arab Studies Quarterly* (Boston); and a columnist for newspapers such as *Dawn* (Pakistan), *Al-Ahram* (Egypt), *Star* (Bangladesh), and *Al-Hayat* in the Arab world. His essays appeared in thirty English-language anthologies, encyclopedias, and books. In the United States, he wrote articles for such publications as the *Washington Post,* the *New York Review of Books, The Nation,* the *Atlantic Monthly, Harper's, Monthly Review, Mother Jones, The New Yorker,* and the *New York Times.* Profiles were done on him by the BBC (London) and the NHK (Tokyo). Before his recent death, he divided his time between the United States and Pakistan, where he was engaged in establishing Khaldunia University, a private institution.

Amrita Basu is professor of political science and of women and gender studies at Amherst College, Amherst, Massachusetts. Some of her recent publications include *Two Faces of Protest: Contrasting Modes of Women's Activism in India* (1992) as well as the collected volumes *The Challenge of Local Feminisms: Women's Movements in Global Perspective* (with C. Elizabeth McGrory, 1995), *Appropriating Gender: Women's Activism and Politicized Religion in South Asia* (1997), and *Community Conflicts and the State in India* (1997). She has written numerous articles for various journals such as the *Journal of Women's History,* the *Journal of Asian Studies,* and the *Harvard International Review.* She currently is working on a book, *Hindu Nationalism: A Movement from Above as Seen from Below.*

Arif Dirlik is Knight Professor of Social Science and professor of history and anthropology at the University of Oregon. His specialty is modern Chinese intellectual and political history; he also works extensively in transnational studies and globalization, Pacific studies, and cultural criticism. His published works include *Revolution and History: The Origins of Marxist Historiography in China, 1919–1937* (1978); *The Origins of Chinese Communism* (1989); *Anarchism in the Chinese Revolution* (1991); *Schools into Fields and Factories: Anarchism, the Guomindang, and the Labor University in Shanghai, 1927–1932* (with Ming K. Chan, 1991); *After the Revolution: Waking to Global Capitalism* (1994); *The Postcolonial Aura: Third World Criticism in the Age of Global Capitalism* (1997); and *Postmodernity's Histories: The Past as Legacy and Project* (2000). Recently edited volumes include *Critical Perspectives on Mao Zedong's Thought* (with Paul Healy and Nick Knight, 1997); *What Is in a Rim? Critical Perspectives on the Pacific Region Idea* (1998); *Chinese on the American Frontier* (with Malcolm Yeung, 2001); *History after the Three Worlds: Post-Eurocentric Historiographies* (with Vinay Bahl and Peter Gran, 2001); *Places and Politics in an Age of Globalization* (with Roxann Prazniak, 2001); and *Postmodernism and China* (with Zhang Xudong, 2001). He serves on the editorial boards of *boundary 2, Interventions, Historical Materialism, Review of Education/Pedagogy/Cultural Studies, Development and Society, Amerasia, China Quarterly, Asian Studies Review, China Review, China Information,,* and *Zhongguo Xueshu* (China scholarship). He has received Fulbright, Foreign Area, National Endowment for the Arts, American Council of Learned Societies, and Chiang Ching-kuo Foundation fellowships.

Arturo Escobar is professor of anthropology and Latin American studies at the University of North Carolina, Chapel Hill. He is a member of the executive board of the Society of Cultural Anthropology and a member of numerous editorial boards for journals such as *Development: The Journal of the Society for International Development* (Rome) and the *Journal of Latin American Anthropology*. His most recent publications include *The Making of Social Movements in Latin America: Identity, Strategy, and Democracy* (with Sonia Alvarez, 1992); *Encountering Development: The Making and Unmaking of the Third World* (1995); *Cultures of Politics/Politics of Cultures: Revisioning Latin American Social Movements* (with Sonia Alvarez and Evelina Dagnino, 1998). He has written many articles for journals such as *Current Anthropology, Development,* and the *International Social Science Journal.* His works in progress include *Estado, capital, y movimientos sociales en el Pacífico Colombiano,* coedited with Alvaro Pedrosa; *Natures: Cultural and Biological Diversity in the Late Twentieth Century,* based on fieldwork carried out in the Pacific Coast rainforest of Colombia in 1993; and *Pacífico, desarrollo o diversidad?*

Sandra E. Greene is associate professor of African history at Cornell University, Ithaca, New York. She served for three years (1997–99) as president of the African Studies Association. Some of her recent publications include *Gender, Ethnicity, and Social Change on the Upper Slave Coast: A History of the Anlo-Ewe* (1996) and numerous articles in published collections of essays and in journals such as *African History, African Studies Review, International Journal of African Historical Studies, Journal of Religion in Africa,* and the *Journal of the International African Institute and Rural Africana.* Her works in progress include *History and Memory, Space and Place: Essays in Anlo History, Village Historians: Narrators and Narrations on Anlo History and Culture,* and *Women and Gender Relations in Precolonial African History.*

Angelique Haugerud is associate professor of anthropology at Rutgers University, New Brunswick, New Jersey. Her publications include *The Culture of Politics in Modern Kenya* (1995) and *Commodities and Globalization: Anthropological Perspectives* (with M. Priscilla Stone and Peter D. Little, 2000). She has received research fellowships from the Social Science Research Council, the American Council of Learned Societies, the National

Science Foundation, and the Rockefeller Foundation. She carried out extensive field research in Kenya and Rwanda during the 1980s and 1990s. She was editor of the scholarly journal *Africa Today* (1996–99) and has been elected to the executive boards of the African Studies Association (1999–2002), the Society for Economic Anthropology (1992–95), and the Association for Political and Legal Anthropology (1997–2000).

Rashid I. Khalidi is professor of Middle East history and the director of the Center for International Studies at the University of Chicago. He was president of the Middle East Studies Association and currently is the president of the American Committee on Jerusalem. In 1991–93, he served as an advisor to the Palestinian delegation to the Madrid and Washington Arab-Israeli peace negotiations. He is the author of *British Policy Towards Syria and Palestine: 1906–1914* (1980); *Under Siege: PLO Decision-Making During the 1982 War* (1986); and *Palestinian Identity: The Construction of National Consciousness* (1997). He is also coeditor of *Palestine and the Gulf and the Origins of Arab Nationalism* (with Camille Mansour, 1982). He has authored more than sixty articles on aspects of Middle East history and policies.

David Ludden is professor of history at the University of Pennsylvania and currently president of the Association of Asian Studies. His research concentrates on agrarian history in South Asia.

Ali Mirsepassi is currently a professor and associate dean at the Gallatin School, New York University. He has published in journals such as *Contemporary Sociology, Radical History,* and *Social Text.* He is the author of *Intellectual Discourse and the Politics of Modernization: Negotiating Modernity in Iran* (2000). He is currently completing a book, *A Good Society? A Sociological Vision of the Iranian Public Culture.*

Timothy Mitchell is professor of politics and the director of the Kagop Kevorkian Center for Near Eastern Studies at New York University. He serves on the board of governors of the American Research Center in Egypt and on the editorial committee of the *Journal of Historical Sociology* and is a contributing editor of *Middle East Report.* His publications include *Colonis-*

ing Egypt (1988); *Egypt in American Discourse* (1992, in Arabic); and *Democracy and the State in the Arab World* (1996, in Arabic); as well as numerous articles in published collections of essays and in journals such as *Cultural Studies, Public Culture, The Ecologist,* and *Muhawirat Al-tanmiya.* His most recent books are *Questions of Modernity* (2000) and *Rule of Experts: Egypt, Techno-Politics, Modernity* (2002).

Doris Sommer is professor of graduate studies in Latin American literature and director of the Harvard Seminar of Latino Cultures at Harvard University. Some of her recent publications include *One Master for Another: Populism as Patriarchal Rhetoric in Dominican Novels* (1984) and *Foundational Fictions: The National Romances of Latin America* (1991). She is also coeditor of *Nationalisms and Sexualities* (with Andrew Parker, 1991) and editor of *The Places of History: Regionalism Revisited in Latin America* (1996) and has written numerous articles for published collections of essays and for journals such as *Modern Languages Quarterly, Signs, Diacritics, Jewish Studies,* and *Latin American Literary Review.* Her work in progress includes *Proceed with Caution: A Rhetoric of Particularism.*

Frederick Weaver is professor of economics and history at Hampshire College. His most recent books are *Inside the Volcano: The History and Political Economy of Central America* (1994); *Latin America in the World Economy: Mercantile Colonialism to Global Capitalism* (2000); and *Economic Literacy: Basic Economics with an Attitude* (2002). His book *Liberal Education: Professions, Pedagogy, and Structure* (1991) won the F. W. Ness Book Award, given each year by the Association of American Colleges and Universities. He has published more than forty journal articles and book chapters and has received grants from the Fulbright Program, the Foreign Area Program, and the Mellon, Whiting, and Spencer Foundations. He is an executive editor of *College Teaching* and a participating editor of *Latin American Perspectives.*

Localizing Knowledge in a Globalizing World

1 Introduction

Knowledge, Power, and Culture

ALI MIRSEPASSI, AMRITA BASU,

AND FREDERICK WEAVER

One day, while devouring the pages of *Hinduism Custom and Ritual,* a newly published anthropological monograph by an earnest American researcher, Annayya's eyes alight on a photograph taken by its author during fieldwork. He recognizes in the photograph the faces of his family: it is the cremation of his own father, news of whose death had not reached him in the library stacks of Chicago. It is an uncanny moment of loss and recognition, like realizing one is looking at light from a long-dead star (Khilnani 1997, 196–97).

The Problematic of Area Studies

The story of Annayya might be read as the story of area studies: a body of knowledge produced mostly by Western scholars for Western audiences about non-Western societies, cultures, and histories. Like Annayya, who learns his family history in the stacks of the University of Chicago library, where scholars will use it as "raw data," "Indians over the past century have come to see themselves in mirrors created by the inquisitive energies of the West" (Khilnani 1997, 196–97). From this perspective, area studies—the organization of teaching and research along the lines of geographical and cultural regions—functions as the intellectual arm of a larger Orientalist enterprise in which Western intellectuals seek to represent the non-West in ways that are convenient, self-congratulatory, and ultimately distorting (Said 1978).

1

2 | ALI MIRSEPASSI, AMRITA BASU, FREDERICK WEAVER

But one might interpret the story of Annayya and of area studies quite differently. In the absence of the detailed knowledge that area studies have generated about regions of the world that are on the peripheries of global capitalism and thus are considered to have no policy relevance, the academy would have been entirely uninterested in Hindu custom and ritual. If area studies scholarship appropriates Annayya's experiences, it also places him and other immigrants, foreigners, and diasporic peoples at the forefront of intellectual inquiry and in so doing reconfigures the relationship between margins and centers. Moreover, by viewing themselves through "mirrors created by the inquisitive energies of the West," Annayya and his fellow students may see images that otherwise would remain in the shadows. The question of how we should interpret the story of Annaya acquires particular significance amidst what is viewed widely as a crisis of area studies.

The post–World War II project of area studies was an attempt by the major centers of academic learning to delineate relatively large geographic regions that possessed some cultural, historic, and linguistic coherence. The area studies map included the former Soviet Union, China (or East Asia), Latin America, the Middle East, Africa, South Asia, Southeast Asia, eastern and central Europe, and, much later, western Europe. It did not include the United States, despite the fact—or perhaps because of the fact—that it was the principal site of area studies scholarship.

Various foundations, in particular the Ford Foundation, lavishly supported the creation of area studies programs, most significantly under the joint auspices of the Social Science Research Council (SSRC) and the American Council of Learned Societies (ACLS). Eleven joint committees administered a highly prestigious dissertation fellowship program, sponsored conferences and publications, and fostered institutional partnerships. By the early 1990s, however, these foundations were withdrawing support from area studies programs, and many scholars were questioning their merits.

This book is a contribution to the current debate on the crisis of area studies as well as an exploration of its revisioning. Like scholars in women's studies, African American studies, and other interdisciplinary programs that have been forced to survive in the niches among academic disciplines, area studies scholars chronically have felt undervalued and under siege. Nevertheless, the current crisis of area studies is of a different order of magnitude. It concerns the very fate of area-based knowledge in a globalizing world.

What do we make of the crisis of area studies? Should we applaud its demise or bemoan its passing?

Area studies have always been sensitive to changing political and intellectual conditions. The major Western powers brought area studies into being in the aftermath of World War II in an effort to understand and influence geopolitical alignments. During the Cold War, area studies scholarship in the United States was hobbled by a climate of anticommunism that determined which areas were studied, which were neglected, and what was designated an area at all. The end of the Cold War ushered in a period of greater intellectual and political freedom, in which area studies scholarship briefly flourished. Today, at the threshold of an era of globalization, many policymakers, universities, and foundations view area studies as anachronistic.

The rise, expansion, and demise of area studies have been associated with changes in the geopolitical context. In order to secure its future as we would want, we must sever the links between knowledge and power. We do not deny the many weaknesses of area studies scholarship. Along with Annayya, we are disconcerted by a model of area studies in which U.S. academics treat the area as the source of evidence for theorizing. However, we equally are worried about theorizing in the absence of knowledge about localities and nations outside the United States and about privileging the supposedly universalizing forces of globalization. After recording the failures and limitations of area studies programs, we suggest the promise of area-based knowledge amidst globalization.

It is impossible to disentangle the project of area studies from its political surround. The Gulbenkian Commission on the Restructuring of the Social Sciences (which included Immanuel Wallerstein) has this to say about area studies: "The political motivations underlying its origins were quite explicit. The U.S., given its worldwide political role, needed knowledge about, and therefore specialists on, the current realities of these various regions, especially since these regions were now becoming so politically active" (1995, 42).

The U.S. government supported area studies programs as a means of achieving knowledge about and control over potential adversaries and allies during the Cold War. Through the 1958 Defense Information Act, it made available substantial funding for the study of the languages, histories, and geographies of remote places. Geopolitical considerations influenced its decisions about which areas of the world to fund. In Asia, for example, enormous funds were lavished on the study first of China and later of Southeast Asia to the neglect of South Asia. Moreover, social scientists' interests in China and the former Soviet Union were dominated by strategic concerns.

Bruce Cumings argues that the Office of Strategic Services created a model for collaboration between intelligence and academe that not only influenced the division of the Central Intelligence Agency (CIA) into research and operations branches, but also laid the foundation for the division between academic disciplines and area studies (1997, 6–26). The CIA collaborated with some of the major foundations, such as the Ford Foundation and the SSRC and hired prominent area studies scholars from the leading research universities to engage in consultation and recruitment. It is now widely recognized that the CIA funded some of the major area studies institutes, such as the Russian Research Centers at Harvard and Columbia in the early 1950s.

The story of area studies fortunately does not end in the dismal period of the 1950s and early 1960s. The very context of the Cold War that produced area studies spokespersons for the state ironically also produced its most ardent critics. For example, by the late 1960s, some of the major opponents of the U.S. role in Indochina were a group of Asian studies scholars who formed the Committee on Asian Studies and published the *Bulletin of Concerned Asian Scholars* (now renamed *Critical Asian Studies*), a forum for dissenting views on the U.S. role in Southeast Asia. These scholars' engagement reflected the fruits of area studies at its best: the knowledge and love of Asia that came from years of language training, foreign residencies, and respect for cultural traditions. Area studies scholars were placed in a position to challenge the official U.S. depiction of Vietnam as having no past or future other than what was imposed by either Western liberals or Soviet communists. Although they may have been few in number, some of them played important roles in making U.S. academia less parochial and U.S. policymakers more accountable.

The quality of area studies scholarship improved significantly in the 1970s and 1980s. By 1981, Ford Foundation funding to China and Korea declined, whereas its funding to South and Southeast Asia grew. Increased support for Southeast Asian scholarship after the Indo-China War indicated the loosening of links between the scholarly and political communities. The prestigious SSRC administered dissertation and postdoctoral fellowships that attracted highly competitive students to area studies. Moreover, several of the joint area studies committees fostered an appreciation of interdisciplinary scholarship and language training. Over time, studies of economic modernization and state formation gave way to more diverse, interdisciplinary themes concerning subaltern resistance, popular cultural practices, gender relations, and ethnic pluralism. Arjun Appadurai argues: "In a society notoriously devoted to exceptionalism and to endless preoccupation with 'America,' this tradition has been a tiny refuge for the serious study of foreign languages, alternative worldviews, and large-scale perspectives on socio-cultural change outside Europe and the United States" (1996, 17).

Yet despite these achievements, the major foundations have withdrawn support for area studies programs, and the major research universities are re-orienting graduate students away from area studies training. The Mellon Foundation stopped funding advanced training and research in area studies in 1993. Shortly thereafter the SSRC and the ACLS dissolved their joint area studies committees. The Ford Foundation similarly engaged in a reorganization that was partially designed to rethink the area studies model. It invested twenty-five-million dollars in a new initiative, "Crossing Borders," which seeks to foster closer links among area studies scholars and among area studies, diaspora studies, and the disciplines ("Remapping Area Studies" 1999, 10–11). The projects it has funded are extremely interdisciplinary but may have more impact and draw more support from historians, anthropologists, and linguists than from economists, sociologists, and political scientists.

The current crisis in area studies arises from the conjunctures of two related developments. The first is the end of the Cold War. With the demise of the Soviet Union and with the unchallenged global dominance of the United States, policymakers became less committed to acquiring area-based expertise. The second is the process of globalization, broadly conceived. The past decade has witnessed increased economic and cultural flows and heightened awareness of these flows across national and regional borders. The growing mobility of capital, commodities, images, cultural forms, and people—tourists, migrants, and refugees—among different world areas has had important implications for area studies. It has meant, as Bruce Cumings notes, a shift in the state's priorities, from potential spheres of influence to potential markets:

> The source of power had shifted in the 1990s from the state's concern with the maintenance of Cold War boundary security to transnational corporations that, as the organized expression of the market, saw no geographic limit on their expression. Sponsors' expectations of area experts likewise changed quickly: a Kreminological opinion about "China after Mao or Deng" was less interesting than informed judgments on China's economic reforms: whither the old state sector and the like. (1997, 6–26)

Several of the major foundations—including Ford, Mellon, MacArthur, and the SSRC—have formed new research programs to study globalization. "The allure of globalization," Peter Hall and Sidney Tarrow note, "has grown just as area-studies programs in many universities have come under pressure from a number of different directions" (1998, B4-B5).

Beyond Area Studies?

The academy has proffered several quite different responses to these developments. We briefly describe three of the most important: formal social science theory, global or globalization studies, and cultural or postcolonial studies. Although these trends predate the crisis of area studies, their growing influence also has contributed to the crisis.

The first trend involves the use of formal models to develop general propositions about the empirical world. Academic disciplines have dominated the organization, financing, and curricula of U.S. colleges and universities since the early twentieth century. The distinction between academic disciplines and area studies is rooted in a narrative of Western modernity. Disciplinary knowledge, which makes supposedly universalistic claims, comes out of the experience of modern European societies. By contrast, area studies knowledge, which makes supposedly particularistic claims, speaks about the non-Western world and thereby stands in a problematic and even contested relationship to disciplinary knowledge.

These differences and tensions have become greater in recent years as the social sciences increasingly have turned to formal modeling and theoretical constructions based on the paradigm of neoclassical economics. The study of history and literature generally remains the study of history and literature of particular times and places. By contrast, economics and psychology historically have been committed to formulating general principles, divorced from time and place. The revival of theories of genetic determination in biology and psychology are closely related to this goal. The hegemony of neoclassical economics, at the expense of even Keynesian emphases on policy and institutions, is evident in most economics departments. Moreover, neoclassical economics also has become paradigmatic for political science, with the growth of rational choice, as well as for sociology, with social choice theory.

With the decline of area studies, the hard social sciences have further hardened, and the intellectual and political influence of the United States has grown. Robert Bates, a Harvard political scientist who was trained as a specialist in African politics, now claims that area studies at best can furnish evidence for broad-based theories in political science. Within political science, the subfield of comparative politics, which was most receptive to area studies in the past, seems to have succumbed to the research agenda and methodology of the subfield of U.S. politics. The U.S. politics field ironically imagined itself to be more theoretical in part because it was supposedly less area based than comparative politics. According to Bates, whereas comparative politics was always "a field in search of a theory," the subfield of U.S. politics "had democratic theory" (1997c, 1). Although comparative politics did not command the authority of U.S. politics within the discipline of political science, its existence was justified by the sheer diversity of the political world. It fell to students of comparative politics to explain why some societies were communist, authoritarian, or democratic and why some economies were command based and others market based.

With the collapse of communism and the rise of formally democratic systems, there appears to be much less diversity today than in the past. We quote from Robert Bates once again, this time at greater length:

Following the recession of the 1980s, authoritarian governments fell, and the collapse of communism in Eastern Europe further contributed to the spread of democracy. This change underscored the broader relevance of the US-oriented research into elections, legislatures, and political parties. The spread of market forces and the liberalization of economic systems high-lighted the broader significance of research conducted on the advanced in-dustrial democracies as well. The impact of economic conditions upon voting, the politics of central banking, the effect of openness upon partisan cleavages and political institutions long studied in Western democracies, these subjects have recently become important and researchable, in the for-merly socialist systems in the North and in the developing nations of the South. As students of comparative politics have addressed them, they have come increasingly to share intellectual orientations and a sense of necessary skills and training with their more "social scientific" colleagues in the disci-pline. (1997a, 167)

In short, Bates suggests that with the turn of countries of the East to the market and of the South to liberal democracy, questions about market democracy that first arose in the United States should become the key con-cerns of comparativists. However, Chalmers Johnson says of Robert Bates:

He is confident that his set of deductive axioms when allied with game the-ory, will lead to scientific progress. But he fails even to acknowledge the ex-istence of evidence that rational choice's key assumption, i.e., that all behavior can be reduced to rational individuals' short-term attempts to maximize their utility, is both wrong and culture bound. This failure is the strongest indicator that rational choice is more an ideological expression of the United States' interest in the post-Cold War period than an attempt at social science. (1997, 171)

We return to this criticism after we discuss the second challenge to area studies.

If one tendency has been toward the creation of more universalistic forms of knowledge and toward increasing homogeneity, another trend has been toward questioning master narratives and privileging the local, the everyday, and the particular. We refer to postmodernism, cultural studies, and postcolonial scholarship. These approaches have complicated implica-tions for area studies. A great deal of postcolonial theory emerges from a close familiarity with particular regions and is committed to interdiscipli-nary, contextually grounded knowledge. However, it also has contributed to dismantling area studies programs by critiquing traditional notions of what constitutes an area and by questioning the connections between area studies and the social sciences.

As national landscapes have changed amidst the growth of immigration, the collapse of old states, and the growth of new ones, postcolonial scholars have turned their attention to diasporas, immigrants, and hybrid identities. They have criticized area studies scholarship on two grounds: for neglecting popular culture in favor of formal political systems and for being unable to adapt to a rapidly changing world in which national boundaries are frequently irrelevant. Arjun Appadurai argues that "the area studies tradition has probably grown too comfortable with its own maps of the world, too secure in its own expert practices, and too insensitive to transnational processes both today and in the past" (1996, 17). While compiling knowledge about the world, area studies scholars need to focus more sharply on the empirical and conceptual problems posed by the "territoriality" of knowledge. Practically speaking, area studies must reformulate the analytical basis for what defines a "cultural area." Using all the technologies and data available, area studies scholars also must demonstrate how societies are defined as both political and cultural territories and must reveal the problems created by rethinking the boundaries between these realms.

However, despite these criticisms, postcolonial scholars are often supportive, even protective of area studies. Some of the reasons are intellectual, and some are autobiographical—the postcolonial origins of these scholars themselves—and some intellectual. Close knowledge of regions outside North America provides a strong basis from which to challenge the Eurocentrism of the academy and the binaries it has created between the West and the Rest. Furthermore, area studies have provided postcolonial scholars with one of the few institutional refuges from the disciplines, where interdisciplinarity and language study are taken seriously.

The dialogue between area studies and cultural studies is an extremely fruitful one. Despite the interest of cultural studies in the everyday and ordinary, its vantage point paradoxically is often the artistic avant garde (Karp 1997). Postcolonial scholarship has not explored seriously culture that is thoroughbred rather than hybrid, rural rather than urban, and national rather than local. Similarly, as Dipesh Chakrabarty notes, there is much to be gained from greater conversation between area studies and diasporic studies:

The conversation between area studies and diasporic studies is then a matter of communication between the politics of different life worlds: On the one side are life worlds produced by travel, (im)migration, battles for cultural recognition, and survival in capitalist consumerist democracies and in postnationalist structures; on the other side are life practices fashioned in the shadow of nationalist struggles against imperialism and in the context of the oppression of nationalisms, in spite of their liberating potential. (1998, 474)

If area studies scholars have tended to confine themselves to the nation-state as the only unit of analysis, postcolonial scholars have neglected the nation-state in favor of local-global connections.

This third challenge to area studies comes from globalization and from the academic industry it has spawned. A vast and ever-growing literature explores the causes, character, and consequences of globalization. Much of this literature exalts advances in science and technology and depicts globalization as natural, inevitable, imminent, and devoid of human volition. By ignoring the growth of regional and class inequalities, these discourses attain an almost utopian quality. Several contributors to this volume contest this perspective, and we concur that some analysts of globalization exaggerate both its magnitude and effects in ways that express ideology and aspiration more than observation. Nevertheless, we also recognize that the heightened international flows of capital, labor, products, information, and technology do have important implications for the intellectual realm of area studies.

It is impossible to identify globalization studies with any one theoretical or normative approach, and every conceivable facet is fiercely debated. In this way, globalization studies are distinct from the emerging consensus in the formal theory portions of the social science disciplines. Nonetheless, there is a fundamental similarity between globalization studies and the social science disciplines. Whereas the disciplines believe that they can assume a universality in human motives and relationships, globalization studies investigate the processes that supposedly are creating those universals through a single, integrated world system with strongly homogenizing tendencies. In their conclusions about area studies, then, the two approaches denigrate the importance of trying to understand regional particularities and thus make area studies scholarship appear to be parochial, insular, and outdated.

This commonality between the disciplines and globalization studies has its roots in their commitment to a Weberian notion of modernization as the faith of our time. The imagined convergence of social, political, and cultural formations of all modernized places also has been accepted in traditional area studies, the legacy of towering Western intellectuals—including Marx, Weber, Habermas, and Giddens—that modernity was identical to the creation of Europeanized societies. As a result, those scholars failed to recognize the different histories and cultural visions of non-European encounters with modernity or had little to say about the ways in which colonization contributed to the European experience of modernity.

Marshall Berman offers a more insightful perspective on theory and practice of modernization. He argues that modernity cannot be reduced either to modernization (a socioeconomic process) or to modernism (merely a cultural vision). For Berman, modernity is the space that mediates between modernization and modernism. Thus, one cannot speak of a universal modernity. Berman's approach to modernity leaves room for the possibility of a more "locally imagined" vision of modernization. He lays out an interpretation of modernity that is grounded in the everyday life experiences of the present:

> There is a mode of vital experience—experience of space and time, of the self and others, of life's possibilities and perils—that is shared by men and women all over the world today. I will call this "modernity." Modern environments and experience cut across all boundaries of geography and ethnicity, of class and nationality, of religion and ideology: In this sense, modernity can be said to unite all mankind. But it is a paradoxical unity, a unity of disunity: it pours us all into a maelstrom of perpetual disintegration and renewal, of struggle and contradiction, of ambiguity and anguish. (1988, 15)

For Berman, a blueprint of modernity is unnecessary: modernity is part of the experience of everyday life, of a life in which "all that is solid melts into air." This experience, Berman contends, is "spread all over the world" and cannot be understood as an essentially Western experience (1992, 37). Indeed, he explicitly argues that people in the "Third World" experience this shared world culture (see Dirlik and Xudong 1997, 2).

The social sciences generally have considered the first of Berman's processes (modernization) as a legitimate area of inquiry for the Third World. The other two aspects of modernity (historical experience of modernization and cultural and intellectual vision) have been defined as exclusively Western. Scholars have assumed that non-Western societies are incapable of articulating a cultural vision that is compatible with their modern experience. This accounts for the separation of intellectual studies, the disciplines, and area studies or the empirical study of non-Western societies.

Berman's distinctions among the different facets of modernization do not reduce modernity in non-Western societies to modernization, a transformation that simply enumerates the economic underpinnings of modernization. These distinctions enable us to think more systematically about both the historical and prospective changes owing to capitalist modernization. It simply is not useful to consider Great Britain, Germany, the United States, Japan, France, Italy, South Korea, and Sweden as having created common social and cultural formations in the process.

These historical experiences with modernization demonstrate that capitalist modernization is consistent with a wide range of social and cultural practices, and the theoretical considerations give us a way to understand these divergent experiences in an intelligent manner. It is imperative, then, for local peoples to formulate and implement their own visions of their own futures because economic modernization need not predetermine those futures. The danger, however, is that without recognizing the possibility for multiple social and cultural outcomes of modernization, the result will be the flattening predicted by conventional social science. In the current intellectual and political climate, there is no question that imagining alternative modernizations is an act of resistance.

The social science vision of comprehensive convergence is an illusion. The appearance of convergence masks significant differences between political economies and regimes. The dismantling of welfare states and the spread of market forces have assumed vastly different forms in the United States and Scandinavia or in East Asia and Latin America. Because different societies appropriate modernity differently, there is an even greater need for the deep study of specific geographies, histories, and languages (Appadurai 1996, 17).

The inescapable conclusion is that area studies, including the learning of languages and the understanding of specific social and cultural processes, are vital, even if one were interested only in economic modernization. Area studies must continue to challenge disciplines and temper their claims to universal truth. First, area studies programs and committees brought together scholars across disciplinary lines to develop curricula, supervise doctoral dissertations, attend conferences, and publish in multidisciplinary books and journals. Such collaborations fostered some understanding and respect for interdisciplinarity. Second, as significant numbers of historians and social scientists who had made their careers studying non-Western regions of the world entered the academy, they forced on the disciplines an awareness of their inability to generalize exclusively on the basis of Western experiences.

The fluid concept of globalization can be made more precise and meaningful only by being grounded in area studies. It is precisely the relationship between global processes and area-based knowledge that opens up new perspectives on globalizing societies, nations, and cultures. Viewing globalization from the vantage point of particular localities necessitates the displacement of totalizing theories of globalization with the recognition that globalization has assumed diverse forms connected by unequal power relations. Already a number of important studies rewrite the history of the global by connecting it to the local. In *The Black Atlantic* (1993, 1–40), Paul Gilroy rewrites relations between Europe, Africa, and the Americas by claiming the history of slavery to be a transnational event, not just part of the field of African American history (see also Cverkovich and Kellner 1997, 20).

Thus, globalization in itself by no means calls for the abandonment of area studies. Rather, it has brought to the fore cultural differences that can be understood only through rigorous place-based knowledge (Ashcroft, Griffins, and Tiffin 1995, 391). The extension of U.S. cultural and economic influence in this era of globalization in fact necessitates a commitment to creating centers of intellectual exchange among international and U.S. scholars; support for U.S.-based graduate students seeking funds for travel; and knowledge of modes of economic, political, and cultural life outside those of the United States. Paradoxically, although globalization demands greater knowledge of the world than ever before, scholars today have less in-depth, committed knowledge than they did in the past.

We have argued that area studies scholarship faces distinct intellectual challenges from formal modelers, globalization scholarship, and cultural studies. Even so, we have argued that all three of these approaches would benefit from more grounding in area-based knowledge. Detailed understanding of the particularities of a region challenges the universalisms of neoclassical economics, rational choice, and social choice theories. Conversely, cultural studies scholarship, with its sights fixed on localities, and globalization scholarship, with its sights fixed on the global, can gain from area studies a greater appreciation of nations and nation-states. In none of these cases can area studies scholarship be said to have become irrelevant.

The Contents of the Volume

The object of the Five Colleges faculty symposium "Global-Local: Revisioning the Area Studies Debate," 16–18 October 1998 at Hampshire College, Amherst, Massuchusetts, was to reflect on the current state of area studies in some of the regions where such studies flourished traditionally. This volume has the same purpose, and although earlier versions of most chapters were presented at the symposium, we have augmented them with additional contributions in order to increase the volume's interpretive and geographical scope. Nonetheless, we were unable to devote equal attention to all regions and had to leave some out entirely.

The authors have revised their original essays for this volume, but it is important to note that all of the essays were completed before 11 September 2001. The event that occurred on that date, which changed so much, has not changed the need for serious attention to area studies. In fact, it has underscored that need in a dramatic and tragic fashion.

The essays in this volume suggest that potential dangers as well as opportunities are entailed in the simultaneous decline of area studies and growth of globalization studies. Among the dangers are a tendency for us to disparage place-based knowledge (Escobar) and to embrace globalization uncritically (Ahmad), thereby disregarding its uneven character (Greene). However, the decline of area studies opens up appreciation of hybrid and multilingual identities (Sommer), as well as the complex character of local-global linkages (Basu). The decline of area studies might contribute either to thinking about place-based identities in less-bounded ways or to falling back on the disciplines as sources of universal knowledge, thereby disregarding their provincialism (Ludden, Mitchell).

The first part of the volume explores ways of conceptualizing the relationship between the local and the global that are richly informed by area studies but seek to move it in new directions. The chapters in this part challenge traditional, sometimes caricatured descriptions of area studies as parochial, insular, and untheoretical. However, they are informed by an appreciation of identities that are local, linguistic, and national. All of these authors have had some form of area studies training.

Chapter 2 by Doris Sommer, "American Baroque," offers a riddle: "What's the best thing about Neo-York?" The answer: "The best thing about it is that New York is so close to the United States." What Sommer loves most about New York is that it belongs to everyone but "standard" Americans. The Neo-York that Sommer loves not only displaces the United States from its hegemonic position but puts in its place a city that is defined by multilingual immigrant populations. This parable of New York provides some ways to rethink American studies. Although American studies have begun to respond to Latino and Asian provocations by including a range of ethnically marked books and instructors, Sommer argues that these steps do not challenge the tendencies to whittle down differences to "leaves of the same grass." The challenge is to seek out a design for both America and American studies that celebrates incommensurability.

Debates on area studies generally have involved historians, anthropologists, political scientists, and sociologists. However, we open the volume with Sommer's essay to suggest how much humanists, in particular linguists, have to contribute. Sommer also suggests some important ways of studying the United States as an area without making it synonymous with the center. This decentering is achieved by a focus on New York rather than on the United States and by a cultural politics that is global in character.

The two chapters that follow, by Arturo Escobar and Angelique Haugerud, respectively, rethink concepts of place and locality in light of globalization and its representations, albeit in very different ways. In chapter 3, "Place, Nature, and Culture in Discourses of Globalization," Escobar examines recent discussions about "place" in geography, anthropology, and political ecology. The most fruitful discussions of globalization in all three disciplines seek to protect place from erasure. He argues that inquiry into place provides a fruitful alternative for thinking about the local and the global. Place is not the same as the local and cannot be defined only in opposition to the global. Broadened as such, it can reinvigorate our thinking about social transformation; significant changes can emerge in places and not only from the supralevels of capital, the state, or the global. Escobar calls for our shifting exclusive attention from "the global" as site of theory and political action. Similarly, this shift entails imagining other forms of "glocality" through which local, regional, and transnational worlds might be in the making.

Where Escobar wants to hold onto locality, Haugerud worries about the dangers that such a project entails. In chapter 4, "The Disappearing Local: Rethinking Global/Local Connections," she analyzes the risks of romanticizing the local. It is not always clear how much the local can be differentiated from the global, and there is a place for broader theoretical analysis that takes history and institutions more seriously than theorists of the local generally do. Furthermore, shortcomings in prevailing conceptions of the local signal deeper epistemological and conceptual challenges, for our analytic vocabulary no longer is equipped to make sense of global changes. Our task now, Haugerud argues, is to move beyond global/local dichotomies and explore the historically contingent ways in which these two domains constitute one another or operate in dynamic tension. An implicit debate runs through the two essays. For Escobar, the danger lies in the false universalisms that come out of development discourse, which is in turn linked to the universalizing traditions of the European Enlightenment tradition. By contrast, for Haugerud the danger lies in the reaction to what Escobar worries about—the tendency among some scholars to idealize the local.

Chapter 5, by Amrita Basu, and chapter 6, by Lila Abu-Lughod, take up Haugerud's challenge to complicate our understanding of local-global relations by interposing nations and states between them. In "Globalizing Local Women's Movements," Amrita Basu argues that much of women's activism is animated by local-level concerns—for potable drinking water, firewood for fuel, and safety in their neighborhoods. At the same time, women's movements are among the most global movements in the world. Particularly since the international women's conference in Beijing in 1995, the slogan "women's rights are human rights" captures a central demand of global women's movements. Questions that flow from juxtaposing women's local and global concerns constitute the focus of her analysis.

Basu suggests that the implications of global influences for local forms of women's activism in the South have changed. In the mid-1970s, women's movements in the South rankled at the attempt by Northern women's movements to define a single feminist agenda. Today women's movements transnationally have come to define their own agendas, and conflicts among global women's movements have subsided. However, the tensions between universalist and particularistic understandings of feminism have not disappeared but simply have assumed new forms. Cross-national alliances of religious nationalists have employed the language of localism or particularism to support their transnational alliances, whereas feminists organizing transnationally and appealing to liberal principles of human rights have adopted global, universalist appeals. Moreover, Basu argues that for many women's movements, including those that form strong transnational alliances, the major locus of activity is the local and national level rather than the transnational level.

In chapter 6, "Asserting the Local as National in the Face of the Global: The Ambivalence of Authenticity in Egyptian Soap Opera," Lila Abu-Lughod explores the relationship between the local and the global in mass media and popular culture. Mass media, especially the most popular, by definition reach large audiences. Although usually produced in one national context, they often cross national and even regional boundaries. The most commonly known example of the global reach of a local national product is the export of U.S. soap operas and films to the rest of the world. However, Mexican soap operas are popular in Russia, Lebanon, and New York City, and Brazil's Globo Television soap operas are popular in Cameroon. Even Egypt, the major producer of Arabic films and soap operas for thirty years, has long exported its programs to the Arab world and now transmits them to Britain and the United States via satellite. Anyone considering the significance of media or the larger theoretical problems of the relationship between the local and the global must assess the impact of this kind of traffic on local mass-media industries; on political, social, and cultural dynamics; and even on individual subjectivities. The case of Egyptian television illustrates crucial features of the cultural dynamics of globalization: the way that certain groups link and mobilize cultural identity and national identity in response to transnationalization.

Basu and Abu-Lughod agree that it is impossible to speak of the local without speaking of the global. An exploration both of media and of movements reveals their close interconnections and reciprocal influences. However, they also agree that exclusive attention to local-global dynamics may obscure the critical influence of the nation-state in women's lives. Their chapters remind us that far from eroding the place of the nation-state, globalizing processes may underscore the continuing significance of the national.

With chapter 7, David Ludden opens the second part of the book, which explicitly addresses the current state of area studies. In his short but provocative intervention "Why Area Studies?" Ludden distinguishes between two principal modalities of knowledge: the universal, which is the principal form of knowledge in the academic disciplines, and the contextual, which is represented by area studies. He qualifies this juxtaposition by acknowledging that universal knowledge depends on contextual knowledge for its raw materials and that Europe and North America constitute the principal areas from which universal knowledge has been drawn. By contrast, he asserts that contextual knowledge in area studies is selected and organized along lines that presuppose underlying theoretical principles embedded in disciplinary work, although often from multiple disciplines.

Despite these qualifications, Ludden suggests that the differences between the modalities of knowledge in area studies and in the disciplines are real and that both are in trouble. The idea of a coherent, identifiable cultural area has been exploded by scholars' realization that upon closer inspection individual cultural areas turn out to have been highly diverse and that increased global integration has further heightened cultural heterogeneity in every region. But the quest for the universal has not fared much better. New approaches to knowledge have undermined the Enlightenment faith in positive knowledge and science, which in turn suggests the existence of a plurality of knowledge and modernities rather than one unified modernity. Ludden argues that, in this untidy situation, area studies research and teaching, including language learning, continue to be vital to an effective knowledge of humanity. But area studies must be reinvented by reformulating the meaning of a cultural area and by emphasizing the historical processes of constant and compelling cultural change that transcend such fruitless dichotomies as that between tradition and modernity.

In chapter 8, "The Multiple Worlds of African Studies," Sandra Greene points out that the general debate about the uncertain state of area studies has a peculiar salience in African studies. Africa's impoverishment and marginalization in the global marketplace may consign both the continent and scholarly work on Africa to oblivion. Greene states that funding agencies and universities have backed away from the very concept of area studies and that universities are becoming less sympathetic to area specialists. She argues that although African studies scholars must respond positively and effectively to the new intellectual and institutional trends within U.S. universities, their attempts may not be sufficient to ensure the viability of the field. In an especially powerful section, she discusses the plight of African universities and the imperative for U.S.-based scholars of Africa to collaborate more with African colleagues in African universities. She also appeals to U.S.-based Africanists to intervene more effectively with policymakers, the media, and those U.S. communities that historically have had an interest in Africa. Both of these dimensions bear directly and immediately on the prospects of African studies as a research and teaching field.

In chapter 9, "Deterritorialization and the Crisis of Social Science," Timothy Mitchell similarly explores the relationship between the disciplines and area studies. However, his critique of the disciplines is even stronger than Ludden's. Mitchell begins by describing what he considers to be the conventional understanding about area studies. As the global movement of commodities, finance, and cultural forms intensifies, area studies—a particular way, in U.S. universities, of organizing expert knowledge about the rest of the world—are thought to be in crisis. Area studies arrived with the Cold War, it is said, and with the passing of that compartmentalized world, area studies must give way to more global forms of expertise. In contrast, Mitchell argues that the origins of area studies lie in a reaction to what happened between the 1930s and 1950s, when each social science discipline invented or redefined an object of study such as the economy, the social system, culture, and so on. The territorial definition corresponded in each case to the borders of the nation-state: the national economy, national cultures, and so on. Since the 1970s, however, the social sciences have abandoned the attempt to define themselves by laying claim to a particular territory of the social world. This deterritorialization of the disciplines, he argues, reflects the larger deterritorializations of contemporary history. Although scholars from within area studies and within the disciplines are calling for a new relationship between the social sciences and area studies, the real challenge facing U.S. universities is to see the limits of social sciences shaped in the image of the nation-state. Where Ludden calls for the revamping of both area studies and the disciplines, Mitchell calls for a collapsing of the disciplines into area studies.

In chapter 10, "The Middle East as an Area in an Era of Globalization," Rashid Khalidi argues that areas have been defined by centers. He shows that in recent years there has been increasing dissatisfaction with the term *Middle East* as a designation for the vast region lying between the Atlantic Ocean, Central Asia, and India. This dissatisfaction results in part from the fact that the term is one of many relics of an earlier, Eurocentric era, when things were "near" or "far" or in the "middle" in relation to the privileged vantage point of Europe.

In the study of the Middle East, complex processes that transcend regions—such as the flow of trade, capital, and labor among countries all around the rim of the Indian Ocean—and that appear to have been quite significant for a very long time have received far less attention than they are owed. This neglect has occurred in part because these processes transcend several fields that have been reified through "Middle East studies," "African studies," and "South Asian studies." Beyond this, little attention has been paid in the Middle East field to what was happening in other branches of area studies. The situation today may indeed be worse than it was before the modern area studies approach was devised.

Part 3 and the last two of the volume chapters combine the themes of the first part of the volume, which focuses on local-global relations, and those of the second part, which explores the crisis of area studies, by critically analyzing the literature on globalism from a perspective informed by area-based knowledge.

In chapter 11, "Culture Against History? The Politics of East Asian Identity," Arif Dirlik explores recent challenges to area studies programs on Asia. He argues that the attack on area studies and in particular on the idea of Asia as an area has come from two very different sources that have more in common than initially might be evident. Both poststructuralists and the large research foundations have sought to supplant area studies with global studies because regionally based knowledge is increasingly irrelevant to a globalized world. As distances are bridged and contact zones multiplied, the expertise of the area studies scholar is rendered less useful. And yet, Dirlik argues, globalism does not do away with the need for area-based knowledge. Open-ended inquiry requires that we keep alive the questions of how to determine significance and relevance. An authentic globalism, similarly, calls for a genuine recognition of difference, not the interpellation of local differences into our theoretical schemes. To either end, the study of concrete places is essential.

In the concluding chapter, we present Eqbal Ahmad's closing reflections on the papers presented at the conference. He begins by registering his qualms about the usefulness of the concept of globalization. His critique suggests that given the strength of earlier global forces, hyperbole about globalization may mask the fact that current tendencies are the product of capital for the benefit of capital and that they reflect a deliberate political project. He illustrates these points with vivid anecdotes. Other major themes in Eqbal Ahmad's comments are why knowledge and its relation to power are so important and how development agencies based in the metropolitan nations have discouraged investments in higher education. He observes that both area studies and globalization scholars tend to ignore class relations and inequality. He also registers qualms about the extent to which there has been a globalization of civil society. For example, he suggests that the transnational scope of some social movements actually have deradicalized them. He concludes with his concerns about the history, politics, and prospects of area studies. He is especially anxious that we continue to be alert about the terms on which resources are available and how those terms will shape the future of area studies.

The contributors to this volume disagree on many issues, including the character of global knowledge and studies, the importance of localities in relation to nationalities and globalities, and the role of the state and private foundations in shaping scholarly inquiry. However, all the contributors share a background in area studies and a commitment to thinking about these areas in new and different ways amidst globalization. Every contribution makes clear that the discussion of area studies cannot be isolated from a larger discussion about knowledge, power, and culture, at home and in the world.

 PART ONE

Rethinking Local-Global Connections

2 American Baroque

DORIS SOMMER

Alejo Carpentier, that quintessential Cuban who was an authority on African strains of national music and a creative master of local histories, lived abroad much of the time. When he came home to the Americas, he would linger lovingly among the buildings, not because they grounded him in a particular style of architecture, but rather because they took liberties with them all, together, in a charmingly undisciplined simultaneity of tastes and traces. This, for him, was the American baroque:

> Nunca he visto edificios tan feos como los que peuden contemplarse en ciertas ciudades nuestras. Hay casas como comprimidas por las casas vecinas, que suben, crecen, se escapan por sobre los tejados aledanos, acabando por cobrar con sus ventanas torturadas por la estrechez, una ferocidad de ogro e dibujo animado, presto a desplomarse sobre quien la comtemple con alguna ironia. . . . En el Vedado de la Habana, zona urbana de la que soy transeunte infatigable, se entremezclan todos los estilos imaginables: falso helenico, falso romano, falso Renacimiento, falso castillo de la Loira, falso recoco, falso *modern-style,* sin olvidar los grandes remedos, debidos a la ola de prosperidad traido por la primera guerra mundial—remedos, a su vez, de otras cosas—. De los que habian edificado en Estados Unidos. . . . Pues bien: desde hace poco esa arquitectura ha empezado a tener encanto y gracia . . . un tanto humilde, patinado y *demode,* que las inscribe, poeticamente, dentro de los caracteres fisonomicos de la ciudad.
>
> [I have never seen buildings as ugly as those you can contemplate in some of our cities. There are houses so squeezed by houses nearby that they rise up, grow, and escape over the bordering roofs to take on the ferocity, because of their tortured windows, of a cartoon ogre ready to pounce on any ironic passerby. . . . El Vedado, Havana, an urban area that I walk tire-

25

lessly, mixes every imaginable style: false Hellenic, false Roman, false Renaissance, false Chateau la Loire, false rococo, false modern style, not to mention the wave of imitations—themselves imitations of other things—from the United States that came with the prosperity from the First World War. . . . Now then, this architecture has recently achieved a certain charm and grace . . . a patina of humility, a bit *demode,* that inscribes it, poetically, into the physiognomy of the city.] (1969, 18–19, my translation)

Compared to the decorative simplicity of European cities such as Brussels, Venice, Rome, Paris, or Toledo, Carpentier concludes, the charming incoherence of American neostyles gives the novelist room to plot surprises. Our great cities do not belong to any one style, people, cultural identity, or even country.

"What's the best thing about Neo-York?" my favorite riddle asks. The best thing about it is that New York is so close to the United States. The City, as we call it both from the center and from the suburbs, or "Nous York" as an Air Canada poster calls it with loving possessiveness, seems to belong to everyone but to "standard" Americans. From some perspectives, the City is the northernmost island of the Caribbean; from others, it's an eastern outpost of Asia's American migrations. It looks and sounds and smells like many places in the world, all together. Some observers probably feel overpowered or at least confused and anxious in the midst of a vitality that has so many different shapes. The variety, after all, can contaminate one's identity and provoke defensive claims to coherence. Languages brush one another with foreign color; musical rhythms mix even when dancers are slow to change partners; and practically everyone eats international cuisine that somebody's mother used to make.

For these same reasons, many New Yorkers, by birth or by choice, permanent residents and addicted visitors, love the City. It is almost literally a utopia, a place that seems to be nowhere in particular and that hardly fits into conventional geography. A center of economic and political power full of peripheral people who don't cluster around any one cultural or social center, no one standard language or value or norm of good taste. The multiplicity makes it impossible for anyone really to fit into the City without noticing the loose ends that also link them elsewhere. No one presumes to go onto a New York street and expect to understand all the languages she will hear; we may feel very clever if we can identify at least some of them by dint of our constant exposure. And because we all fit badly, we all fit *"a nuestra manera,"* some with more success than others, admittedly, but all with the consciousness of our limitations. This is the paradoxically democratizing charm of incommensurable identities in New York and in Miami, Los Angeles, Chicago, Havana, Buenos Aires. These are dense and fissured spaces, where the loose ends of postmodern subjects can slip through the cracks. Those who defend a tidier American identity have caused more problems than they have cleared away.

"How does it feel to be a problem?" is what white people are always asking black people who can't manage to be simply American, says W. E. B. Du Bois at the beginning of *Souls of Black Folk* (1965, originally published in 1903). They ask it when feeling compassionate or vicariously outraged at things "that make your blood boil." Du Bois reduces his own boiling point to a simmer, as he puts it, in order to ventriloquize for whites who don't dare to ask the question outright and don't worry about constructive answers. So Du Bois asks it boldly and responds: Feeling yourself to be a problem, he says, "is a peculiar sensation, this double-consciousness, this sense of always looking at one's self through the eyes of others, of measuring one's soul by the tape of a world that looks on in amused contempt and pity. One ever feels this twoness,—an American, a Negro; two souls, two thoughts, two unreconciled strivings" (1965, 215).

Double consciousness is a double-bind for Du Bois, as it generally has been for minorities in the United States, the "Neither nor" in the poem by Sandra María Esteves. The problem, of course, supposes that coherence is better than heterogeneity. Why suppose this anymore, after so much postmodern provocation along with projections that doubly American Latinos will soon be the major minority population of the United States? The fact is that daily practices no longer suppose a monoculture, now that bilingual-language games will soon take over a whole television network as they have taken some streets ("Telemundo" 1998) and given the patriotic feelings that can belong to more than one country ("A Shuttle Between Worlds" 1998). Today, we are puzzles with pieces left over, says Giannina Braschi. They are excesses that interrupt anyone's cultural identity to make space for some movement. They also might free up some space in the imploding field of American studies to cultivate more variety where equalizing and infinitely repeatable Whitmanian rhizomes still dominate. The problem with rhizomes is that they level the field by overcoming everything in their way.

American studies have begun, slowly, to respond to Latino and Asian provocations by including a range of ethnically marked books and instructors. These moves are steps forward, no doubt, but they don't disturb the rhizomatic design that whittles differences down to leaves of the same grass. The challenge will be to formulate a different design, one that features the democratizing charms of incommensurability. Why, for example, have we left bilingualism to political and pedagogical debates? Doesn't it have aesthetic and philosophical specificities? Bilingual-language games show a metalinguistic sophistication and creativity that might intrigue even monolingual conservatives. But bicultural aesthetics is a discourse that has yet to be invented. The same goes for a philosophy of language that acknowledges more than one code at a time. Even Austin's and Wittgenstein's respect for context and usage stops at the border between one language and another, missing the games played in counterpoint. "What happens," Wittgenstein asks, when you express an idea or a feeling in words? Or when an English expression comes, and you try to hit on the German equivalent? He doesn't mention the possible relief from hitting on German for a moment, thanks to the English interruption. One symbolic order may be as limiting as the other, but shifting codes opens some room for maneuver: "sonriéndose se empina el bato la botella and wagging chapulín legs in-and-out le dice algo a su camarada dy los dos avientan una buena carcajada y luego siguen platicando mientras la amiga, unaffected masca y truena su chicle viéndose por un espejo componiéndose el hairdo" (Vigil 1982).

Double codes and double consciousness need not bind us in the self-destructive contradictions that frustrated Du Bois. On the contrary, and this is my point today. They may be our best cultural safeguard for democratic practice because doubleness will not allow the meanness of one thought, one striving, one measure of value. Democracy prizes nonnormative procedure over political substance. In the seam between particular cultures that fit badly together, democracy can work procedurally to define universal rights and obligations. Good fits leave little room for serious play. But differences that are admitted and continue to strain against one another show the gap where debate and procedure can work. Du Bois himself opens leads in this direction when he refuses to "bleach his Negro soul" in order to fit into white America. But *Souls of Black Folk* complains mostly that seeing double means losing focus. Ralph Waldo Emerson's double consciousness amounted to social bankruptcy for blacks, who were pulled in opposite directions and getting nowhere.

For Emerson, it was the principle of coordination between opposing forces, the productive tension between nature and freedom, between racial inheritance and universal purpose. He formulated this mixture of optimism and resignation during the troubled decade before the Civil War, just after the war that annexed half of Mexico to the United States. Rather than remedy a condition that we would call schizophrenia today, Emerson commissioned monuments to the grand American solution. "Why should we fear to be crushed by savage elements, we who are made up of the same elements?" (1860, 816).

This is not a rhetorical question for everyone. Those who are crushed ask it differently. Emerson himself thanked his luck for belonging to the winning race. "We like the nervous and victorious habit of our own branch of the family"; and "Cold and sea will train an imperial Saxon race, which nature cannot bear to lose, and, after cooping it up for a thousand years in yonder England, gives a hundred Englands, a hundred Mexicos. All the bloods it shall absorb and domineer: and more than Mexicos,—the secrets of water and steam, the spasms of electricity, the ductility of metals, the chariot of the air, the ruddered balloon are awaiting you" (1860, 808). Meanwhile, other races deteriorate when you dislodge them, literally becoming fertilizer for the heartier race: "The German and Irish millions, like the Negro, have a great deal of guano in their destiny. They are ferried over the Atlantic, and carted over America, to ditch and to drudge, to make corn cheap, and then to lie down prematurely to make a spot of green grass on the prairie" (1860, 801).

Need I insist on our responsibility to affirm these "disposable" particularisms today, as long as they respect the procedures of civility? Without interrupting triumphal Americanism—in, for example, the video *The Global Tongue: English* (Crystal 1998)—our fellow citizens may remain loyal priests of the Saxon race. Fifty years after Emerson's rhapsody on Fate, freedom began to feel like another form of bondage for blacks, and a frustrated Du

Bois protested that no amount of equestrian skill could save the black rider of Emerson's contending horses. Blacks are crushed between the furious hoofs as race consciousness collides with racist national consciousness, or they are torn apart as the strains of a divided consciousness pull in contrary directions.

Ever since then double consciousness has been the curse of American minorities. In its structural duplicity, this is an unhappy consciousness by definition. To feel oneself as a problem breeds the kind of self-hatred that members of any minority group are likely to experience to the degree that they also belong to the majority group that hates them. Doubleness has not always been a predicament, though. A long history of some premodern societies is instructive. Nor does doubleness necessarily mean trouble for a postmodern society, where the overload of cultural differences demands, as I said, an empty, public space for coordination. Consider medieval England, where Normans were wise enough to know that they ruled a nation of foreigners. Jews, Germans, Danes, and others could not "speak the same language" in any literal way, but they were enjoined to deal fairly with one another. Prudent listening for the "differend" was a medieval practice long before it became Lyotard's postmodern hope. A medieval mixed jury, which combined local subjects and foreigners as members of the same tribunal, would hear cases between culturally different litigants who could not be subject to one existing rule.

Now that our postmodern nations are adjusting to culturally mixed populations, unstoppable waves of immigration, the continuing sounds of different languages in public places, we might take a lead from the Normans and from the Moors in Spain, to cite one more example. The Moors used to tax thriving infidels rather than eliminate them as so much guano. More rational than Christian tradition has portrayed them, Muslim empires have been hosts to the cultural differences that Christendom does not abide. Spanish modernity came with cultural and political coherence: the consolidation of reluctant and even embattled kingdoms, the expulsion of miscreants, and the continued surveillance of private devotions by public authority. Modernity drove England to overcome internal differences, too: a uniform Common Law replaced the ad hoc mixed jury, and Jews were expelled (as elsewhere) because they preferred double consciousness over the coherence of one intolerant culture.

Today, universal rights are an idea that parts company with what Europeans had assumed to be a universal culture. Ernesto Laclau argues provocatively, along with some critical legal scholars, that universalism is promising today because it depends on difference.[1] It has survived classical philosophy's dismissal of particularity as deviation, and it has outlived a European Enlightenment that conflated the universal (subject, class, culture) with particular (French) incarnations. Today's universalism is a paradox for the past because it is grounded in particularist demands that unmoor it from any fixed cultural content and keep it open to an "always receding horizon" (Laclau 1995, 107).[2] Precisely because citizens cannot presume to feel or to

1. Citing Robert Paul Wolff's "Beyond Tolerance" (in Wolff, Moore, and Marcuse 1969, 4, 17), Neil Gotanda (1991, 53) defends racial-cultural diversity as a positive good in the polity, rather than as something to be merely tolerated and benignly overlooked. He also quotes Justice Brennan, whose decision in *Metro Broadcasting v. FCC* draws from *Regents of University of California v. Bakke:* "Just as a 'diverse student body' contributing to a 'robust exchange of ideas' is a 'constitutionally permissible goal' on which a race-conscious university admissions program may be predicated, the diversity of views and information on the airwaves serves important First Amendment values. The benefits of such diversity are not limited to the members of minority groups . . . ; rather, the benefits redound to all members of the viewing and listening audience" (1991, 57). Thanks to Susan Keller for directing me to this article.

2. Judith Butler cautiously agrees that universality can be a site of translation: "the universal is always culturally articulated, and . . . the complex process of learning how to read that claim is not something any of us can do outside of the difficult process of cultural translation [but definition is in the process of defining, *el camino se hace al caminar*]. . . . [T]he terms made to stand for one another are transformed in the process, and where the movement of that unanticipated transformation establishes the universal as that which is yet to be achieved and which, in order to resist domestication, may never be fully or finally achievable" (Benhabib et al. 1995, 130). See also Butler's forthcoming article "Sovereign Performatives in the Contemporary Scene of Utterance," where she argues for the efficacy of "performative contradictions" in the contestatory translations of the term *universal. Performative contradiction* is a term Habermas (1987, xv) used to discredit Foucault's critique of reason via reason. I'm not sure, however, how different in practice is Butler's project of open-ended translation from Habermas's pursuit of the universal as an ideal (1987, 198). Who could ever reach an ideal? And yet, in the heuristic spirit of Seyla Benhabib's work, how can one have a political engagement without imagining ideals? In *The Location of Culture* (1994), Homi K. Bhabha also makes translation the site of the moveable nature of modernity in general(see especially 32, 242). Translation is the favored strategy for keeping the promise of modernity usably alive.

think or to perform alike, their ear for otherness makes justice possible.[3] That is why political philosophy and ethics, from Benjamin and Arendt to Bakhtin and Levinas, caution against empathy, which plays treacherously in a subject-centered key that overwhelms unfamiliar voices to repeat solitary sounds of the self (Benjamin 1969, 256).[4]

This is no time to lead the horses of double consciousness in one direction, with Emerson's agile Anglo-Saxons driving others aground. Nor is this the time to follow Du Bois in vicious circles as race and nation dig each other into a ground that requires acculturation but does not permit it. Today we might notice that double consciousness is a normal and ever more universal condition of contemporary subjects. It is also, I have been saying, a structure of democratic feeling. The difference between acculturation and this syncretic program that Du Bois preferred may be lost on some American readers because we have been trained to value assimilation as the process of becoming American. We hardly know how to name his reluctance to cut and to choose when different cultures claim him. What does one call the cultural process of amalgamation that embraces difference but apparently absorbs it in a new homogeneous mix?

Latin Americans know several names for *"lo junto y revuelto." Mestizaje* is probably the most familiar. In English, the counterpart would be *miscegenation,* and the clumsy translation is a sign of the bad fit between the

3. This is a commonplace of political philosophy, one that Mari Matsuda develops for the practice of law. John Rawls argues that "liberalism as a political doctrine supposes that there are many conflicting and incommensurable conceptions of the good, each compatible with the full rationality of human persons" (1985, 248). And Milton Fisk writes, "There has to be at least a conflict based on an actual lack of homogeneity for what is distinctive about justice to become relevant" (1993, 1). See also Dahl 1982 and Benhabib 1992, 2.

4. In thesis VII of "Theses on the Philosophy of History" (1969, 253–264), Benjamin disdains historicism for cultivating empathy, that lazy attachment to the past that has survived in documents, necessarily to the oppressive winners. In Arendt 1963, see the long section in chapter 2, "The Social Question," 69–90. Because compassion abolishes the distance where politics can happen, it is irrelevant for worldly affairs (81), and, worse, speaking for (weak) others may be a pretext for lust for power (84). See also Bakhtin 1990, 64, 81, 88; Levinas 1969, 1981. For a proceduralist critique of grounding politics in positive feeling, see, for example, Dahl 1982, especially chapter 7, "Changing Civic Orientations," 138–64. Dahl writes, "To love a member of one's family or a friend is not at all like 'loving' abstract 'others' whom one does not know, never expects to know, and may not even want to know" (147).

codes.[5] *Miscegenation* has been pronounced with mistrust or revulsion, whereas Latin American racial mixing has often been an official slogan in Spanish and Portuguese. *Mestizaje* endorses the particularity of New World peoples through a rhetoric of national brotherhood that is meant to ease racial tensions, not necessarily to address material equity. Latin Americans would recognize immediately Du Bois's manifesto for merging as a conventional banner of cultural pride. It was, for example, the standard of the independence movement throughout the continent, when Simón Bolívar proclaimed that Spanish Americans have many fathers, but only one mother, that they are neither Spanish nor Indian nor Black, but all of these. A century later, to mention just one more of many examples, *mestizaje* reaffirmed Mexico as a modern country with *la misión de la raza iberoamericana*, the subtitle for José Vasconcelos's *La raza cosmíca* (originally published in 1925, translated in 1979). Whites and Indians would be joined by blacks and Asians in the unprecedented culmination of one "cosmic race." This would happen in Mexico because no other country was as free from the racial prejudice that obstructs human progress. Anglo-Saxons seemed to prosper by divine will, but "they committed the sin of destroying those races, while we assimilated them, and this gives us new rights and hopes for admission without precedent in History" (Vasconcelos 1979, 15).

In 1940, Fernando Ortiz proposed a new word for merging, *transculturation,* to take account of the pain and the costs (mostly to blacks), even when the end product was an admirable Cuban culture. Understandably, transculturation (along with *mestizaje* and the "cosmic race") has come under criticism lately as an official ideology that amounts to control.[6] What difference can difference make if it becomes a comfortable part of the self, neutralized and melted down?

Nevertheless, Du Bois probably yearned for this kind of stabilized merging. He was troubled by the incommensurability of both a black and an American consciousness. Until very late in his life, he aspired to bilateral creativity. Everything seemed to hang on establishing the mutual respect of really enlightened whites and gifted blacks. But I want to risk a less likely

---

5. See Werner Sollors's book *Neither Black nor White Yet Both* (1997), for example.

6. I am referring primarily to debates among authors of the *New Cultural History of Latin America,* being prepared under the leadership of Mario Valdés and Linda Hutcheson.

reading of Du Bois and to reread other Hegelian-American ideologues along the way. Among them is Richard Rodriguez, who is an assimilationist, he says, not because he's "American" but because he's Mexican and mestizable. "I don't hate or fear Americas," he added in a talk I heard. "I love them, so much that I eat them alive and make them part of myself." I could have quoted the "Manifesto antropofago" by Oswald de Andrade, about Brazilian America being a cultural vacuum cleaner, and Roberto Schwarz's corollary, "National by Subtraction," which mocks the resistance to foreign bodies. But I'm more interested in the moment before we take them in, the point before differences merge, while they remain ill-fitting partners. This is the point where Gertrudis Gómez de Avellaneda leaves her hero Sab, whose three races stay visible and juxtaposed, without melding into mulatto. It's where Nestor García Canclini detains us, to consider the *multitemporal heterogeneity* of hybrid cultures, colored by a certain melancholy for the losses we neither forget nor entirely forgive. They survive in Du Bois's scorn for the requirement to bleach one's soul and to ignore racial antagonism. That scorn is an expression of pride in one's difference, and it is the energy that keeps one cultural particularity in productive tension with others. Thanks to this tension—to incommensurability itself when one thinks of history, taste, preferences—the empty space opens up for a truly universal, nonnormative public sphere of rights and obligations. This is postmodernity's response to the dialectics of modernization: to appreciate the emphasis on procedure in modern politics and to value cultural variety (that demands tolerance and flexibility) over modernity's taste for normalization.

If you allow me to pose a perhaps impertinently personal question, I might ask if you would cure your double consciousness if you could. Or would you prefer to continue under its burden? Suppose that you could wake up tomorrow no longer a Jewish American, lesbian American, Latino, African, Asian, gay, Muslim American, or any other particular variation but simply American or Mexican or Cuban or Peruvian. Would you do it? If you could suppress the hyphen of your oxymoronic, more than single "identity," would you want to? Well . . . would you? Almost everyone else I ask answers "no," even when they seem surprised. What would predict the resistance when so much of our civic and cultural training in the Americas demonizes the doubleness? Perhaps we sense, sometimes without saying it, that the cure is worse than the complaint.

Some contemporary theorists do say it, urgently and boldly. I mentioned Ernesto Laclau, an Argentine in France, who defends an empty nonnormative universality cleared away by the bad fit of cultural particularities. I should mention Mari Matsuda, too, a Japanese Hawaiian legal scholar who also defends the play of cultural differences. Without that play, the promise of fairness stays mired in the monocultural intolerance of the courts (Matsuda 1991, 1329–407).[7] This is certainly not an argument for a Tower of Babel that will quake and crumble with the frustrations of incomprehension. Instead, I want to defend code switching as one of democracy's most effective speech-acts, along with translation and speaking English through heavy accents, because they slow down communication and labor through the difficulties of understanding and reaching agreement.

To these theorists and others, one might add a variety of authors who live happily on the hyphen, cultivating the space for personal self-fashioning and for political flexibility. Gustavo Pérez Firmat (delighted with the paradox) easily becomes American *because* he already is Cuban, transculturated, but with a postmodern difference that refuses sublations. "The Cuban-American way" (Pérez Firmat 1994) doesn't fuse contending cultures but braces them together, on either side of a spacing device that leaves room for creativity. Coco Fusco continues the game in *English Is Broken Here* (1996), a manifesto for keeping the country fractured linguistically and open to the play of difference. And Roberto Fernández disguises one language with another to enjoy the misalignment (" 'Thanks! for the boniato,' says Mrs. Olsen as she rushes Barbarita out. 'For nothing,' answers Barbarita" [1997, 86]). Even Richard Rodríguez boasts that he "might surprise, even offend you by how inconveniently Mexican I can be." Is this an unhappy consciousness that troubled Du Bois? Or is it more defiant to monoculturalism than disappointed at not fitting in?

Double consciousness may indeed be a challenge today for the United States and for other countries reluctant to let go of the dialectical dream of coherence. But it is no longer a rush of contrary forces that human progress should gradually coordinate, as it was for Emerson. Instead, double consciousness is the challenge to develop stamina for the incoherence. Matsuda

7. Matsuda celebrates cultural difference beyond the tolerance that liberals such as Richard Rorty defend. I am grateful to Professor Susan Keller for this reference.

and others will not be satisfied by mere tolerance for different accents in the courtroom, different flavors of food on street-corner stands, and complicated personal webs of belonging and sympathies. America needs to value these differences, to celebrate them as the fissures that keep the country from congealing into the meanness of one standard style.

Does double consciousness block responsible conversation in a vertigo of particular self-hatred and universal contempt for misfits? There is good reason to believe the opposite: that it enables conversation between parties who respect the differences that separate them because they acknowledge stubborn discords that fissure their own identities. On the crowded streets of big cities, those cracks multiply in unpredictable ways, interrupting a single-mindedness that is less than democratic. Thanks to double and multiple consciousness, we gratefully can tolerate difference. Anyone who imagines that tolerance means dismissing difference as irrelevant rather than revering it as a condition of today's democracy is surely more afflicted by an unhappy consciousness than those of us who learn to love the hyphens. My favorite is the hyphen implied in New York's borrowed and baroque name, an identity doubled between the old world and the new. In its capacious fissure, the City multiplies itself to become ours in French, to go tropical as "El Gran Mango" in Spanish, and to respond to lovers in who knows how many languages. The fissure at its core, like the water that floats it off the mainland, keeps New York discreetly discontinuous from any one thing called America.

3 Place, Nature, and Culture in Discourses of Globalization

ARTURO ESCOBAR

On Place and Culture

The question of "place" has been raised newly in recent years from a variety of perspectives—from its relation to the basic understanding of being and knowing to its fate under economic globalization and the extent to which it continues to be an aid or a hindrance for thinking about culture. This questioning is, of course, not coincidental. For some, placelessness—a "generalized condition of homelessness," as some have called it—has become the essential feature of the modern condition and a very acute and painful one in many cases, such as those of exiles and refugees. Whether celebrated or decried, the sense of utopia seems to have settled in. This seems to be as true in Western philosophy, where place has been ignored by most thinkers (Casey 1993), in theories of globalization that have effected a significant erasure of place (Dirlik 2001), or in debates in anthropology, which have seen a radical questioning of place and place making. Yet the fact remains that place—as the experience of a particular location with some measure of groundedness, sense of boundaries, and connection to everyday life, even if its identity is constructed and never fixed—continues to be important in the lives of many people, perhaps most. There is an "implacement" that counts for more than we want to acknowledge, which makes one ponder if the idea of "getting

This chapter owes much to the work of and dialogue with Arif Dirlik, Julie Graham, and Mexican ecologist Enrique Leff, whose support and interest I greatly appreciate. It owes as much to Libia Grueso, Yellen Aguilar, and Carlos Rosero, of the Process of Black Communities (PCN, its Spanish acronym) of the Pacific Coast of Colombia, to whom I am deeply grateful for sharing with me their sophisticated knowledge and understanding of PCN's political ecology, discussed in part 3.

back into place," to use Casey's title, or a defense of place as project, in Dirlik's case, are not so irrelevant after all.

To be sure, the critique of place in anthropology, geography, communications, and cultural studies of recent times has been both essential and important and continues to be so. New metaphors of mobility—deterritorialization, displacement, diaspora, migration, traveling, border crossings, nomadology, and so on—have made us aware of the fact that the principal dynamics of culture and economy have been altered significantly by unprecedented global processes. Yet there has been a certain asymmetry in these debates. As Dirlik (2001) argues, this asymmetry is most evident in discourses of globalization, where the global is equated with space, capital, history, and agency, and the local with place, labor, and tradition. Place, in other words, has dropped out of sight in the "globalization craze" of recent years, which has profound consequences for our understanding of culture, knowledge, nature, and economy.[1] It is perhaps time to reverse some of this asymmetry by focusing anew—and from the perspective afforded by the critiques of place themselves—on the continued importance of place and place making for culture, nature, and economy.

This is, indeed, an increasingly felt need of those working at the intersection of environment and development. Not only are scholars and activists in environmental studies confronted with social movements that maintain a strong reference to place, but they also are faced with the grow-

---

1. Consider, for instance, the role of place in Manuel Castells's first volume on the "Information Age," *The Rise of the Network Society* (1996), a magisterial and in many ways essential book for understanding today's economy and society. For Castells, the rise of a new technological paradigm based on information, electronic, and biological technologies is resulting in a network society in which the "space of flows" overtakes the "space of places" and where "no place exists by itself, since positions are defined by flows. Places do not disappear but their logic and meaning become absorbed in the network, structural meaning disappears subsumed in the logic of the metanetwork" (412). In this new situation, places may be switched off, leading to their decline and deterioration; people and labor are fragmented in the space of places, as places get disconnected from each other ("elites are cosmopolitan, people are local" [415]). Although Castells, of course, seems to maintain a certain nostalgia for places where face-to-face interactions and local actions count (such as the Belville, who saw him come of age as a young intellectual), it is clear that the new paradigm is here to stay. This is one of the many instances of the asymmetry in globalization discourse about which Dirlik writes.

ing realization that any alternative course of action must take into account place-based models of nature with their accompanying cultural, ecological, and economic practices and rationalities. Debates on postdevelopment and political ecology are a hopeful arena for reintroducing a place-based dimension in discussions of globalization, perhaps even for articulating a defense of place. Said differently, a reassertion of place, noncapitalism, and local culture against the dominance of space, capital, and modernity, which are central to globalization discourses, should result in theories that make visible possibilities for reconstructing the world from the perspective of place-based practices.

This reassertion should be of interest to anthropology and cultural studies, which saw in the 1990s a powerful critique of conventional notions of culture as discrete, bounded, and integrated. This critique has been accompanied by a series of innovative inquiries into the relation between space, culture, and identity from the perspective of transnationalized processes of cultural and economic production. It has its roots in earlier developments in political economy and in the critique of representation, particularly during the 1980s; it has produced an important theoretical momentum of its own, constituting what is undoubtedly one of the most vibrant instances of anthropological debate and innovation today. Taking as a point of departure the problematic character of the relation between place and culture, these works emphasize that places are historical creations to be explained, not assumed, and that this explanation must take into account the ways in which the global circulation of capital, knowledge, and media configure the experience of locality. The focus thus shifts to the multiple links between identity, place, and power—between place making and people making—without naturalizing or constructing places as the source of authentic and essentialized identities.[2]

Always clear in this anthropological critique was the fact that places continue to be important for both the production of culture and its ethnogra-

2. It is not the point to recast these debates here. Some of the landmarks in the anthropological literature are Appadurai 1990, 1991; Gupta and Ferguson 1992; Hannerz 1989. These debates are recaptured in Gupta and Ferguson 1997, on which the remarks in this section are based. This collection constitutes the most important collective intervention on these issues to date.

phy (Gupta and Ferguson 1992). However, a certain, perhaps necessary, discursive excess in the argument has led to deemphasizing issues of groundedness, boundaries, meaning, and attachment to places that also constitute part of the experience of people and culture making. Is it possible to envision a defense of place without naturalizing, feminizing, or essentializing it, one in which place does not become the source of trivial processes or regressive forces? Can one reinterpret places as linking up to constitute networks, deterritorialized spaces, even rhizomes? Places that allow for traveling, border crossing, and partial identities without completely disabling notions of groundedness, boundaries, and belonging?

In the last instance, the goal of the present chapter is to examine the extent to which our frameworks do or do not allow us to visualize actual or potential ways of reconceiving and reconstructing the world embodied in manifold place-based practices. Which new forms of "the global" can be imagined from this perspective? Can we elevate place-based imaginaries—including local models of nature—to the language of social theory and project their potential onto novel types of globality so that they appear as alternative ways of organizing social life? In sum, to what extent can we reinvent both thought and the world according to the logic of place-based cultures? Is it possible to launch a defense of place with place as the rallying point for theory construction and political action? Is it possible to find in place-based practices a critique of power and hegemony without overlooking their embeddedness in circuits of capital and modernity?[3]

In what follows, I try to articulate the rudiments of a defense of place, on the one hand, by relying on works in postmodern geography as well as in poststructuralist and feminist political economy that explicitly address the question of place and, on the other hand, by reinterpreting from a place perspective some recent trends in ecological anthropology that document cultural models of nature. Part 1 of the chapter reviews the most recent works on local knowledge and models of nature in ecological anthropology and the anthropology of knowledge, rereading them from the perspective of place. With this background in mind, part 2 introduces a handful of recent

3. In other words, it is possible to approach places from an opposite direction—not from the side or its critique but from its affirmation, not from the side of the global but of the local. This is precisely what ecology allows you—indeed, forces you—to do.

works, particularly in postmodern and feminist geography and political economy, that self-consciously articulate a defense of place and place-based economic practices. I argue here that much as we need to overhaul conceptions and categories of the local, place and place-based knowledge continue to be essential for approaching globalization, postdevelopment, and ecological sustainability in socially and politically effective ways. Part 3, finally, brings the first two sections together by attempting to provide some guidelines for a place-based defense of local ecosystems and models within contexts of globalization and rapid change. I briefly outline the role of social movements and political ecology in the articulation of a defense of place. I leave out much that would have to be considered for a more substantial defense of place, including important issues such as the impact of digital technology (in particular the Internet) on place; the connections between place and class and gender; the linking up of places into networks; and the broader implications of the repatriation of place into anthropology, ecology, and area studies for conceptions of culture and nature. At the end, however, I briefly discuss the implications of the analysis for concepts of globalization, modernity, and area studies.[4]

1. The Place of Nature: Local Knowledge and Models of the Natural

The question of "local knowledge," in particular knowledge of natural systems, also has been raised newly in recent years from various perspectives (cognitive, epistemological, ethnobiological, and anthropological) and in connection with a variety of issues, from native taxonomies and biodiversity conservation to territorial politics and social movements. Attention has been focused on aspects such as the mechanisms by which local knowledge operates, including whether "local knowledge" itself is an appropriate label for the cognitive and experiential mechanisms at play in people's relation to nonhuman environments; the existence and structuring of cultural models of nature, in which local knowledge and classification systems themselves

4. A refined outline of the concept of "place" is beyond the scope of this paper. See Casey 1993 and 1997 for such an attempt within philosophy. I take "place" in an empirical and analytical sense—that is, as a category of thought and as a constructed reality.

would be immersed; and the relation between local and modern expert forms of knowledge in concrete ecological and institutional settings—for instance, in the context of development and conservation programs, particularly in tropical rain forest areas. Growing out of earlier concerns in ethnobotany, ethnoscience, and ecological anthropology, inquiry into local knowledge and cultural models of nature can be said to have come of age. This resurgence has yielded increasingly sophisticated accounts of people's constructions of nature and has provided us perhaps with the possibility of finally doing away with the binarism between nature and culture that has been so prereviewent and detrimental to ecological anthropology and related fields.[5]

Anthropologists, geographers, and political ecologists have been demonstrating with increasing eloquence that many rural communities in the Third World "construct" nature in strikingly different ways from prereviewent modern forms; they signify and thus use their natural environments in very particular ways. Ethnographic studies in Third World settings unveil a significantly different set of practices of thinking about, relating to, constructing, and experiencing the biological and the natural. This project was formulated some time ago and has achieved a remarkable level of sophistication in recent years. In a classic article on the subject, Marilyn Strathern (1980) made the case that we cannot interpret native (nonmodern) mappings of the social and the biological in terms of our concepts of nature, culture, and society. For many indigenous and rural groups, " 'culture' does not provide a distinctive set of objects with which one manipulates 'nature' . . . nature is not 'manipulated' " (174–75). "Nature" and "culture" thus need to be analyzed not as given and presocial but as cultural constructs if we wish to ascertain how they function as devices for cultural constructions, from human society to gender and the economy (MacCormack and Strathern 1980).

There is, of course, no unified view on just what characterizes local mod-

---

5. I have in mind the following volumes in particular: Descola and Pálsson 1996; Gudeman and Rivera 1990; Hobart 1993; MacCormack and Strathern 1980; Milton 1993; Milton 1996; Restrepo and del Valle 1996. Descola and Pálsson 1996 in particular is dedicated exclusively to examining cultural models of nature and to debunking once and for all the nature/culture dichotomy.

els of nature, although most ethnographic studies share some common features, including the following: a concern with epistemological questions, including the nature of the cognitive devices at play in cultural models of the
natural world and the commensurability or not of diverse models; the overall mechanisms through which nature is apprehended and constructed, in
particular the existence or absence of general schemes for nature construction, whether universal or not; and the nature of local knowledge, including
whether this knowledge is embodied and developed through practice or is
explicit and developed through thought processes of some kind. Perhaps the
most well-established notion today is that local models of nature do not rely
on a nature-society dichotomy. In addition, and unlike modern constructions with their strict separation between biophysical, human, and supernatural worlds, it is commonly appreciated that local models in many
non-Western contexts often are seen as predicated on links of continuity
among the three spheres. This continuity, which might nevertheless be experienced as problematic and uncertain, is established culturally through
symbols, rituals, and practices and is embedded in particular social relations
that also differ from the modern, capitalist type. In this way, living, nonliv-
ing, and often supernatural beings are not seen as constituting distinct and
separate domains, certainly not two opposed spheres of nature and culture,
and social relations are seen as encompassing more than humans. Descola,
for instance, argues that "in such 'societies of nature' plants, animals and
other entities belong to a socioeconomic community, subjected to the same
rules as humans" (Descola and Pálsson 1996, 14).

A local model of nature may exhibit features such as the following,
which may or may not correspond to the parameters of modern nature or
only partially: categorizations of human, social, and biological entities (for
instance, what is human and what is not, what is planted and what is not,
what is the domestic and what is the wild, what is produced by humans and
what is produced by forests, what is innate or what emerges from human action, what pertains to spirits and what pertains to humans, and so on);
boundary settings (differentiating, say, humans from animals, forest from
settlement, men from women, or among various parts of the forest); systematic classification of animals, plants, and spirits; and so on. It also may contain mechanisms for maintaining the good order and balance of the
biophysical, human, and supernatural circuits; or circular views of the time

and of biological and social life, ultimately validated by Providence, gods, or goddesses; or a theory of how all beings in the universe are "raised" or "nurtured" out of similar principles because in many nonmodern cultures the entire universe is conceived of as a living being with no strict separation between humans and nature, individual and community, community and the gods.[6]

Although specific formulae for arranging all of these factors vary greatly from group to group, they tend to have certain features in common: they reveal a complex image of social life that is not necessarily opposed to nature (in other words, one in which the natural world is integral to the social world) and that can be thought about in terms of particular cultural logics and social relations such as kinship, extended kindred, and vernacular or analogic gender. Local models also evidence a particular attachment to a territory conceived of as a multidimensional entity that results from many types of practices and relations; and they establish links between symbolic/cultural systems and productive relations that can be highly complex.[7]

This brings us fully into the issue of local knowledge. In recent anthropological approaches to local knowledge, there seems to be a certain convergence in treating knowing as "a practical, situated activity, constituted by a past, but changing history of practices" (Hobart 1993, 17)—that is, in assuming that local knowledge works more through a body of practices than through a reliance on formal system of shared, context-free knowledge (see also Ingold 1992, 1996). A related trend emphasizes the embodied aspects

6. This particular formulation is at the core of the work of the Peruvian group Proyecto Andino de Tecnología Campesina (PRATEC). See Apffel-Marglin and Valladolid 1995; E. Grillo 1991.

7. Is it necessary to say that not all local practices of nature are environmentally benign and that not all social relations that articulate them are nonexploitative? The extent to which local knowledge and practices of nature are "sustainable" or not is an empirical question. Gudrun Dahl has perhaps best summarized this point: "All people of necessity maintain ideas about, and of necessity act on, their natural environment. This does not necessarily mean that those who live as direct producers have great systematic insights, although on the whole subsistence producers have detailed knowledge about the working of many small aspects of their biological environment. Much of this knowledge has from experience proved to be true and efficient, some is misconceived and counterproductive, and some is incorrect but still functions well enough" (1993, 6).

of local knowledge, this time appealing to phenomenology. For Ingold (1995, 1996), the most articulate of these proponents, we dwell in a world that is not separate from us, and our knowledge of the world can be described as a process of enskillment in the context of practical engagement with the environment. Humans, in this view, are embedded in nature and engaged in situated, practical acts. For anthropologist Paul Richards (1993), local agricultural knowledge must be seen as time- and context-specific improvisational capacities rather than as a coherent "indigenous knowledge system," as earlier literature suggested. For others, local models are "experiments in living"; they are "developed through use" in the imbrication of local practices with larger processes and conversations (Gudeman and Rivera 1990, 14). This proposal suggests that we can treat practical, embodied knowledge as constituting a somewhat comprehensive model of the world. It is in this sense that the term *local model* is used in this chapter.

The consequences of this rethinking of local knowledge and local models are enormous. There exists, of course, the danger of reinscribing local knowledge into hierarchical constellations of knowledge forms and of recasting anew the dreviewuation, stigmatization, and subordination that has characterized it in much discussion on the subject (including in ethnobiological debates linked to biodiversity conservation). However, the displacement effected by this ethnographically oriented rethinking offers hope in a variety of ways. Perhaps the most important for our purposes is that the new thinking contributes to debunking the dichotomy between nature and culture that is fundamental to the dominance of expert knowledge in epistemological and management considerations. If this is the case, we must accept that the common view of distinct domains of nature and culture that can be known and managed separately from each other is no longer tenable.

What about place and its relation to the new views of local knowledge and cultural models just described? In general terms, what is most important about these models from the perspective of place is that they can be said to constitute ensembles of meanings and uses that, although existing in contexts of power that increasingly include transnational forces, can be neither reduced to modern constructions nor accounted for without some reference to grounds, boundaries, and local culture. Cultural models and knowledge are based on historical, linguistic, and cultural processes that, although never isolated from broader histories, nevertheless retain certain place specificity. Many aspects of the natural world stand in places. In addition, many of the mechanisms and practices at play in nature constructions—boundaries, classifications, representations, cognitive apprehensions, and spatial relations—are significantly place specific. Notions of performativity, enskillment, enactment, and practice also suggest important links to place. That place-based practices continue to be socially significant perhaps is stated more clearly by Gudeman and Rivera (1990), whose peasant models retained a place-based character despite the fact that they are the result of long-standing "conversations" and engagement with globalizing markets and economies. In their work, we find a nonglobalocentric view of globalization seen from the perspective of place and the local.

2. The Nature of Place: Rethinking the Local and the Global

Local knowledge is a mode of place-based consciousness, a place-specific way of endowing the world with meaning. Yet the fact remains that in our concern with globalization place has dropped out of sight. A few recent works try to move beyond this paradox by working through some of the epistemological traps that constrain theories of globalization. At the same time, they provide elements toward thinking beyond development—that is, for a conceptualization of postdevelopment that is more conducive to the creation of new types of languages, understanding, and action.[8] Novel debates on economy and place seem particularly useful in this regard. In these works, place is asserted against the dominance of capitalism as an imagery of social life.

Let us start with an enlightening critique of capitalocentrism in recent discourses of globalization, emerging out of certain trends in poststructuralist and feminist geography. For geographers Julie Graham and Catherine Gibson, most theories of globalization and postdevelopment are capitalo-

---

8. The notion of "postdevelopment" is a heuristic for relearning to see and reassess the reality of communities in Asia, Africa, and Latin America. Is it possible to lessen the dominance of development representations when we approach this reality? Postdevelopment is a way to signal this possibility, an attempt to carve out a clearing for thinking other thoughts, seeing other things, writing in other languages (see Crush 1995; Escobar 1995).

centric because they situate capitalism "at the center of development narratives, thus tending to dreviewue or marginalize possibilities of noncapitalist development" (Gibson-Graham 1996, 41). More generally, these authors present a powerful case against the claim, shared by mainstream and left theorists alike, that capitalism is the hegemonic, even the only, present form of economy and that it will continue to be so in the foreseeable future. Capitalism has been endowed with such dominance and hegemony that it has become impossible to think social reality differently, let alone to imagine the suppression of capitalism; all other realities (subsistence economies, Third World forms of resistance, cooperatives and minor local initiatives, hybrid economies) thus are seen as opposite, subordinate, or complementary to capitalism, never as sources of a significant economic difference. By criticizing capitalocentrism, these authors seek to liberate our ability for seeing noncapitalisms and for building alternative economic imaginaries.[9]

This reinterpretation challenges the inevitability of capitalist "penetration" that is assumed in much of the literature of globalization:

> In the globalization script . . . only capitalism has the ability to spread and invade. Capitalism is resented as inherently spatial and as naturally stronger than the forms of noncapitalist economy (traditional economies, "Third World" economies, socialist economies, communal experiments) because of its presumed capacity to universalize the market for capitalist commodities. . . . Globalization according to this script involves the *violation* and eventual death of "other" noncapitalist forms of economy. . . . All forms of noncapitalism become damaged, violated, fallen, subordinated to capitalism. . . . How can we challenge the similar representation of globalization

---

9. The argument is more complex than presented here and entails a redefinition of class on antiessentialist grounds that builds on Althusser's work and on the poststructuralist Marxism of Resnick and Wolff (1987). Briefly, at issue is both a reinterpretation of capitalist practices as overdetermined and the liberation of the economic discursive field from capital as a single overarching principle of determination. Coupled with a transformed definition of class that focuses on the processes of producing, appropriating, and disturbing surplus labor, this reinterpretation yields a view of the economy as constituted by a diversity of class processes— capitalist and noncapitalist—thus making visible a variety of noncapitalist practices by women wage earners, peasants, households, communal and self-help organizations, cooperatives, subsistence economies, and so on.

as capable of "taking" the life from noncapitalist sites, particularly the "Third World"? (Gibson-Graham 1996, 125, 130, emphasis in original)

Not everything that emerges from globalization can be said to conform to the capitalist script; in fact, globalization and development might propitiate a variety of economic-development paths, which can be theorized in terms of postdevelopment so that "the naturalness of capitalist identity as the template of all economic identity can be called into question" (Gibson-Graham 1996, 146). Gibson and Graham's goal is to provide an alternative language, a new class language in particular, for addressing the economic meaning of local practices. In the same vein, the goal of the postdevelopment literature is to make visible practices of cultural and ecological difference that might serve as the basis for alternatives. It is necessary to acknowledge that these goals are linked inextricably to conceptions of locality, place, and place-based consciousness.

Yet, as Arif Dirlik (2001) has pointed out, place and place-based consciousness have been marginalized in debates on the local and the global. This marginalization is doubly regrettable because place is central, on the one hand, to issues of development, culture, and the environment but is equally essential, on the other, for imagining other contexts for thinking about the construction of politics, knowledge, and identity. The erasure of place is a reflection of the asymmetry that exists between the global and the local in much contemporary literature on globalization, in which the global is associated with space, capital, history and agency while the local (Dirlik 2001, 17), conversely, is linked to place, labor, and tradition as well as with women, minorities, the poor, and, one might add, local cultures.[10] Some feminist geographers (Chernaik 1996) have attempted to correct this asymmetry by arguing that place also can lead to articulations across space—for instance, through networks of various kinds. To this important corrective must be added an inquiry into the relation between place and grounded experience.

10. This is very clearly the case in the environmental discourses of biodiversity conservation, for instance, where women and indigenous people are credited with having the knowledge of saving nature. Massey (1994) already has denounced the feminization of place and the local in theories of space. For a good example of the asymmetry Dirlik talks about, see the quotes from Castells 1996 in note 1, p. 38.

More fundamental perhaps in Dirlik's analysis are the consequences of the neglect of place for current categories of social analysis such as class, gender, and race (and we should add the environment here), which make such categories susceptible of becoming instruments of hegemony. To the extent that contemporary notions of culture are sundered significantly from place in the "globalization craze" of "deterritorialized identities" and in much discourse that privileges traveling, mobility, displacement, and diaspora, they do not manage to escape this predicament, for they tend to assume the existence of a global power to which the local necessarily is subordinated. Under these conditions, is it possible to launch a defense of place in which place and the local do not derive their meaning only from their juxtaposition to the global? Who speaks for "place"? Who defends it? As a first step in resisting the marginalization of place, Dirlik summons Lefebvre's distinction between space and place (between first and second space, in Lefebvre's work), in particular his notion of place as a form of lived and grounded space, the reappropriation of which must be part of any radical political agenda against capitalism and against spaceless and timeless globalization.

Politics also, in other words, is located in place, and not only in the supralevels of capital and space. Place, one might add, is the location of a multiplicity of forms of cultural politics—that is, of the cultural becoming political, as has become evident in rain forest and other ecological social movements. Can place be reconceived as a project? For this to happen, we need a new language. To return to Dirlik, *glocal* is a first approximation that suggests equal attention to the localization of the global and the globalization of the local. This two-way traffic is complex. Even "the local" of social movements against capital and modern natures are often a result of global processes in some ways—for instance, to the extent that social movements borrow metropolitan discourses of identity and the environment (Brosius 1997). Conversely, many forms of the local are offered for global consumption, from kinship to crafts and ecotourism. The point here would be to distinguish those forms of globalization of the local that can become effective political forces in defense of place and place-based identities, as well as those forms of localization of the global that locals can use to their own ends.

To turn place-based imaginaries into a radical critique of power and to align social theory with that critique require that we venture into other terrains. *Place* and *local knowledge*, to be sure, are no panaceas that will solve the world's problems. Local knowledge is not "pure" or free of domination; places might have their own forms of oppression and even terror; they are historical and connected to the wider world through relations of power and in many ways determined by them (Massey 1994, 1997). The defense of local knowledge proposed here is both political and epistemological, arising out of the commitment to an antiessentialist discourse of difference. It will be necessary, however, to expand the inquiry into place to consider broader questions, such as the relation of places to regional and transnational economies; place and social relations; place and identity; place and boundaries and broader crossing; hybridity; and the impact of digital technology, in particular the Internet, on places. What changes do occur in particular places as a result of globalization? Conversely, what new ways of thinking about the world emerge from places as a result of such an encounter? How do we understand the relations between biophysical, cultural, and economic dimensions of places?

What also emerges from these works, a point I take up in part 3, is the ability to differentiate further between place and "the local." The global and the local are scales, processes, or even levels of analysis, but certainly not places or locations as discussed here. The theorization of scale and scalar politics in geography of recent times has been very useful in this regard (Peck 2000; Swyngedouw 1998). Nevertheless, it is impossible to provide a definition of place that works from all and for all perspectives. As indicated earlier, in this chapter *place* refers to the experience of and from a particular location, with some sense of boundaries, grounds, and links to everyday practices. At the risk of being redundant, it is necessary to reiterate that all of these elements are constructed and not only by place-based processes. Boundaries and links to places are certainly neither natural nor fixed, and although boundaries do not exist in a "real" sense, their construction is an important aspect of the active material and cultural production of place by groups of people that, albeit heterogeneous and diverse, do share what Virilio (1997, 1999) calls the *hic et nunc* (here and now) of social practice. They do share many other things with "absent others" as well, as Giddens (1990) put it, and increasingly so. And as Ingold (1993) so perceptively has discussed, places can have boundaries only in relation to the activities of the people (the "taskscapes") or of the animals, for whom they are recognized and experienced as such. Even "natural boundaries" such as rivers and mountains follow this logic of construction. Finally, that places are also constituted by capital and "the global" should be clear by now—more on this issue in the part 3.

3. The Defense of Place: Political Ecology and Alternative Modernities

The defense of place can be linked to the practice of a number of actors, from social movement activists to historical archaeologists, ecological anthropologists, environmental psychologists, and political ecologists. A full exploration of these links is beyond the scope of this chapter; rather, in this last section, I present some general considerations for future research. To start with, many social movements—those of rain forest people in particular—invariably emphasize four fundamental rights: to the movements' identity, to their territory, to their political autonomy, and to their own vision of development. Most of these movements are conceived explicitly in terms of cultural difference and on the ecological differences that this difference makes. They are not movements for development and the satisfaction of needs, even if economic and material improvements are important for them. They are movements of cultural and ecological attachment to a territory. For them, the right to exist is a cultural, political, and ecological question. They necessarily are open to certain forms of the commodity, market exchange and to technoscience (for instance, through engagement with biodiversity conservation strategies), but they resist complete capitalist and scientific valorization of nature. They thus can be seen as advancing through their political strategy a tactics of postdevelopment and alternative ecological rationality, to the extent that they forcefully voice and defend discourses and practices of cultural, ecological, and economic difference.

In Colombia, black activists of the Pacific rain forest region progressively have articulated conceptions about territory and biodiversity in their interaction with local communities, state authorities, nongovernmental organizations (NGOs), and academic sectors. The territory is seen as a fundamental and multidimensional space for the creation and re-creation of the social, economic, and cultural values of the communities. The relationship between meanings and practices and the social relations in which they are embedded are being transformed today by the developmentalist onslaught that brings with it loss of knowledge and territory and that renders nature into a commodity. The demarcation of the collective territories granted to the region's black communities by the country's new Constitution (1991) has led activists to develop a conception of the territory that highlights articulations between patterns of settlement, use of spaces, and practices of meanings-uses of resources. This conception is validated by recent anthropological studies that document the cultural models of nature that exist among black river communities (Restrepo and del Valle 1996).[11]

Activists have introduced other important conceptual innovations, some of which have come about in the process of negotiation with the staff of a government biodiversity conservation project with whom they have maintained a difficult and tense, but in many ways fruitful relation. The first innovation is the definition of *biodiversity* as "territory plus culture." Closely related to it is a view of the Pacific as a "region-territory" of ethnic groups, an ecological and cultural unit—that is, a space that is constructed laboriously through the daily cultural, ecological, and economic practices of the black and indigenous communities. The region-territory could be said to be a management category of the ethnic groups that points toward the construction of alternative life and society models. It is a conceptual unit and a political project. It entails an attempt at explaining biological diversity from inside the ecocultural logic of the Pacific. The demarcation of collective territories fits into this framework, even if government dispositions—which di-

11. These comments are based chiefly on my knowledge of the social movement of black communities of the Colombian Pacific Coast that emerged in 1990 in the context of the reform of the national Constitution, which granted collective cultural and territorial rights to the black and indigenous communities, and of the increased pace of the activities by capital and the state. Important in the conformation of the movement, particularly since 1993, has been the national and international attention given to the region because of its rich biodiversity and genetic resources. It is not my purpose to describe and analyze the movement in depth in this chapter. I only want to indicate the most relevant aspects of the movement for my argument about place and cultural models of nature. I discuss the cultural politics of biodiversity in another piece (Escobar 1997), with a focus on the Pacific region. The development of the black movement is chronicled and analyzed in Grueso, Rosero, and Escobar 1998; the political ecology articulated by the movement as its members encounter issues of biodiversity conservation and sustainable development is presented in Escobar 1998. For background on the movement and the Pacific Coast in general, see Escobar and Pedrosa 1996.

vide up the Pacific region among collective territories, natural parks, areas of utilization, and even areas of sacrifice where megaprojects are to be constructed—violate this framework. The issue of territory is considered by community activists, organized as the Process of Black Communities (or PCN, its Spanish acronym), as a challenge to developing local economies and forms of governability that can support its effective defense. Strengthening and transforming traditional production systems and local markets and economies; pressing on with the collective titling process; and working toward organizational strengthening and the development of forms of territorial governance—all are important components of an overall strategy centered on the region.[12]

It is clear that the political ecology crafted by these social movements entails a defense of identity, place, and region that does not take for granted place and identity, even if it is couched as their defense. A collective construction of identity is, of course, crucial in this regard. In fact, this political ecology has been arrived at in the encounter with national and transnational forces and discourses—from the new forms of mining, timber, and agroindustrial capital moving into the Pacific region to biodiversity conservation strategies originally conceived by Northern environmental NGOs and international organizations—and in the context of a "national" space that is beginning to leak on all sides, causing a painful de- and recomposition of identities and regions. If territory is to be thought of as "the ensemble of projects and representations where a whole series of behaviors and investments can pragmatically emerge, in time and in social, cultural, aesthetic and cognitive space" (Guattari 1995, 23)—as an existential space of self-reference where "dissident subjectivities" (24) can emerge—then it is clear that this project is being advanced by the social movements of the Pacific.

The notion of territory being worked out by social movement activists and political ecologists can be said to enact a relation between place, culture, and nature. Similarly, the activists' definition of biodiversity as "territory plus culture" is another example both of place-based consciousness and of

12. This presentation of the political ecology framework developed by the PCN is based chiefly on conversations and in-depth interviews with key PCN activists conducted in the period 1994–97, in particular Libia Grueso, Carlos Rosero, and Yelen Aguilar; it is elaborated more extensively in Escobar 1998.

place and culture becoming a source of political facts. The local models of nature equally can be reinterpreted as constitutive of a variety of noncapitalist practices, many of which, albeit not all of them, are ecological. Ensembles of meanings-uses of the natural can be seen, for purposes of the present analysis, as at least potentially endowed with noncapitalist economic meaning. Community economies are grounded in place (even if not bound to place because they participate in translocal markets), and they often rely on holding a commons consisting of land, material resources, knowledge, ancestors, spirits, and so on (Gudeman 1996; Gudeman and Rivera 1990).

The implications of a place perspective for ecological anthropology are also substantial. Ethnographically, the focus would be in documenting meanings-uses of the natural as a concrete statement of place-based knowledge. From a multiplicity of ensembles of meanings-uses, ecological anthropologists might posit a defense of place couched as the possibility of redefining and reconstructing the world from the perspective of manifold place-based cultural logics. This is a question they seem to shy away from, but one that they need to tackle head on in order to articulate a discourse of ecological difference. Social movement activists and political ecologists, as we saw, are engaged with this task already. Environmental psychologists have begun to develop ecosystem-management tools based more clearly on the concept of place. Going beyond the dominant instrumental conception of management and inventories, these scholars emphasize the cultural meanings through which places—and, indeed, ecosystems—are constructed. In thus viewing ecosystems as socially constructed places, they conclude that "the heart of ecosystems management is to guide decisions affecting a place using a rich understanding of its natural and cultural history" (Williams and Patterson 1996, 18). Similarly, "resource decisions should be guided by an understanding of all the social processes that define, structure and alter the meaning of landscapes" (Williams and Patterson 1996, 20). This position is a far cry from conventional views driven by an instrumental or commodity paradigm.

Is it possible, then, to accept that places are always being defended and re-created and that different economies are always on the rise? That alternative ecological practices not only can be documented but have always been struggled for in many localities? Daring to give serious consideration to these questions certainly supposes a different politics of reading on our part as analysts, with the concomitant need to contribute to a different politics of representation of reality. It also supposes that postdevelopment is already (and has always been) under continuous (re)construction (Rahnema and Bawtree 1997). It is in the spirit of postdevelopment that we can rethink sustainability and conservation as key aspects of the politics of place.

A fundamental question remains, of course, regarding the conditions of possibility for the defense and strengthening of place. Through real and virtual networks of all kinds, through social movement coalitions, and through heterogeneous alliances of diverse actors such as scholars, activists, NGOs, and so on, it is clear that place-based struggles are beginning to create supraplace effects and realities. How can these realities be conceptualized? What are the real effects on the local and the global? Do they have a real opportunity for redefining power and at what levels? What particular coalitions seem most promising? I devote the last few pages of this chapter to this burning question.[13]

At the level of knowledge, the question is deceptively clear: How is local knowledge to be translated into power and this knowledge-power into concrete projects and programs? How can local knowledge-power constellations build bridges with expert forms of knowledge when necessary or convenient, and how can they widen their social space of influence when confronted, as it is most often the case, with detrimental local, regional, national, and transnational conditions? An anthropology of globalization predicated on the need to identify both socially significant discourses of difference (cultural, ecological, economic, political) and the ways in which they can operate as discourses of articulation of alternatives would examine the manifold ways of constructing culture, nature, and identities today. It also would look at the production of differences through historicospatial processes that are not solely the product of global forces—whether capitalism, new technologies, market integration, or what have you—but that also are linked to places and their defense. It is important to make visible the manifold local logics of production of cultures and identities, economic and

13. I analyze in some detail the politics of networks, in particular those facilitated by the Internet, in another piece focused on women's and ecology networks (Escobar 1999).

ecological practices, that are emerging ceaselessly from communities world-wide. To what extent do they pose important and perhaps original challenges to capitalism and Euro-centered modernities?

Once place-based practices are visible, however, what would be the conditions that would allow them to create alternative structures that would give those structures a chance to survive, let alone grow and flourish? This last aspect of "the question of alternatives" remains largely intractable. For Dirlik, the survival of place-based cultures will be ensured when the globalization of the local compensates for the localization of the global—that is, when symmetry between the local and the global is reintroduced in social and conceptual terms and, we need to add, when noncapitalism and different cultures similarly are rendered into centers of analysis and strategies for action. In the last instance, however, the imagination and realization of significantly different orders demand "the projection of places into spaces to create new structures of power . . . in ways that incorporate places into their very constitution" (Dirlik 2001, 39). It also calls for the release of noncapitalist imaginaries into the constitution of economies and economic structures as well as for the defense of local cultures from their normalization by dominant cultures so that they can become effective political and life forces. For this to happen, places must "project themselves into the spaces that are presently the domains of capital and modernity" (Dirlik 2001, 39). Some social movements are pointing the way with their redefinition of the relation between nature and society, the cultural and the political.

It is clear that places increasingly are subjected to the operations of global capital, even more so in the age of neoliberalism and downsizing of the nation-state. This situation, however, only gives poignancy to the question of regions and localities. Networks such as those of indigenous people, environmentalists, NGOS, and other social movements are becoming more numerous and influential at local, national, and transnational levels. Many of these networks can be seen as producing place-based yet transnationalized identities. They also can be thought of as producing "glocalities" alternative to those of global capital, media, and culture. All glocalities are both local and global, but they are not local and global in the same way (Dirlik 2001). It is important to consider those that enact a cultural politics in the defense of place and nature. These glocalities might propitiate visible reorganizations of space from below and the reconquering of space out of their very place attachment. The making of "areas" and regional worlds is becoming an increasingly salient and contested process with growing globalization. Emerging actors, practices, and identities shape the double-sided process of socionatural and sociocultural regional world making. And although networks of sociocultural and socionatural world making increasingly are tied to networks of economy and technoscience (Castells 1996), place-based social actors increasingly are adept at negotiation in the entire world-making process.

It should be emphasized again that this process in no way entails reifying places, local cultures, and forms of noncapitalism as "untouched" or outside of history. To speak about activating local places, cultures, natures, and knowledge against the imperializing tendencies of space, capitalism, and modernity is not a deus ex machina operation, but a way to move beyond the chronic realism fostered by established modes of analysis. Surely places and localities are brought into the politics of commodification and cultural massification, but the knowledge of place and identity can contribute to the production of different meaning—of economy, nature, and each other—within the conditions of capitalism and modernity that surround that knowledge. Alternative ecological public spheres might be opened up in this way against the imperial ecologies of nature and identity in capitalist modernity.

It is at the intersection of place-based models of nature and economy, on the one hand, and the theorization of alternative productive rationalities, on the other, that we might find a broader framework in which to situate debates on cultural and ecological sustainability. This broader framework necessitates new ways of thinking about global-local intersections, such as those contributed by the theories of place; by alternative views of local knowledge and innovation and their relation to formal, global knowledge; by a reinterpretation of the political claims of social movements in terms of the defense of local models of nature and biological territories with specific cultural-biological productivities (Varese 1996); and by notions of grassroots forms of governance based on ecological ethnicities, protection of communities from certain aspects of the market, and a simultaneous revitalization of ecology and democracy (Parajuli n.d.).

Finally, this broader framework has implications for how we think about globalization, modernity, and area studies. If it is true that globalization is characterized most by connectivity (the narrowing down of both physical and cultural distance with the concomitant transformation of local orders), it is also patently clear by now that the ideas and practices of globalizing modernity are appropriated and reembedded in locally situated practices, giving rise to a plethora of modernities through the assemblage of diverse cultural elements (see, for instance, Arce and Long 2000). And if it is true that globalization weakens the ties of culture to place (deterritorialization), and locals lose the power to define the terms of their existence, it is also true that this process is met sometimes by countertendencies to restore the power of place over the definition of locality, even if within an increasingly global horizon (Tomlinson 1999). What this means is that places continue to be of importance for thinking about modernity, globalization, areas, and regions. "Areas," to be sure, are the result of active processes of construction, but the elements that go into such construction range across scales, from the local to the global. The contribution of place-based social actors to the construction of areas and regional socionatural worlds is often not negligible. It is necessary to imagine multiple modernities from multiple place perspectives; even if all of these perspectives are immersed in global horizons, the genealogies of the cultural, ecological, and economic practices that determine each of them are certainly different. These genealogies of place-based practices are crucial for imagining areas and regional worlds, given the connections to forms of power they necessarily continue to maintain, however weakened by the will of globalization.

What redefinitions of meanings and practices of the economy, nature, and social relations are necessary to advance the project of imagining alternatives to development and to unsustainable and unequal ecological practices? What types of research and what political practices by intellectuals, social movements, and communities are required to give social force to such a project? Whose definitions of the local and the global, of place, nature, culture, and economy one uses is, indeed, crucial. The critique of the privilege of space over place, of capitalism over noncapitalism, of global cultures and natures over local ones is as much a critique of our understanding of the world as of social theories on which we rely to derive such understanding. This critique is also an attempt to bring social theory into line with the views of the world and with the political strategies of those who exist on the side of place, noncapitalism, and local knowledge—an effort to which anthropologists and ecologists usually are committed. If it is true that forms of postdevelopment, noncapitalism, and alternature are always under construction, there is hope that they may get to constitute new grounds for existence and significant rearticulations of subjectivity and alterity in their economic, cultural, and ecological dimensions. In many parts of the world, we are witnessing an unprecedented historical movement of economic, cultural, and biological life. It is necessary to think about the political and economic transformations that may make such a movement a hopeful turn of events in the social history of cultures, economies, and ecologies.

In the latter instance—suggested at least by a utopian imagination as the critique of the current hegemonies—the question becomes: Can the world be reconceived and reconstructed according to the logic of local practices of culture, nature, and economy? Which regional worlds and which forms of "the global" can be imagined from other, multiple local perspectives? Which counterstructures can be set into place to make them viable and productive? What notions of politics, democracy, development, and the economy are needed to release the effectiveness of the local in all its multiplicity and contradictions? What role will various social actors—including technologies old and new—have to play in order to create the networks on which manifold forms of the local can rely in their encounter with the multiple manifestations of the global? Some of these questions will have to be given serious consideration in our efforts to give shape to the imagination of alternatives to the current order of things.

4 The Disappearing Local

Rethinking Global-Local Connections

ANGELIQUE HAUGERUD

Inscriptions such as "Queen of Sheba," "Smooth Criminal II," "Eden," "Let God Decide," "Good Morning Meru," "Michigan Choice," "Candle in the Wind," and "Monica" appear in radiant colors on Kenya's *matatu,* the ubiquitous minibuses and minivans that operate as private taxis in town and countryside. A centerpiece of popular culture and complaint, *matatu* often play the latest African or European music, are overloaded with passengers, and operate in less than optimum mechanical condition.[1] These vehicles' bright exteriors offer lively evidence of transnational cultural flows, illustrating the incorporation into Kenyan popular culture of the Lewinsky scandal, Princess Diana's death, the Bible, Hollywood films, and North American geography. The pathways by which such cultural symbols travel the globe cannot be depicted in tidy maps or flow diagrams. Nor can the effects of such symbols on the imaginations or the social and moral maps of people in Africa be assessed easily. Furthermore, global economic, financial, or political connections and flows are no easier to model or track than are

I am grateful to Frank Holmquist and Ron Kassimir for extremely helpful suggestions on an earlier version of this chapter. I also thank the anonymous reviewers and the participants in the October 1998 conference at Hampshire College from which this volume originates, part of the Ford Foundation's program "Crossing Borders: Revitalizing Area Studies."

1. Such vehicle slogans are found elsewhere in Africa as well. For example, see Lawuyi's (1997) discussion of Yoruba taxi slogans and Chinua Achebe's description in *Anthills of the Savannah* (1987) of a bus popularly known as "Luxurious," which carries a fleeing political dissident from the capital to a remote part of the countryside; this bus "had inscribed on its blue body in reds, yellow and whites three different legends: . . . *What a man commits . . . All Saints Bus . . . and Angel of Mercy*" (186).

cultural flows. All of these forms of globalization signal profound changes in the world that academics are only beginning to understand. In such a world, is the term *local* any longer definable or meaningful?

The "local" is construed in contradictory ways: as a residual category overtaken by development, as a haven of resistance against globalization, or as a historical or cultural construct. Each of these images conveys partial truths, but all are problematic as means of understanding global-local connections. These notions of the local tend to erase it, romanticize it, or essentialize it. Such shortcomings signal deeper epistemological and conceptual challenges to understanding globalization as profound world changes race beyond our familiar analytic vocabularies.[2] This chapter explores contradictory scholarly images of the local and argues that notions of both the "global" and the "local" need to be problematized. More productive than reinvocations of global-local dichotomies—and their reinscription in false oppositions between social science theory and area studies—is exploration of the historically contingent ways in which these two domains constitute one another or operate in dynamic tension.

The Disappearing Local?

There are at least two senses in which the local sometimes appears to disappear. The first is in the familiar (and now declining) postwar development paradigm of modernization theory, nation building, import substitution, and a belief in technological progress under nationally managed economic growth modeled on a "Western" path (McMichael 1996).[3] Scholars such as Escobar (1995), Ferguson (1990), and Sachs (1992) argue that a monolithic development apparatus erases the local by imposing uniform categories, assumptions, programs, and policies. Thus, a nation such as Lesotho

2. As Prewitt puts it, "we have only begun to explore the true meaning and significance of phenomena that have raced beyond the vocabularies to which we have grown accustomed" (1996, 35). Or, as Rosenau writes, we are at an "early stage in a profound ontological shift, a restless search for new ways of understanding unfamiliar phenomena" (1997, 360).

3. On shifts in postwar development theory and policy, see also Rapley 1996 and Leys 1996; the latter notes that "By the mid-1980s the real world on which 'development theory' had been premised had . . . disappeared. Above all, national and international controls over capital movements had been removed, drastically curtailing the power of any state wishing to promote national development" (7).

becomes a generic "Less-Developed Country," whose deficiencies are defined to correspond to the kinds of technical interventions development agencies can administer anywhere (Ferguson 1990). The World Bank's country report on Lesotho falsely casts it as a generic place of "primordial isolation," an aboriginal, ahistorical, " 'traditional' society somehow untouched by the modern world" (Ferguson 1990, 32)—an image that overlooks the country's long history of agricultural commercialization and migrant labor. In addition to homogenizing the local, development discourse often naturalizes poverty, as in the construction of Egypt as object of development in U.S. Agency of International Development (USAID) reports, whose narratives focus on nature, geography, and demography rather than on politics, power, and economic inequality (Mitchell 1991a). In short, as the "local" is homogenized or naturalized in development agency reports, it takes on a generic form that suggests the location in question will benefit from an array of standardized interventions or "blueprint development" (Roe 1991).

Objections to or critiques of standard development narratives (such as the tragedy of the commons) on the basis of location-specific information may increase uncertainty among policy decision makers, but critiques do not displace these narratives or eliminate development blueprints. Indeed, microlevel uncertainty merely heightens development planners' desire for "broad explanatory narratives that can be operationalized into standard approaches with widespread application" (Roe 1991, 288). The only effective replacement for a faulty blueprint narrative, Roe (1991) suggests, is either a new counternarrative or a modified version of a standard narrative. That is, development planning demands compelling stories with universal programmatic implications. A focus on local diversity and unpredictability simply confuses things and paralyzes the development enterprise.

States, too, prefer simplifications of local complexities in the societies they govern (Scott 1998).[4] That preference, Scott (1998) argues, helps to explain development disasters or why schemes intended to better the human

4. Scott notes as well that in this era when states have had to curtail their ambitions dramatically, "large-scale capitalism is just as much an agency of homogenization, uniformity, grids and heroic simplification as the state is, with the difference being that, for capitalists, simplification must pay" (1998, 7–8).

condition often have turned out to be deadly. The state's simplifications are both necessary and dangerous. They are necessary in order to bring into sharp focus and to render legible forms of reality that otherwise are complex and unwieldy—such as customs of personal naming, land tenure, or forestry. Simplification makes these phenomena more amenable to "careful measurement and calculation on the one hand and to control and manipulation on the other" (Scott 1995, 29). Thus, permanent last names were created, weights and measures standardized, cadastral surveys and population registers established, freehold tenure created, language and legal discourse standardized, cities designed, collective farms set up, field and plantation layouts regularized (Scott 1998, 2). Codifications such as state cadastral maps do not merely describe (in idealized or simplified fashion) a system of land tenure; they create the very system imagined by giving the new categories the force of law (Scott 1998, 2). Lost in the process are a myriad of informal practices, forms of local knowledge, and improvisations that enable people to cope with unpredictability. Without uncritically valuing local knowledge and practices, Scott (1998) makes a case for the resilience and advantages of both social and natural diversity (noting, for example, the dangers of monocropping). He also suggests, but deliberately leaves undeveloped, the notion that his argument could be turned as well against "a certain kind of reductive social science" (1998, 7). That is, just as large institutions such as states must simplify reality in order to govern, so too "scholars simplify the societies they study" (Scott 1995, 36). I return later to this idea about reductionism in social science knowledge.

A second sense—from an entirely different theoretical orientation—in which the local appears to disappear is when it is viewed as a historical or cultural construct.[5] That is, the "local" is not a fixed, bounded, or natural geographic space. Instead of assuming that localities or regions are natural units to be discovered, attention shifts to how they are produced and for what strategic purposes they are invoked in particular historical struggles. If space is a useful metaphor, it now must be imagined in non-Euclidean terms, "with unbounded, often discontinuous and interpenetrating sub-spaces" (Kearney 1995, 549). Gone are yesterday's metaphors of neatly specified

---

5. This paragraph draws heavily on Haugerud in press.

"levels" of analysis (local, regional, national, global) or tidy maps of peoples and cultures fixed to well-bounded localities (see Gupta and Ferguson 1997a; Malkki 1997). Instead of spatially fixed identities or clearly marked centers and peripheries, we have diaspora, hybridity, interstitiality, imagined localities, local-global continua, and peripheries imploding into centers.[6] Our attention is drawn to borderlands, frontiers, and "a world of disjunctive global flows" (Appadurai 1996, 47). Corresponding to these new understandings of space are nonteleological notions of historical time and development (see Cooper and Packard 1997; Escobar 1995; Ferguson 1990). Cultural forms, moreover, now are better conceived as polythetically overlapping, rather than possessing two-dimensional "Euclidean boundaries, structures or regularities" (Appadurai 1996, 46). Culture is less global mosaic than global ecumene (Hannerz 1997, 164); the demarcation of cultural units appears to be more arbitrary than natural. To capture various dimensions of global cultural flows, Appadurai (1996) has coined the neologisms *ethnoscapes, mediascapes, technoscapes, financescapes,* and *ideoscapes.* He intends the suffix *-scape* to highlight the "fluid, irregular shapes of these landscapes, shapes that characterize international capital as deeply as they do international clothing styles;" in addition, these *-scapes* are perspectival constructs rather than "objectively given relations that look the same from every angle of vision" (33). Thus, they take on different shapes from the vantage points of states, multinational corporations, diasporic communities, subnational groups, villages, neighborhoods, and families.

In short, many believe that understanding globalization requires us to overturn earlier assumptions—to address deterritorialized identities, nonteleological development, and nonspatial regions.[7] The local in this view is a historical product, one that both shapes and is shaped by global processes. The local is no longer to be equated with "pristine cultures" or with the

6. The latter notion is from Kearney, who refers to "the implosion of peripheries into centers, affected by transnational migration, global marketing, electronic media, and tourism" (1995, 550).

7. See Kearney's (1995, 552–53, 557) discussion of various forms of deterritorialization as well as Sivaramakrishnan and Agrawal's (in press) discussion of regions as both discursive and spatial entities.

parochial, the traditional, or the static, but rather with "complex and specific negotiations between history and globality" (Appadurai and Breckenridge 1995b, 16). Analysis, then, may focus on how to engage the global in local sites, how global cultural flows are received and transformed locally (Appadurai and Breckenridge 1995a, viii), and the historical processes that link local sites to one another.[8]

Thus, when "Monica" and "Candle in the Wind" are painted on Kenyan *matatu,* their meanings are inflected locally, remade, and embedded in local moral discourses and debates. Globalization of the local as well as localization of the global require attention; global cultural traffic does not follow unidirectional paths from "center" to "periphery." Cultural cross-fertilization (between North America and Africa) is apparent, for example, in the music of Hugh Masekela and in Paul Simon's *Graceland* (Hannerz 1997, 166, 169; see also Erlmann 1997). Indistinct local-nonlocal boundaries are evident as well in Kenyan national political culture, which is not a disembodied entity overhanging discrete "local" cultures (Haugerud 1995). There is cultural continuity as well as discontinuity across the worlds of kin group elders, appointed chiefs, district and provincial commissioners, cabinet ministers, president, and foreign dignitaries. The political language of the state and that of localities are not discrete domains. As Parkin notes more generally, there is a "cross-fertilization of ideas transacted across constantly shifting cultural boundaries" (1990, 195).

Thus, critiques of notions of the "local" point to its fuzzy, nonspatial boundaries so that global and local processes or identities are not necessarily even distinguishable. The boundaries of the local are more political, rhetorical, or social than natural or geographical (Forbes 1996, 31; Hannerz 1997, 164; McMichael 1996, 51). It is not the local as entity but rather the local in its historically constructed relational field that makes global restructuring processes concrete (McMichael 1996, 51). Space and locale have not become irrelevant to individual experiences, but rather analytical attention has shifted to "how spatial meanings are worked, reworked, and fought over . . .

8. Appadurai refers to a strategy for "engaging the global modern in a specific site" (1996, 201 n. 2).

how space is 'reterritorialized' " under contemporary conditions (Watts 1992, 18).[9] Local transformation is an integral part of globalization; what happens in one urban neighborhood is likely to be affected by faraway world money and commodity markets. The resulting changes are apt to be contradictory rather than unilinear; for example, a complex network of global economic relationships may causally link enrichment of an urban area in Singapore to the impoverishment of a Pittsburgh neighborhood no longer able to sell its products competitively on world markets (Giddens 1990, 64–65). That is, paths of local change cannot be predicted mechanically from a universal global script. The global script itself is influenced by local transformations.

Reimagining the Local, Resisting Development

If the local is obliterated or homogenized by the dominant postwar development paradigm or understood as a constructed rather than naturally bounded unit, it nonetheless reemerges as a singular entity among some who imagine a postdevelopment era. In a reversal of modernization theory's assumption that "traditional" communities pose obstacles to development or change, some scholars and activists now celebrate community as the locus of participatory development initiatives and valuable "local" knowledge and practices. Globalization has brought new attention to identity politics, self-determination, ideas of local cultural recovery or preservation of "indigenous" knowledges, and a search for local protections against marginalization by global markets. Thus, Escobar (1995) critiques the illusion of a homogeneous Third World and imagines a postdevelopment era that avoids universalizing paradigms and respects local heterogeneity, hybridity, resistance, knowledge, political mobilization, popular culture, and collective action. Al-

9. Watts also observes that "the nonlocal processes driving capital mobility are always experienced, constituted and mediated locally. . . . If the local is to be theorized, then this should be undertaken in such a way that external determinations are articulated with internal agency, with locally shared knowledges and practices, with shared but socially differentiated meanings and experiences" (1992, 6).

though acknowledging the dangers of uncritically celebrating place,[10] critics of development see hope in the emergence of a new politics wherein "the local can inform the global," where the local becomes an "important source of critique and change" (Escobar and Harcourt 1998, 4; see also Crush 1995 and Escobar 1995).[11]

The state decentralization and privatization occurring under neoliberal reform programs may open new opportunities for local political and economic renewal, some argue (see McMichael 1996, 42). Under the globalization paradigm that succeeded developmentalism during the 1980s debt crisis,[12] some localities may carve out specialized—and precarious—economic niches in a global economy (McMichael 1996). Indeed, the unpredictable dynamics of such economic specialization (which includes marginalization) define the way capitalism is stabilized under globalization.[13] Such local differentiation may be contrasted with the universalist project of replication under the earlier developmentalist paradigm, wherein external influences were assumed to be benign and all nations were to replicate a "Western" path to modernity. Today many regard the latter notion of development as an illusion; such "[d]evelopment has evaporated," declares Sachs (1992, 22), arguing that it is time to recognize the structural impossi-

10. See Giddens's discussion of the distinction between *space* and *place*. "Place", he says, is "best conceptualized by means of the idea of locale, which refers to the physical settings of social activity as situated geographically. In pre-modern societies, space and place largely coincide, since the spatial dimensions of social life are, for most of the population, and in most respects, dominated by 'presence'—by localised activities. The advent of modernity increasingly tears space away from place by fostering relations between 'absent' others, locationally distant from any given situation of face-to-face interaction" (1990, 18).

11. Escobar observes that "the Third World should in no way be seen as a reservoir of 'traditions' " (1995, 215). Neither should grassroots movements that resist development be seen as essentialized identity construction; rather, "these processes of identity construction [are] . . . flexible, modest, and mobile, relying on tactical articulations arising out of the conditions and practices of daily life" (215).

12. McMichael (1996), among others, discusses how the globalization paradigm brought a turn toward export production and away from protectionism or import substitution. In addition, norms of efficiency and discipline in a global economy displaced national economic priorities such as welfare and equity. See also Leys 1996.

13. This sentence and the next are points made by McMichael (1996).

bility of a universal realization of the material goals of development.[14] Instead, he suggests, politics must be renewed at the grassroots level. As another contributor to Sachs's edited volume *The Development Dictionary* puts it, most people on earth must resist development, "disengag[e] from the economic logic of the market," turn to the local, and reconstitute village or neighborhood life "on their own terms," creating a "new commons" (Esteva 1992, 20–21).

Postdevelopment approaches tend to view states as simply the agents of brutal or failed modernization rather than as possible vehicles of democratization and beneficial access to markets.[15] A turn to the local, however, may be as likely a prescription for poverty as for improved livelihoods. The postdevelopment approach raises questions about the circumstances under which "local" people might prefer a state that works for them rather than state withdrawal.

Deromanticizing the Local,
Resisting Resistance to Development

There are a number of drawbacks to the idea of the local as a haven of resistance against development. Watts, for example, in analyzing the struggles of Ogoni peoples in southeastern Nigeria, argues that calls to localism or appeals to cultural identity entail "nothing necessarily anti-capitalist or particularly progressive. . . . [C]alls to localism can produce Hindu fascism as easily as Andean Indian cooperatives" (1998, 6).[16] That is, there is a danger in uncritically privileging or romanticizing the local, place, culture, "the people," or popular discourse from below without acknowledging "the potentially deeply conservative, and occasionally reactionary, aspects of such

14. By the late 1980s, altered global economic circumstances (including deregulation of capital markets, rising debt burdens, growing economic inequality, and reduction of the state's role in development) were reflected in the scaling down of official development goals so that even the "basic needs" of the poor were to be sacrificed (Leys 1996, 25–26).

15. My thanks to Frank Holmquist for raising the issues mentioned in this paragraph.

16. Page numbers cited for Watts 1998 are from the prepublication manuscript. Although extreme versions of localism or cultural essentialism have become the basis of apartheid (Hannerz 1997, 164) or of genocide, antiessentialist grassroots movements nonetheless are possible, as Escobar (1995, 215) suggests.

local particularisms" (6). Furthermore, Watts says, such invocations of the "local" often overlook the ways that "the 'local' is never purely local, but is created in part by extra-local influences and practices over time" (6).[17] Watts then notes that the ostensibly unified Pan-Ogoni organization Movement for the Survival of the Ogoni People (MOSOP) relies on no Pan-Ogoni myth of origin and encompasses some Ogoni subgroups that are more loyal to local identities than to Ogoni nationalism. Indeed, one such subgroup sometimes argues that they are *not* Ogoni. In addition, there are divisions among MOSOP leaders, traditional clan leaders, the vigilante MOSOP youth wing, and state government leaders and civil servants. What Ken Saro-Wiwa did, Watts suggests, "was to build upon over fifty years of Ogoni organizing and upon three decades of resentment against the oil companies, to provide a mass base and a youth driven radicalism—and it must be said an international visibility—capable of challenging state power" (1998, 11–12). Rather than an idealized grassroots movement and unproblematic invocation of authentic cultural identity, MOSOP might as well be seen as a fractious, unstable, hybrid entity—"a much more complex sort of social movement than the postdevelopment literature might admit" (12).

It may be an illusion to imagine that a "pristine postdevelopment era" is possible (Agrawal 1996, 466). The concept rests in part on dubious distinctions that favor so-called indigenous knowledges and communities, local peoples, nonparty politics, or nongovernmental organizations (NGOs), whose transformative capacities poststructuralist theorists may overestimate (Agrawal 1996, 475).[18]

Effective NGOs, for example, may owe their success less to their "local" identity than to their global or international capabilities. For example, a special issue of *Cultural Survival Quarterly* (fall 1996) focuses on the question

---

17. William Fisher states that "we need to realize that [local situations] are neither good nor bad. . . . [We need to] recognize the presence of unequal relationships of power locally even as we expose them globally" (1996, 139). He also suggests that Escobar verges on romanticizing the local and that we need to recognize that resistance does not necessarily spring from unified motives. He emphasizes the need to explore how local and transnational, center and periphery, Third World and First World are intertwined or inextricably linked.

18. See also Agrawal 1995 on problems with the category "indigenous knowledge" and Agrawal and Gibson (forthcoming) on difficulties with notions of community "as a small spatial unit, as a homogeneous social structure, and as shared norms."

"Who's local here?" in relation to participatory development approaches and the micropolitics of development. Contributors point to the dangers of assuming an unproblematic community and suggest that analytic attention be shifted "away from a search for the legitimate 'local' toward an understanding of the processes by which different identity claims are employed to achieve different strategic ends" (Forbes 1996, 32). Thus, one would recognize that NGOs' claims to "localness" are important legitimizing strategies in an era when local participation and indigenous knowledge have become "buzzwords of authenticity" (Forbes 1996, 31). Such claims to localness should neither be taken at face value nor cynically dismissed. Rather, analysis should focus on the strategic uses and consequences of such claims and on the various local and nonlocal histories and networks in which they are embedded. Two Nepali NGOs that opposed the World Bank's proposed construction of a hydropower project in Arun were made up of human rights activists, lawyers, engineers, economists, management experts, and journalists. Though describing both organizations as "local" was important in mobilizing international opposition to the project, their leaders readily admitted that the claim of "localness" could be contested easily (Forbes 1996, 31). Moreover, the effectiveness of Nepali NGOs "depends on their skills in moving across boundaries, not on their ability to claim a fixed identity attached to one particular place" (Forbes 1996, 31). It is thus important to trace global-local connections and networks and their political significance in the development enterprise, rather than to reify any particular entity or organization as simply "local."

The 1994 Chiapas rebellion in Mexico is another illustration of how global and local are intertwined in resistance to particular forms of development and of how peasant protests may be inspired less by a desire for local autonomy than for a state that works for them.[19] The Chiapas protest, sparked in part by the grievances of small farmers in the region, had larger causes beyond the region as well. The latter included inequalities associated with the coincident implementation of the North American Free Trade Agreement (NAFTA), which to the Chiapas rebels "completed the undermining of the revolutionary heritage in the Mexican national Constitution

---

19. Frank Holmquist raised the latter point. This discussion of the Chiapas rebellion is drawn from McMichael 1996, 43–45.

of 1917" (McMichael 1996, 43). Peasants opposed the Mexican government's 1992 opening of communal or *ejido* lands for sale to domestic and foreign agribusinesses, as well as NAFTA's proposed deregulation of markets for commodities such as maize, a local staple food. The Zapatistas pressed for inclusion in the political process, challenged old patterns of local patronage politics, and demanded ecologically sustainable local development projects. The rebellion took on a Pan-Mayan identity rather than a locally specific ethnic one. In coinciding with the implementation of NAFTA, this revolt contributed to long-term opposition to new global economic rules (e.g., the General Agreement on Tariffs and Trade [GATT] Uruguay Round) and helped to destabilize the monetary system (as in the December 1994 Mexican peso crisis), contributing indirectly to new efforts to stabilize world monetary relations. All of these connections illustrate the interpenetration of global and local processes (McMichael 1996, 45). Globalization is characterized by such unpredictable and contradictory processes, not by an inevitable homogenization of the world's diverse social landscapes.

In addition to carrying dangers of essentialization or romanticization of the local, an emphasis on resistance to development and invocation of a postdevelopment era reinforces the dichotomous images of a monolithic development industry and its hapless victims.[20] Depictions of development as a monolithic, top-down enterprise risk overlooking the ways individuals operate not as passive recipients (or victims) of development but rather as agents who actively shape outcomes. Thus, we may call attention to historical processes of active engagement with rather than mechanical enactments of a Western construct of development or modernity, "so that those who are supposedly subjected to development can emerge as subjects of development" (Sivaramakrishnan and Agrawal in press). That is, "local" people can influence "global" processes. Moreover, within the development apparatus itself, ideas, assumptions, and practices vary significantly (R. Grillo 1997, 21; see also Cooper and Packard 1997). Thus, William Fisher (1996, 139) notes that in addition to the problem of objectifying the local, there is the problem of objectifying and homogenizing the development apparatus. As Cooper and Packard put it, "It is thus too simple to assert the emergence of

20. See Sivaramakrishnan and Agrawal's introduction in *Regional Modernities: The Cultural Politics of Development in India* (in press).

a singular development discourse, a single knowledge-power regime. The appropriations, deflections, and challenges emerging within the overall construct of development—and the limits to them—deserve careful attention" (1997, 10).

Celebrating the local carries the dangers not only of romanticizing it or essentializing it, but also of allowing it to be co-opted by states and international development institutions whose commitment to participatory or alternative development or empowerment may be primarily rhetorical.[21] Thus, mainstream development practitioners may adopt rhetorics of sustainability or participatory development without altering their practices. Of course, co-optation need not proceed only in one direction (Agrawal 1996, 476). As the cases of Nepali NGOs and the Ogoni movement suggest, the language of the local or rhetorics of sustainability or human rights can be highly effective strategies to mobilize international support for "local" resistance to state policies or projects (see Kearney 1995, 560). Change and co-optation therefore are not confined to only one side of "the familiar dualisms of local and global, indigenous and western, traditional and scientific, society and state" (Agrawal 1996, 476). Rather than give up on the state or international development agencies as lost causes, "it may be time to think about how to coopt 'development' " (Agrawal 1996, 476).

In short, the development apparatus is not as monolithic, the state is not as hopeless, objects of development are not as inert, and the local is not as homogeneous, as easily identified, or as politically benign as sometimes portrayed. Some notions of the local as haven of resistance against globalization or development verge toward the uncritical and romantic. Attention is better directed to the varied sites and forms of engagement among actors involved in development at multiple "levels" of social agency. Such a focus acknowledges the advantages of problematizing the power of Western knowledge and revaluing alternative experiences and ways of knowing (Crush 1995, 4) without necessarily privileging an essentialized local or overly dichotomizing the local and the nonlocal.

21. See Rahnema's (1992) discussion of why governments and development institutions became very interested in participatory development and how they have tried to co-opt the notion of participation for other ends.

Local and Global: A False Opposition?

Notions of the global as well as the local can be overly objectified, reified, homogenized, or naturalized. What is globalization,[22] and is the global any easier to identify than the local? Global flows of capital, commodities, people, technologies, and ideas, of course, did not appear suddenly in the last few decades but have existed for centuries.[23] Long-term processes such as the Agricultural Revolution and industrial and postindustrial transformations have sustained globalization (see Rosenau 1997). What is new are the volume and velocity of such flows and the financial mobility and speculation associated with deregulation of financial institutions, which some believe has correspondingly diminished state monetary authority.[24] That is, globalization and the retreat of the state have been propelled by the accelerated mobility of capital and technological change, especially new information and

22. Globalization is often subdivided into financial, political, economic, and cultural subtypes. Here I take *globalization* to mean the intensification of worldwide social, economic, and political relations that "link distant localities in such a way that local happenings are shaped by events occurring many miles away and vice versa. This is a dialectical process" (Giddens 1990, 64). Giddens further suggests that sociologists' earlier reliance on the notion of "society" as a bounded system "should be replaced by a starting point that concentrates upon analyzing how social life is ordered across time and space—the problem of time-space distanciation" (1990, 64). Leys observes that economic globalization entails historical movement toward a "unified global capitalist economy—and one regulated, if at all, only by institutions reflecting the interests of transnational capital" (1996, 19).

23. See Wallerstein 1974 and a debate on the novelty of globalization between Davis (1998) and Kassimir (1998) in *Africa Today*. Krugman argues that world trade has increased significantly in recent decades but that international capital movements, although larger in the mid-1990s than in 1990, "are not so large compared with world income as those of the pre-1913 world" (1997, 9).

24. McMichael observes that "precisely because of the nonterritorial character of financialization, all states are constrained to manage their finances according to global criteria" (1996, 28). Panitch, on the other hand, argues that globalization has not necessarily diminished the role of the state and suggests that "today's globalisation both is authored by states and is primarily about reorganizing, rather than bypassing, states" (1994, 63). Keller and Pauly similarly suggest that "markets . . . are not replacing states as the world's effective government" (1997, 370).

communication technologies (Strange 1997, 367). Also recent is globalization as an ordering vision held by new global elites—regulators, business executives, political leaders, managers of multilateral institutions (International Monetary Fund [IMF], World Bank, World Trade Organization [WTO]), and financial specialists from both the North and the South (McMichael 1996, 31). Though economic globalization has a wide impact and sometimes is viewed as a juggernaut, its real reach in some respects is limited; for example, by one estimate approximately "80 percent of the more than five billion people in the world live outside global consumer networks" (McMichael 1996, 27).[25] In any case, globalization produces highly unequal effects in different parts of the world, with global competition impoverishing some areas and enriching others (see Leys 1996, 23). Africa, Asia, and Latin America now have a substantially smaller share of world trade than they did in 1913.[26] And for the first time in history, an entire subcontinent—Africa—has been "relegated to the margins of the global accumulation process" (Leys 1996, 193). The average income share that industrialized countries allotted to official development assistance to poorer nations dropped from 0.5 percent in 1960–61 to 0.34 percent in the mid-1990s.[27] At the same time, the world has become accustomed to previously unimaginable levels of starvation, violence, and cruelty in Africa and elsewhere.[28]

Rather than take the global processes that have produced these changes

25. Heredia offers figures on inequalities both among and within nations, noting that "Between 1989 and 1992 . . . 72 percent of total FDI [foreign direct investment] flows to developing countries went to only ten countries (China, Mexico, Malaysia, Argentina, Thailand, Indonesia, Brazil, Nigeria, Venezuela, and South Korea). . . . The poorest countries have seen little profit from the recent boom in international financial flows, while suffering a great deal from major cuts and reorientations in aid flows from advanced nations" (1997, 385). As for inequalities within countries, Heredia notes that "poverty . . . has increased in both absolute and relative terms in much of Africa and Latin America" (386) since the 1980s.

26. Glyn and Sutcliffe (1992, 90–91), quoted in Leys 1996, 22–23.

27. These figures and the point made in the next sentence are drawn from Leys 1996, 194.

28. Many economic observers accept that global competition must produce winners and losers; some even take "free-market" models to imply that the competition is somehow fair or just, equating it with "natural selection," as if economies operate according to the rules of the biological world.

as natural or inevitable contexts for local processes, it is more useful to examine how both global and local entail historically specific projects, institutions, ideological relations, and social forces (McMichael 1996, 26–27, 50–51). It also may be helpful to define more specific foci such as regions (see Sivaramakrishnan and Agrawal in press). In any case, economic globalization need not be taken as inevitable context; it should be problematized so that we can consider how the contemporary restructuring of economic and political relations "conditions the options faced by particular communities and regions" (McMichael 1996, 50–51).[29] Lowe makes a similar point in proposing that rather than take globalism (in its free-trade or other guises) as an uncriticized starting point, a critical global study would "take global relationships to localities and regions as a problematic focus of study, from regionally grounded perspectives" (1997, 305–6). Local and regional foci, then, would not be "narrow" or parochial histories to be discarded but rather the pivotal point of inquiry into global-local connections.[30]

Globalizing and localizing processes often are seen to be at war with one another, with a common assumption that only one—most likely globalization—will win out (Rosenau 1997, 362–63; see also T. Friedman 2000). Some suggest that if these two contradictory tendencies are to accommodate one another, individuals will have to recognize that their search for psychic comfort in collectivities can occur simultaneously in local, national, and transnational domains (Rosenau 1997, 364). Analysts, of course, differ on the principal fault lines in the world today. Whereas some critics of globalization on the right view conflicting interests between American workers and their foreign counterparts as a principal division in the world economy, many on the left are less concerned with tensions among countries and more interested in struggles between the world's workers and international capital

29. According to Leys, "what has demobilized development theory is a retreat from politics in the face of the seemingly irresistible success of capital in subordinating everything to the arbitration of 'global market forces.' But a broader, more historical view of development shows that no such victory is ever really irresistible" (1996, vi).

30. For example, see Edelman's (1998) innovative study of a transnational peasant movement in Central America. He shows how peasants in seven countries in the region constituted a cooperative movement that reflected common problems of economic and political marginality while at the same time encompassing national particularities and subnational distinctions among the landless, squatters, smallholders, and cooperativists.

(Tonelson 1997, 359). Others on the left oppose greater global economic integration and favor instead more national and subnational self-reliance (Tonelson 1997, 359).

The sheer uncertainty of specialists' understanding of global connections and processes is striking. Scholars are searching for clarifying metaphors or analogies (e.g., spider's webs, networks, commodity chains, flow diagrams, footloose capitalism, Asian contagion). Financial experts contemplating what began as the "Asian crisis" admit that they have "lost [their] ability to predict" (Fishman, Garten, and Greider 1998, 41), and they speak of negative shock waves from the Asian crisis "moving around the world in subterranean fashion" and being hidden from view "in the heads of investors and in managers' order books" (Fishman, Garten, and Greider 1998, 40). Garten observes that the "top bankers or corporate CEOs . . . know that we are more linked to the rest of the world than we can document. . . . Everybody is involved in every loan. We don't fully understand the connections, and there's great nervousness" (Fishman, Garten, and Greider 1998, 40). The complexities of financial globalization (volatility of exchange rates and investments as well as the sheer rapidity of electronic financial transactions) indicate that mechanical models of interactions between neatly specified "levels" of analysis—local, regional, global—are of little use. In short, even the experts describe financial globalization as a domain of unpredictability, incomprehensibility, and invisibility.

As we address the great analytical challenges of linking these poorly understood global forces to local dynamics, many call for a reinvention of area studies. Challenges to area studies (as discussed in the introduction to this volume) have emerged from the disparate domains of formal social science theory, globalization studies, and cultural or postcolonial studies. Scholars such as Rafael (1994, 1999), for example, urge recognition of European and North American biases (including imperialist underpinnings) in the very definition of world regions and call attention to the contingent positionings of "us" versus "them" distinctions ("American" versus "indigenous" scholars or "centers" versus "margins"). Others who critique area studies invoke dichotomies between supposedly narrow or parochial area specialists, on the one hand, and universalizing theorists on the other (e.g., Bates 1997b). The latter distinction, though useful in some academic turf wars, is misleading and overstated.

Globalization and Area Studies

Without rehearsing the debates over the future of area studies,[31] I wish to emphasize that grappling with the dynamics of the "local" and the "global" are equally challenging endeavors and that—contrary to some stereotypes—most scholars doing area studies work have long taken explicit account of global models and have addressed general disciplinary theory.[32] Much U.S. scholarship on Africa since the 1950s, for example, has addressed how local and global are mutually constituted and has been carried out under globalizing frames of reference such as modernization and underdevelopment theories; articulation of modes of production; African diaspora; structural adjustment; and theories of globalizing markets, democratization, and postcoloniality (Lowe 1997). Although recent debates might suggest the reverse, area studies were founded in order to deparochialize some academic disciplines, and that need remains.[33]

The post-Cold War era and the challenges of globalization surely call for a broadening rather than a narrowing of theoretical, methodological, and disciplinary approaches. Given all that is "hidden" from view in the global domain—even from global finance experts—and given the complexities of global-local interactions, there is little reason to privilege the supposed "rigor" of any existing analytical approach or paradigm. Current academic turf wars need not harden the stereotypical divide between supposedly particularizing and universalizing disciplines (anthropology and history versus

31. Among multiple sources, see the special issue of *Africa Today* 41, no. 2 (1997), titled *The Future of Regional Studies;* Guyer 1996; Harbeson 1997; Heilbrunn 1996; Hershberg 2000; Prewitt 1996; Zeleza 1997; and the special issue of *PS: Political Science and Politics* 39, no. 2 (1997).

32. For example, the 1993 volume *Africa and the Disciplines,* edited by Bates, Mudimbe, and O'Barr, effectively illustrates the many contributions of African research to disciplinary theory.

33. For example, the disciplines that tend to constitute the largest shares of applications to and awards from the Social Science Research Council's international doctoral research fellowship program are history and anthropology, followed by political science and then much smaller percentages of economics, sociology, and psychology (see Haugerud and Cadge 2000.)

political science, economics, and sociology) or between qualitative and quantitative approaches (Guyer 1996, 72).

Today rich traditions of area-based scholarship are threatened by vocal advocates of a "one-sided globalism," by social scientists who invoke misleading analogies to the natural sciences,[34] and by those who favor reductionist formal models, such as rational choice (Lowe 1997, 300).[35] Though the latter have generated much heat in the area studies controversy, debates about the usefulness of formal modeling approaches such as rational choice theory of course do not arise from conundrums about how to conceptualize the local and the global. Rather, rational choice theorists' attacks on area studies are an externalization of a debate in political science about the relationship of the subdiscipline of comparative politics to the rest of the discipline.[36] Disagreement centers on hegemonic claims that only rational choice theory is capable of producing rigorous, scientific, causal, cumulative, and generalizable knowledge, and that the subdiscipline of comparative politics is weak because not enough of its members have the analytical tools, incentives, or desire to do rigorous "science."

In spite of this attempt to depict those who do not use rational choice theory or formal models as atheoretical, unscientific, and parochial, even the discipline most wedded to formal models—economics—has critics from within. Robert Kuttner (1985), for example, characterizes his discipline as having inadequate intellectual diversity (compared to other social sciences), a fear of dissension, avoidance of empiricism, and adherence to a "suicidal formalism."[37] And a 1991 panel of twelve eminent economists concluded that this discipline is in danger of producing a generation of *"idiots savants,* skilled in technique but innocent of real economic issues"* (Cassidy 1996, 60)—a finding that appears to have had little, if any, effect on the discipline. Yet formalism and scientism (in economics and now in other social sciences)

34. Kuttner, on the other hand, observes that "The difficulty is that economic phenomena are neither so universal nor so predictable as physical phenomena" (1985, 76).

35. See the critique by Green and Shapiro (1994).

36. Thanks to Ron Kassimir for raising this issue and for suggesting the formulations of it offered in this sentence and the one that follows it. See also the 1997 symposium in *PS: Political Science and Politics* 30, no. 2.

37. See also the work of economist Donald McCloskey (1985).

threaten to take precedence over the careful empirical research that enables critical evaluation and modification of theory (Lowe 1997, 300). Many fear that shifts in funding priorities and scarce resources now favor shorter, shallower field research and that superficial fieldwork will become handmaiden to overvalued formal models.

The data simplifications or reductions required for such models can be both useful and dangerous. Formal models are useful in sharpening the focus of inquiry and in systematizing comparisons. On the other hand, as Scott observes, "if you see the world only through your instruments, then it is likely to be a world that is hard to broaden and that may very well be poverty stricken. These instruments define the conclusions you can reach" (1995, 37). Similarly, Kuttner states that devotion to the deductive method in economic science "creates a professional ethic of studied myopia" and "drives out empiricism" (1985, 77). Scott offers his fellow political scientists a maxim: "If half your reading is not outside the confines of political science, you are risking extinction along with the rest of the subspecies. Most of the notable innovations in the discipline have come in the form of insights, perspectives, concepts, and paradigms originating elsewhere" (1995, 37). Thus, the narrow reliance on formal models that Bates (1997b) advocates is the intellectual equivalent of monocropping—and we know well the dangers of such narrow specialization in the agrarian world.[38]

Furthermore, recent global financial crises and associated debates about "Who lost Russia?" or "Who lost Asia?" have called attention to the severe limitations of economists' formal models. Observers have pointed directly to the IMF's political tone deafness, its "inability to understand and reckon with the national politics of countries in need of national reform" (Sanger 1998, A1). The *New York Times,* for example, reports that it was apparent to all except IMF managing director Michel Camdessus that Indonesian president Suharto had no intention of fulfilling the IMF agenda. The *Times* links

38. Contrary to what Bates (1997b) argues, area specialists are as likely to be trendsetters as resisters to new trends in the discipline. Indeed, Harbeson suggests that in many departments it is precisely the narrow specialists in new formal modeling techniques who are likely to dismiss the legitimacy and importance of the work of others. Such disparagement based on inaccurate stereotypes "should be replaced by more efforts on all sides to learn from our colleagues" (1997, 30–31).

the IMF's political ignorance to a staff made up almost entirely of Ph.D. economists: "there are few officials with deep experience in international politics, much less the complexities of Javanese culture that were at work in Indonesia. . . . As a result the fund had only a rudimentary understanding of what would happen if its demands were met and all Indonesia's state monopolies were quickly dissolved" (Sanger 1998, A10). In short, economists need area studies, and other social scientists should not overly emulate the reductionist models of economics.

As we address the epistemological and conceptual challenges of globalization, turf wars over area studies and social science disciplines risk becoming an unproductive distraction. Misleading images of area studies reinforce false oppositions between the local and the global as well as between description and theory. Our task now is to move beyond global-local dichotomies and to explore the historically contingent ways in which these two domains constitute one another or operate in dynamic tension.

Trends toward localization are as worthy of study as globalization. Localizing initiatives (boundary accentuation or closing of borders) may provoke globalizing reactions (boundary expansion or transgression) and vice versa.[39] Notions of both the "global" and the "local" need to be problematized, and other analytical foci such as region[40] or nation interposed.

There is no reason to assume that any one discipline or theoretical approach should lead the way as scholars grapple with globalization. Well-timed accusations about "parochial" or "prescientific" area studies should be recognized as legitimizing strategies and rhetorics, not as revealed truths about one ideal path of theory and method, whether rational choice or any other approach (Haugerud 1997, 117). Indeed, the social sciences already are reacting against "the imperial quest of rational-choice theorists for a simplified and unified social science" (Bender 1997, 29). The rational choice crusade has stimulated a reengagement with explicitly historical approaches

39. See Rosenau's (1997) discussion of countervailing forces of fragmentation and integration and of how dynamics of localization and globalization are linked.

40. See, for example, Sivaramakrishnan and Agrawal's (in press) discussion of why a focus on "regional modernities" is useful.

that reject any quest for timeless behavioral laws (Smith 1997). In economics and political science, there is new interest in institutional approaches and more complex models (Bender 1997, 29). Ambitious new theorizing is necessary, and a starting point might be to make explicit the higher-level theoretical assumptions it has become fashionable to obscure in the current "mininarratives" that have replaced discredited metanarratives.[41] Global theoretical visions demand pluralistic approaches that combine attention to politics, economics, culture, and history. The "local" is in no danger of disappearing. Scholars' attention to the global has sharpened understanding of why that is so.

41. A suggestion made by Leys (1996, 28–29), who is author of the term *mininarratives* in this context. Part of the reason for the contemporary influence of rational choice theory may be that it fills a near vacuum created by skepticism about grand theories or metanarratives. Whatever the merits of rational choice theory, however, there are large questions it cannot address, especially those concerning processes of social change or the historical origins of any particular set of institutions.

5 Globalizing Local Women's Movements

AMRITA BASU

The changing relationship between two nondisciplinary yet well institution-alized fields of study—namely, area studies and women's studies—is highly informative in considering debates about the future of area studies and the relationship of the local to the global. At a time when the disciplines are re-linquishing their ties to area studies and their interest in area-based knowl-edge, women's studies scholarship has come to take international perspectives and global-local relations very seriously. This has not always been true. The field of women's studies emerged from the Western academy and a close relationship with Western feminism, historically tending to de-fine itself in global terms and to identify women as universal subjects. One of the many tensions that inevitably resulted, both within and across North-South lines, centered on the importance of place and context to women's lives.

The field of women's studies has arrived at a new juncture as it has shed its association with Western feminism. Some of the most exciting new schol-arship concerns locally based ideas, practices, and movements in Brazil, South Africa, India, and Australia and comes from transnational and dias-poric communities in these countries and elsewhere. The very foundations that have been reorganizing or dismantling area studies programs are seek-

I presented earlier versions of this essay at the October 1998 conference at Hampshire College and subsequently as the Jackie Pritzen Lecture at Amherst College in April 1999. I am grateful for helpful discussions with Mary Katzenstein, Mark Kesselman, Ritu Menon, Bina Agarwal, Sonia Alvarez, Carol Cohn, and Valentine Moghadam. I published an earlier version of this essay under a different title for *Meridians: Feminism, Race, Transnationalism* 1, no. 1 (autumn 2000).

ing to invigorate the study of women, gender, and sexuality. The Ford Foundation, for example, has invested lavishly in college and university programs that would strengthen ties between area studies and women's studies.

These scholarly trends reflect tendencies within movement politics. There are closer links between women's movements locally, nationally, and transnationally than at any other time in the past. Both scholars and activists find themselves confronting a range of questions about the relationship of national particularities to global universalities. To what extent has the transnationalization of women's movements displaced nationally based movements? To what extent do women from the South see transnational groups and ideas as aiding or derailing them? What impact has transnationalism had on local forms of organizing within a particular national context?

This chapter explores the implications of the growth of transnational networks, organizations, and ideas for women's movements in the South. It asks how North-South tensions around the meaning of feminism and the nature of women's movements have changed. What new opportunities have emerged and what new tensions have surfaced? What is the relationship between the transnationalism of the 1990s and the global feminism of the 1960s and 1970s that Robin Morgan aptly and controversially termed "sisterhood is global"?

My point of departure is my edited anthology *The Challenge of Local Feminisms: Women's Movements in Global Perspective* (Basu and McGrory 1995). In that work, my coeditor and I found ourselves attempting to navigate twin dangers: on the one hand, resisting the tendency to equate women's movements narrowly with autonomous urban, middle-class feminist movements or, on the other hand, defining women's movements so broadly that they include virtually all forms of women's activism. We highlighted the local origins and character of women's movements cross-nationally and argued that women's movements must be situated within the particular political economies, state policies, and cultural politics of the regions in which they are active.

The question I propose to explore now is whether we need to rethink the relationship between local and global feminisms. Is it possible that the 1995 Beijing women's conference, which the aforementioned book was designed to commemorate, in fact marked the coming of age of transnational feminism and the eclipse of locally based women's movements? This question is prompted by the appearance of more transnational women's movement activity than ever before.

Before proceeding, a word about the terms I use: I am aware that *local* can connote the supposed particularism, provincialism, and primordialism of the "Third World," whereas *global* may connote the breadth and universality that is often associated with Western feminism. I use the term *local* to refer to the indigenous and regional, and *global* to refer to the transnational. I employ these terms because they correspond to the levels at which a great deal of women's activism is organized—namely, at the grassroots and transnational levels. As I discuss later in the chapter, it is also important to inject attention to the national level into this dynamic.

There is considerable controversy about the significance of transnational movements, nongovernmental organizations (NGOs), networks, and advocacy groups. Although some scholars speak of the emergence of a global civil society, others are more skeptical.[1] How to evaluate the transnationalization of women's movements is no less complicated. From one perspective, it represents a signal achievement—particularly for women in the South. For example, Valentine Moghadam (1996a, 111–25) argues that transnational networks are organizing women around the most pressing questions of the day: reproductive rights, the growth of religious "fundamentalism," and the adverse effects of structural adjustment policies. She also comments favorably on the recent emergence of networks, which she believes have a broader and more far-reaching impact than local movements. From another perspective, as women's movements have become more transnational, their commitment to grassroots mobilization and cultural change has diminished (Alvarez 1997, 1998). Sonia Alvarez argues that women's movements are becoming increasingly bureaucratized as they have come to work more closely with NGOs, political parties, state institutions, and multilateral agencies. What explains the differences in these two perspectives? Which is correct?

It is inaccurate to depict local women's movements as simply being subsumed by global ones or as engaging in sustained, overt resistance to global influences. Rather, we have a more complex and varied situation in which

---

1. For a sampling of the debates on global civil society, see Keck and Sikkink 1998; Lipschutz 1992; Wapner 1995.

local and transnational movements often exist independently of one another and experience similar challenges and dilemmas. Furthermore, although transnational ideas, resources, and organizations have been extremely successful around some issues in some regions, their success is more circumscribed elsewhere. After discussing these questions within the global context, I address them in the case of the Indian women's movement.

Women's Movements in Global Perspective

The international women's conferences that took place in Mexico City (1975), Copenhagen (1980), Nairobi (1985), and Beijing (1995) provide a fruitful opportunity to explore changing relationships among women's organizations transnationally. The two-tier system of conferences—namely, official conferences of heads of states convened by the United Nations (UN) and the nongovernmental conferences convened by women's groups and movements—provide insights into the workings of the international state system and of what some describe as a burgeoning global civil society.

International feminism might be periodized as comprising two broad phases. The first phase, between 1975 and 1985, was marked by bitter contestation over the meaning of feminism and over the relationship between the local and the global. The second phase, which began with the Nairobi conference in 1985 and culminated in the Beijing conference in 1995, was marked by a growth of networks linking women's activism at the local and global levels.

Fierce contestation over the meaning and significance of feminism took place at international women's conferences of activists and policymakers from 1975 to 1985. Some of these debates identified the South with the local and the North with the global. A typical scenario was one in which women from the South argued that women's major priorities were both local and material—for example, for potable drinking water, firewood for fuel, and more employment opportunities. Meanwhile, women from the North typically focused on women's broad, transnational identities and interests.

It would be inaccurate to imply that tensions along North-South lines had disappeared entirely by the time of the 1995 Beijing women's conference. Even today the organizations that sponsor campaigns to extend women's civil and political rights typically are based in the North, whereas groups that are more apt to address poverty, inequality, and basic needs are based in the South. Esther Ngan-ling Chow notes, "Even when they agree on the importance of an issue such as human rights, women from various world regions frame it differently. While Western women traditionally have based their human rights struggles on issues of equality, non-discrimination and civil and political rights, African, Asian and Latin American women have focussed their struggles on economic, social and cultural rights" (1996, 187).

But these differences were less striking than the significant areas of agreement that women established across North-South lines. Charlotte Bunch and Susan Fried argue that the entire Beijing Plan of Action was an affirmation of the human rights of women: "The incorporation of women's human rights language and concepts by governments and organizations from all parts of the world and in all manner of ways indicates more than a rhetorical gesture. It represents a shift in analysis that moves beyond single-issue politics or identity-based organizing and enhances women's capacity to build global alliances based on collective political goals and a common agenda" (1996, 203).

One important explanation for the diminution of tension among women's movements in the North and South is the increasingly important influence of women of color in shaping debates about North American feminism. Recall that some of the earliest and most important critiques of feminist universalism came from African American and Latino women in the United States. Years later, in preparation for the 1995 Beijing women's conference, women of color in the United States formed a coalition with women from the South and drafted language for the platform document about women who faced multiple forms of discrimination (Chow 1996, 189).

At the same time, women from the South increasingly have worked to correct nationalism's exclusions by formulating nondiscriminatory policies in newly formed states. Namibia's Constitution, thanks to the influence of its women's movement, forbids sex discrimination, authorizes affirmative action for women, and recognizes only those forms of customary law that do not violate the Constitution. The South African Constitution similarly provides equal rights for women and prohibits discrimination on grounds of sexual orientation. Palestinian women have drafted a bill of rights and have sought legislation protecting women from family violence.

Furthermore, with the end of the Cold War, the character of international gatherings changed quite significantly. The early meetings, such as the Mexico City conference in 1975, were dominated by national political leaders who sought to use these forums to pursue their own agendas. Whereas many of the delegates attending this conference were the wives, daughters, and widows of male politicians, the delegates for the 1985 Nairobi conference included many women who were powerful in their own right. Even more important was the growth of women's movements globally and their increasingly important roles relative to those of nation-states.

As nongovernmental organizations and movements have multiplied, they have become more diverse, and divisions that crosscut the North-South divide have become more salient. There has been a growth of transnational networks of feminists and conservative activists alike. For example, a coalition of conservative Islamic groups and Christian anti-abortion activists sought to shape the agenda of the Cairo Conference on Population and Development in 1994 and to influence the World Plan of Action at the Beijing conference a year later (Moghadam 1996b). The coalition included some powerful NGOs, such as the International Right to Life Committee and Human Life International, as well as religious bodies, such as the Vatican, and some states, most preeminently the Islamic Republic of Iran. Like women's organizations, this coalition functioned at local, national, and transnational levels.

The growth of transnational networks of the religious right has reduced North-South polarization. Some of the staunchest opponents of feminism are North American and European, but its staunchest supporters are Asian, African, and Latin American. The ability of Muslim, Protestant, and Catholic groups to transcend national differences and to arrive at common positions on motherhood, pornography, abortion, homosexuality, and premarital sexuality has encouraged feminist groups also to seek out areas of agreement.

Charting the Terrain

It is tempting to treat international conferences as synonymous with transnational women's movements because they have grown simultaneously. However, to conflate them would underestimate the extent to which new forms of transnationalism emerge from civil society and include a diverse array of organizations, including NGOs, social movements, identity networks, project coalitions, and issue-based campaigns.

The growth of transnational women's movements entails the spread and increased density of groups as well as the greater linkages among groups within civil societies transnationally. It also refers to a flow of resources, generally from the North to the South, to support women's organizations. Southern-based NGOs have come to rely heavily on financial support from Northern affiliates, foundations, and academic institutions. But it is not just individuals, groups, and currencies that cross borders with greater ease and frequency than in the past. Certain discourses—and this is a second dimension—have acquired greater importance among women in both the North and the South. One of the most significant changes in discourse is that the violation of women's rights is now considered a human rights abuse. Thus, women's movements can be said to have become increasingly transnational when they appeal to universal principles of human rights and seek redress in global arenas.

The past few years have witnessed the growth of all these dimensions of transnational activism. There also has been a vast expansion in the number of NGOs that engage in international networking, from 114 that attended the NGO Forum in Mexico City in 1975 to 3,000 that participated in the Beijing NGO Forum in 1995. Today tens of thousands of NGOs participate in international conferences and gatherings. Many of them are organized at the regional level by women activists from the South, independent of both the United Nations and national governments.

In keeping with the multifaceted character of globalization, transnational women's movements are themselves extremely diverse. A minority among them seek to challenge the feminization of poverty and class inequality that globalization entails. For example, researchers and activists formed Development Alternatives with Women for a New Era (DAWN) in 1984 to promote alternative approaches to state-sponsored macroeconomic policies. At first based in Bangalore and now in Rio de Janeiro, DAWN includes membership from the Caribbean, Latin America, Africa, South and Southeast Asia, and the Middle East.

A much larger group of women's organizations has sought to extend women's civic and political rights, particularly to address violence against women and the denial of women's rights by religious nationalists. An important example is the coalition of 130 women's and human rights groups— including the National Organization for Women, the Feminist Majority, Human Rights Watch, the National Political Congress of Black Women, and the Women's Alliance for Peace and Human Rights—that organized a campaign to protest the repressive measures the Taliban took against Afghan women when it assumed power in Kabul in September 1996 and to urge the international community to deny the Taliban both investments and recognition. It organized a Web site documenting the Taliban's abuses, a petition campaign and demonstrations, and various fund-raising activities. Among other victories, it dissuaded Unocal, a U.S. oil company, from building a pipeline through Afghanistan.

The amount of international funding available for women's organizations, women's studies programs, and women's movements has grown dramatically over the past decade. Grants by major U.S. foundations to groups working on women's rights and violence against women increased from $241,000 in 1988 to $3,247,000 in 1993 (Keck and Sikkink 1998, 182). The Ford Foundation underwrote almost half of this amount. The large majority of women's NGOs in India receive foreign funding.

As far as transnational discourses are concerned, neither conventions on international human rights nor the campaign for women's human rights are new. What is relatively new is the extent to which coalitions of transnational women's organizations have lobbied to demand recognition for women's rights as human rights. 1993 marked a turning point for the women's human rights movement, for in that year both the Vienna Human Rights Declaration and Program of Action and the UN Declaration on the Elimination of Violence Against Women recognized violence against women as a human rights abuse and defined gender violence to include public and private violence against women. Women's human rights activists consolidated their gains at the Beijing conference and increasingly have employed human rights appeals since then. With the collapse of communism and the decline of the organized left, democratic movements have taken the place formerly occupied by socialism, and liberal principles of human rights have become hegemonic.

What are the implications of the transnationalization of women's movements for women in the South? Does the diminution of overt North-South tensions at the Beijing conference and other international forums reflect the increasingly important leadership and agenda-setting roles of women from the South? Or, conversely, are Southern-based organizations less able to oppose Northern domination because of their greater dependence on Northern funding sources? There is no one simple response to these questions.

It would be inaccurate to see transnational networks and movements simply as vehicles for Northern domination. Networks such as DAWN are organized by and for women from the South. Although they may accept external funding, they formulate their objectives independently of donor organizations. Furthermore, certain problems may be addressed more effectively at the transnational level rather than at the local level. A good example concerns the consequences for women of the growth of religious "fundamentalism." Afghan women's groups are subject to such extreme repression that they needed outside support to organize effectively. Moreover, transnational feminist networks have been a vital counterweight to transnational networks of the religious right.

The campaign against the Taliban also illuminates the possibilities of combining global and local appeals. Although the campaign made extensive use of the Web site and e-mail petition campaigns, it also organized demonstrations locally, including one in Amherst, Massachusetts, where women marched through the town commons with banners in their hands and pieces of mesh fabric pinned to their lapels to evoke the *burqa* (veil). Terming the campaign an attempt to stop "gender apartheid" in Afghanistan, the coalition identified the crimes against Afghan women with the evils of apartheid in South Africa. This simple, indeed simplistic, characterization provided an effective means of generating support for the campaign.

Another tool that the campaign against the Taliban and other campaigns against religious "fundamentalism" have employed is to record the stories of women who are stoned, beaten, or publicly humiliated for having worked, married, divorced, or simply existed. These individual narratives not only permit a personal identification with the victims but also invite activism against those who perpetrate abuse. The coalition against sexual apartheid in Afghanistan distributed a video entitled *A Shroud of Silence*, which recounts these stories in a vivid form.

The very conditions for the success of global campaigns such as the one against the Taliban in Afghanistan also suggest some of the limitations of such campaigns. Global campaigns are much more likely to succeed when women's civil and political rights rather than their economic rights (food, shelter, housing) have been violated. They are more effective in challenging physical violence than structural violence against women. Although this same problem exists locally, it is much more significant at the transnational level.

Struggles opposing violence against women are nested more within the context of women's class and sometimes ethnic identities at the local level than at the transnational level. In India, for example, struggles against marital abuse often have emerged amidst social movements of the urban and rural poor. Women who protest the complicity of the state and illicit liquor producers in Andhra Pradesh, for example, readily appreciate the connections between violence against women and unemployment, state corruption, and a range of other issues. By contrast, when women come together in global forums as victims of gender violence, their identities as Bosnian, African American, and poor women often are muted.

Women's groups most enthusiastically have supported transnational campaigns against sexual violence where the state is repressive or indifferent and women's movements are weak. Conversely, transnationalism has provoked more distrust in places where women's movements have emerged, grown, and defined themselves independently of Western feminism. Indeed, one explanation for the differences between the positions of Valentine Moghadam and Sonia Alvarez is that they examine such different contexts. Moghadam's optimism about the role of transnational networks may be born of the pessimism she feels about women's movements in face of the growth of Islamic "fundamentalism" in the Middle East. By contrast, Alvarez expresses concern about co-optation because women's movements in Latin America historically have been strong and closely tied to left-wing parties and human rights movements.

It is precisely in situations where women's movements are grappling with how to organize more inclusively to overcome social hierarchies that transnational linkages may pose the greatest challenge. In such situations, transnationalism may deepen divisions between globalized elites, who belong to transnational networks, and the large majority of women, who do not. The result may be a deradicalization of women's movements. Or greater rifts may grow between those who have access to international funding and those who do not. In this event, some activists will become more mobile, whereas others will remain stuck at the local level. Transnational activists' dependence on the Internet, which requires specialized skills and technology, further accentuates class divisions among activists.

With these questions in mind, I turn to India. Although there is a rich literature on Indian women's movements, little has been written on global-local linkages. India provides an ideal context in which to consider the interplay of the local and the global because it has a long history of women's activism, with its roots in anticolonial nationalism. At the same time, Indian women's movements have a long history of interaction with the West and with universalist principles.

The Women's Movement in India

The feminist movement in India, also known as the autonomous women's movement, in many ways resembles women's movements in the United States and western Europe. It is similarly composed primarily of educated, middle-class women whose attention has focused on gender inequality. Indeed, their central concern has been the question of violence against women, which they have addressed in the context of the so-called dowry deaths (the murder of brides by in-laws and husbands seeking larger dowries after the time of marriage), the rape of women in police custody, and a few incidents of sati (the burning of women on their husbands' funeral pyres).

Given these commonalities, one might assume that Western feminism formed the crucible from which the Indian women's movement emerged. Although global feminism undoubtedly has influenced the Indian women's movement, a similar point can be made about the U.S. women's movement—namely, that it, too, has absorbed the influences of women's movements across the world. Indeed, U.S. feminism in the 1990s is intertwined deeply with global developments. The Feminist Majority campaign against the Taliban in Afghanistan tells us as much about how the U.S. women's movement has chosen to define itself as about the situation of Afghan women. And yet ultimately the women's movement in India, as in the United States, is more a product of national influences than of global influences.

The Indian women's movement not only comprises a number of movements but has emerged through its association with other important movements in India: the social reform movement of the late nineteenth century, the nationalist movement of the early to mid-twentieth century, the civil liberties movement of the mid-1970s, and the grassroots struggles of the rural and urban poor from the late 1970s on. It was mostly male social reformers who first sought to raise the age of marriage for girls, to prohibit sati, to permit widow remarriage, and to educate women. These reforms identified the key deterrents to gender equality in religion and the family. The nationalist movement that followed provided the first opportunity for women's mobilization. Whatever the blind spots of nationalist politics, and there were many, it encouraged women's activism and laid the foundations for women's professional and political advancement.

The contemporary women's movement also can be traced back to the civil liberties movement of the mid-1970s, which emerged in the aftermath of the state's flirtation with authoritarian rule. Prime Minister Indira Gandhi imposed a state of emergency for two years (1975–77) because she claimed there were threats to political stability. Opposition parties and democratic movements grew in jail cells and in underground networks and finally found expression in the Bharatiya Janata Party (BJP), which defeated Congress at the 1977 polls for the first time since independence. Many key features of the women's movement—its commitment to civil rights and liberties, its opposition to unjust state practices, and its critique of the male-dominated left and of democratic politics—emerged during this period.

However, it would be wrong to identify the contemporary Indian women's movement exclusively with the activities of urban middle-class women. What is termed *the* Indian women's movement comprises a number of diverse rural and urban movements that foster women's activism and protest against sexual inequality: the Shramik Sangathana in Dhulia District; the Maharashtra, a movement of tribal landless laborers against the exploitation of Hindu landowners; the Self-Employed Women's Association in Gujarat, which organizes women who work in different trades to protest low wages, poor working conditions, and lack of access to credit; and the Chipko movement in northern India, which opposes deforestation and the displacement of subsistence farming by commercial agriculture. The activities and demands of all of these movements are consistent with even the most stringent definitions of feminism; in all these cases, large numbers of women play leadership roles and fight exploitation of themselves as women.

The segment of the Indian women's movement most influenced by Western feminism was an autonomous, middle-class movement that focused on violence against women. However, even here we should not readily assume similarities. Women's movement activists employed the term *violence against women* to describe diverse practices cross-nationally, Keck and Sikkink (1998) argue, in order to assert the global dimensions of a single problem. The further implication of their argument is that this inventive strategy masked considerable cross-national variation in the meanings of *violence against women*. The danger of naming such varied practices as battering, incest, individual and mass rape, and female genital mutilation or circumcision as *violence against women* is that the term masks important differences in the ways activists interpret and resist these practices in different regions of the world.

If the distinguishing feature of the U.S. women's movement was its immersion in cultural politics, the Indian women's movement was distinguished by its commitment to the broad goal of transforming the state. This is particularly ironic in light of Uma Narayan's (1997) contention that violence against women often is assumed to be a religious and cultural matter in India but a political question in the United States. The Indian women's movement demanded the passage of laws for the greater accountability of the police and the courts in deterring families from providing dowries at the time of marriage and in punishing dowry-related murders and rape. Similarly, in addressing the question of contraception and abortion, the women's movement sought to pressure the state to ban the use of Deproprovera and amniocentesis for purposes of feticide. Compared to their U.S. counterparts, Indian activists were less interested in exploring alternatives to the family, establishing battered women's shelters, addressing questions of sexual orientation, and engaging in consciousness raising.

Despite having expanded its focus significantly to a range of other issues, the Indian women's movement continues to focus on the state. It has worked closely with some parliamentarians and political parties to support the passage of a bill that would reserve 33 percent of seats in Parliament for women. Support for this bill brings the women's movement into a closer relationship than ever with state institutions.

Similar debates about reservations and quotas do not figure as prominently in North American feminist circles. If, as I have been arguing, the Indian women's movement should be located at the nerve center of Indian politics, why is the charge that it is excessively Westernized the most damning charge that it faces? One reason has to do with the notions not only that the women who form the autonomous women's movement are Westernized elites, but that appeals to women's rights pit them against women who are defined primarily by their religious, caste, and ethnic identities. One of the best examples of the latter notion concerns the supposed sati of a woman named Roop Kanwar in Deorala District, Rajasthan, in September 1987. The Rajput community to whom Roop Kanwar belonged alleged that the feminists who protested her death were disparaging their Rajput Hindu identity. A powerful pro-sati campaign developed to "defend" Hinduism from opponents of sati. Hindu nationalists, including some activists from the Shiv Sena and the BJP, extended this campaign to target those women who represented a challenge to "traditional" values. The campaign around sati entailed a significant setback for the women's movement (Kumar 1995, 82).

The irony of this charge became apparent when the Hindu nationalist BJP became a major proponent of the Uniform Civil Code, which would supplant the religious laws that currently govern the family with secular laws. In order to challenge Muslim family law, the BJP appropriated feminists' commitment to women's rights as individuals rather than just as communal beings. The charge that a commitment to individual rights and secular law is Western in inspiration cannot be sustained when religious nationalists and feminists alike put forward that position. Furthermore, debates about women's rights date back to the nineteenth-century social reform movement. More important than tracing the origins of rights discourse is determining the purposes for which it is deployed.

Funding by Northern donor organizations to NGOs, some of which are connected to social movements, also has popularized the charge that the Indian women's movement is highly Westernized. In the past, the question of whether NGOs and voluntary agencies should accept foreign funding was extremely fraught with controversy. Some prominent leftists sharply condemned the compromises that accepting foreign funding entailed. Although social movements continue to debate the ethics of foreign funding, these debates have become less acrimonious. Vast amounts of money are now available for research, documentation, and publication and even for organizing. Many donors allow recipients more latitude in determining how funds will be spent than they did in the past.

However, the very benefits that women's organizations derive from foreign funding also pose new challenges and problems. Transnational networks exacerbate tensions between those who acquire funds to attend conferences, undertake research projects, and build organizations and those who do not. The orientation of particular groups may be shaped by the imperatives of undertaking or completing particular projects. Most important, what initially may appear to be an extraordinary opportunity—to get paid to engage in activism—actually may become a liability when activists find their work becoming increasingly professionalized and bureaucratized. Some organizations actually have found it more difficult to sustain the commitment of their members when funds dry up than they did before those funds became available.

It would be naïve to attribute to foreign funding alone any tendencies toward professionalization and bureaucratization. The focus of the Indian women's movement on transforming the state has been responsible for its increasing reliance on institutional and legislative means rather than on grassroots mobilization. For different reasons and in different ways, both state agencies and international donors seek to fund organizations that can deliver the goods, whether this delivery takes the form of policy recommendations, reports, or development projects. The very success of women's organizations at achieving these tasks can divert them from movement activities.

How should we evaluate the transnationalization of women's movements? To what extent is transnational activism overcoming the tensions that bedeviled women's movements from the North and South? Are new networks, coalitions, and alliances addressing the key issues that women face transnationally? These questions are of more than academic relevance. The major funding organizations are committed to strengthening civil society both locally and cross-nationally and have identified women's movements as key to this endeavor. For women's movement activists in the South, the question of what kind of transnational alliances to forge and resources to accept is a key concern.

Transnational networks, campaigns, and discourses seem to be most effective where support for a particular demand exists locally but its expression is constrained, where the state is either indifferent or repressive toward women, and where the violation that is being protested involves physical violence and redress can be found by asserting women's civil and political rights. Examples of such situations include the mass rape of Bosnian women, Taliban violence against Afghan women, and the plight of East Asian comfort women during the Second World War. By contrast, transnational networks, campaigns, and discourses have been less effective in strengthening women's movements where strong local movements already exist. Furthermore, activists derive less benefit from transnational connections when the state concedes, however partially, to their demands.

Yet there is a danger of both crediting and blaming transnational networks too much. In India as in many other places, the principal location of the women's movement is the national level, where its priority is to influence the state. As Elizabeth Friedman (n.d.) aptly notes, attention to the impact of international organizing on the national level reveals that although transnational organizing has provided positive opportunities for the development of national movements, it also has exacerbated tensions in national movements, introduced foreign agendas that may be irrelevant to national concerns, and distributed increased external support unequally. In Venezuela, the Beijing conference increased tensions between activists who feared co-optation by the state and those who sought closer ties to it. The availability of external funding skewed the movement's efforts away from urgent priorities. Thus, although the United Nations conferences may have had beneficial consequences at the regional and transnational levels, their impact on the national level was more mixed.

In all contexts, however, transnational linkages are likely to be most effective when redress can be sought by asserting women's civil and political rights rather than their economic well-being and when those linkages are not designed primarily to provide economic resources. The extent to which women's organizations in the South have come to depend on Northern funding has impeded the open-ended two-way flow of ideas that has been so critical to the development of feminism. Economic reliance on Western foundations fosters the ever-present possibility of dependence and resentment. These problems are quite independent of the intentions of Northern-based funding organizations, many of which have become quite sensitive to such issues.

Meanwhile, women's economic situation remains perilous. Women constitute 70 percent of the 1.3 billion people living in absolute poverty and approximately 67 percent of the world's illiterate population. Accordingly, the Beijing Plan of Action calls on women's NGOs to strengthen antipoverty programs and to improve women's health, education, and social services. It calls on those NGOs to take responsibility for ensuring women's full and equal access to economic resources, including the right to inheritance, ownership of land, and natural resources. Interestingly, the only recommendation that NGOs have taken up seriously is to provide women with greater access to savings and credit mechanisms and institutions. Important as microcredit schemes are in allowing women a larger share of the pie, they do not contribute to rethinking the implications of macroeconomic policies for women (Lynch 1998, 149–73).[2]

Extremely telling is the evidence from the Beijing Plus Five meeting that was convened by the United Nations in New York in June 2000 to assess the extent to which national governments have implemented the provisions of the Beijing women's conference. The Beijing Plus Five meeting concluded that certain problems, such as the challenge that globalization presents to women, have become increasingly pressing since the 1995 conference. It noted that more open trade and financial flows, privatization of state-owned enterprises, and lower public spending have had often devastating consequences for women, particularly in less-developed countries. And yet although the situation of women in poverty ranks at the top of the Beijing Plan of Action list of critical areas of concern, it ranked low on the list of government priorities in the years that followed the conference.

An umbrella organization of activist groups named U.S. Women Connect (USWC) produced a report card for the U.S. efforts to implement the Beijing Plan of Action for Women. It gave the United States an F for its efforts to alleviate poverty rates among women, noting that the number of

2. Lynch points to the ineffectiveness of social movements in confronting globalization.

women (but not of men) in poverty had grown. The 1996 welfare reforms actually had reduced the average income of female-headed households by 35 percent. It gave the United States a C– for its efforts to improve women's roles in the economy. Women still earn only 70 percent of each dollar that men earn. By contrast, the U.S. government performed better in its efforts to end violence against women (B–) and to bring women into government (B) (Chow 1996, 187).

Even if we dispute the fairness of these grades and share Donna Shalala's belief that the USWC is a hard grader, it is clear that the U.S. government has made fewer strides in tackling poverty and economic rights than in supporting women's civil and political rights. If the problems this imbalance creates are serious in the United States, they are even more serious in those regions of the world where much larger numbers of women are in poverty and many fewer resources are available to confront this poverty.

Transnational networks and activists are most effective when the basis for mobilization is sexual victimization. Moreover, the victims who generate the most sympathy are generally women from the South who experience genital mutilation, stoning, and public humiliation. Important as campaigns such as the coalition against gender apartheid in Afghanistan may be, they draw sympathy in part because of pervasive anti-Muslim sentiment in the United States—a sentiment that is gendered. Muslim women often are considered the victims of the Islamic faith and the misogyny of their community. The dissemination of pieces of mesh fabric to signify the *burqa* by the coalition against the Taliban certainly implies that purdah is inevitably associated with the degradation of women, thereby inadvertently exacerbating anti-Muslim sentiment.

That there is an alternative to the choice between a religious politics that undermines women's rights and a universalist, liberal feminism that undermines women's religious and nationalist loyalties is illustrated by the network Women Living Under Muslim Law (WLUML). Established in 1985, it provides information, solidarity, and support to women in Muslim countries and to Muslim women living elsewhere. The network was formed in response to the rise of religious "fundamentalist" movements and to the attempt by certain states to institute family codes that would deny women full citizenship rights. By making Muslim women both its objects of concern and its leaders, and by showing how Islam provides both sympathetic and adverse characterizations of women's rights, the WLUML avoids disparaging characterizations of Muslim women.

Several essays in this volume note the decline of area studies. However, this decline may be most serious from a disciplinary perspective, for area studies have been dwarfed by the hardening of the hard social sciences. By contrast, area studies have become more rather than less significant to certain interdisciplinary fields such as women's studies and, in some cases, American studies and black studies, which have begun to include diasporas and migrants. Indeed, the pressure that the field of women's studies has faced to take serious account of cross-cultural perspectives has revitalized it.

Before celebrating the globalization of women's studies, however, recall that 1970s feminism was also global in its aspirations. It is only when global scholarship and activism are grounded in local realities that the dangers of excessive universalism can be confronted. Otherwise, there is the ever-present danger of feminism becoming linked to Western universalism or to its antithesis—religious nationalism.

The additional challenge is to recognize the vital place of the national context for studying and organizing women. No attempts at transnational organizing or scholarship have been able to do away with it.

Both points suggest the vital importance of area-based knowledge to the study of women and to the politics of women's movements. They also suggest the importance of cross-disciplinarity. Although anthropologists have been at the forefront of analyzing local-global dynamics, political scientists have taken on the task of analyzing the nation-state. It falls to women's studies to make the global local and the local global and to appreciate the mediations of the national within this complex dynamic.

6

Asserting the Local as National in the Face of the Global

The Ambivalence of Authenticity in Egyptian Soap Opera

LILA ABU-LUGHOD

Any regional specialist who comes to realize the importance of mass media and popular culture and decides to study these phenomena is confronted immediately with the problem of how to relate the local and global. By definition, mass-media products, especially the most popular, reach large audiences. Although usually produced in one national context, they often cross national and regional boundaries. The most commonly known example of the global reach of a local national product is the export of U.S. soap operas and films to the rest of the world. However, Mexican soap operas are popu-

I am indebted to a humbling number of people for help with this article. Faruq al-Rashidi at the Higher Institute of Cinema in Cairo and Sahar Tawila and Don Heisel at the Social Research Center at the American University in Cairo made it possible to focus on *I Won't Live in My Father's Shadow*. Others who contributed in various ways to the research include Iman Farid Basyouni, Elwi Captan, Khaled Fahmy, Timothy Mitchell, Mustafa Muharram, Sonali Pahwa, Omnia Shakry, Elizabeth Smith, Mohammad Tabishat, Usama Anwar 'Ukasha, Dalia Essam Wahdan, Jessica Winegar, and the Cairo working women, Fatma, Sabrine, Samira, Sa'diyya, and Zaynab, who shared their thoughts and insights with me. Audiences at Hampshire College, Duke University, New York University, the University of California at Los Angeles, and the University of Karlsruhe helped sharpen my thoughts. I want to single out Purnima Mankekar, Anne Allison, and Amrita Basu and the other editors of this volume for the special help they gave to me. For material support for research and writing, I am deeply grateful to the John Simon Guggenheim Foundation and the National Endowment for the Humanities. An affiliation with the American Research Center in Egypt and kind permission of the Ministry of Higher Education made it possible for me to do research in Egypt in 1996–97. A longer version of this essay will appear in *Melodramas of Nationhood* (University of Chicago Press, forthcoming).

lar in Russia, Lebanon, and New York City, and Brazil's Globo Television soap operas are watched in many countries around the world, including the Cameroons. Even Egypt, which has been the major producer of Arabic films in the twentieth century and of Arabic-language television soap operas for more than thirty years, has long exported its programs to the Arab world and now, via satellite, to London and the United States.[1] Anyone considering the significance of media, on the one hand, or the larger theoretical problems of how to think through the relationship between the local and the global, on the other, has to assess the impact of this kind of traffic on local mass-media industries, on local political, social, and cultural dynamics, and even on individual subjectivities.[2]

There is another way, however, in which local and global dynamics work themselves out in media, as they do in other arenas where political and cultural life are ordered. Rather than looking at the global circulation of television soap operas, I want to explore the impact of political economic processes and cultural movements that might be glossed as global or transnational on the content and intents of nationally produced soap operas. Studying Egyptian television of the 1990s leads me to argue that as the nation seems to become more "hollow" because of the increasing power and appeal of the transnational, the cultural products of state media seek more and more to assert a local authenticity (see also Hannerz 1996). This assertion is not unproblematic, as I show, with the soap opera messages about a national culture being received ambivalently by many viewers within Egypt. But the case of television in Egypt illustrates crucial features of the dynamics of globalization: the way that cultural identity and national identity become linked and the way that both are mobilized by certain groups in response to processes of transnationalization.[3] As Sassen has noted, "global processes materialize within national territories" (2000, 119), and it is the nation, I argue, that is still the crucial frame for the workings of and imaginative responses to global processes.

1. For discussions of satellite broadcasting in the Arab world, see Boyd 1999.

2. This is apart from general concerns about media's possible roles in such processes as deterritorialization, modernity, and transnational civil society. For good discussions of these debates, see Sreberny-Mohammadi 1996 and Tomlinson 1999.

3. There is a good literature on identity and global processes. Work by Hannerz and Appadurai is cited elsewhere, but see also J. Friedman 1994.

The nation I deal with is Egypt; the historical moment is the 1990s. For Egyptians, the last two decades of the twentieth century brought radical transformations in everyday life. The "open-door policies" begun in the 1970s reversed the processes of nationalization and state production and the policies of restricting imports so central to Gamal Nasser's programs of the 1950s and 1960s. With so-called economic liberalization, the ideological appeals to Arab unity and socialism also ended. Egypt was opened to foreign investment, returning landowners and businessmen, a huge U.S. government presence, and multinational companies, making especially visible in the world of consumption what is glossed as globalization. Escalating in the last decade, these processes have put McDonalds' arches, Pizza Hut's roofs, and Jeep Cherokees in and around the fancy neighborhoods of Cairo. They have filled new, exclusive shopping centers and tourist resorts with clothing boutiques that are branches of French and Italian companies. More recently, they have improved dramatically the production values of television commercials that now use rap music to sell Coca-Cola and local film stars to capture women for competing brands of laundry soap manufactured by Unilever and Palmolive.

Coinciding with these political economic processes that have benefited the families and classes able to take advantage of the business opportunities (but have meant serious economic and social decline for the growing majority of the poor) has been another transformation, as noticeable on the streets of Cairo as the new BMWs but reaching far more widely into the everyday lives of people across Egypt. This is the growing hegemony of a self-conscious Islamic identity along with the practices (prayer, religious lessons, meetings, and anti-Christian rhetoric) and paraphernalia (clothing, mosques, books, and cassettes) that enact, embody, and inculcate it. Alongside this Islamization has been the strengthening of Islamic organizations, some militant, and the shift in leadership of the professional syndicates (for lawyers and medical doctors, for example) to those with strong convictions about religious identity.

The relationship between these apparently contradictory trends is complex and tangled. Analysts have focused on a wide variety of political, economic, social, and cultural events and processes. All I note here is that there is a dialectical relationship between these processes but that each also has its own logic and compulsions, internal and external.

For anyone analyzing public culture, however, one of the most interesting aspects of such contradictory national developments is how they have positioned Egypt's intelligentsia—its writers, its artists, and, arguably most significant given the widespread popularity of television, its producers of television drama. They are educated people who usually take on for themselves the role of social commentators and architects of understanding and for whom the past two decades have been a time of great concern. One powerful response has been, as I show, to try to negotiate for their public a cultural identity that is particularly Egyptian, somewhere between the (Western-oriented) cosmopolitanism embraced by the elites, old and new, and the Pan-Islamic (anti-Western) identity implied by the Islamists and charismatic religious authorities who have a wide and mass-mediated audience. This effort can be seen especially clearly in the television serials of the 1990s, two of which I discuss in this essay.

In seeking to articulate an Egyptian cultural essence of authenticity, as did intellectuals in an earlier period of anticolonial nationalism, the producers of such serials (with the official approval implied by their ability to speak through state-run television) are trying to shape popular consciousness about Egypt's contemporary situation. They are, in Appadurai's words, engaged in producing the cultural—constituting in their serials "the diacritics of group identity" (1996, 14). This is not, as in so many culturalist movements around the world today, a process of creating identities to counter the national, but rather the rearguard action of an identity politics meant to shore up the nation-state. What these intellectuals—by and large secular and products of education under a strongly nationalist regime—are seeking to undermine are, on the one hand, the postnational identities of a cosmopolitan business elite who work within the framework of economic liberalization and, on the other, the Islamists. Islamism can be considered postnational in its "prenational" religious definition of community (the *umma*) and in its divisiveness for the nation-state, producing as it does both communal strife (divisions between Muslims and Christians) and threats to the integrity and legitimacy of the state apparatus. Although these television producers may draw on a stock of images from Egyptian literature, print media, and film, the current contexts and audiences as well as the producers' own views of the current situation give these television dramas a particular cast.[4]

4. For excellent discussions of Egyptian cinema, with which television serials have continuities, see Armbrust 1996 and Shafiq 1998. Armbrust demonstrates strong continuities in the issues dealt with by print media and cinema, especially about leisure and consumption, in his essay "Bourgeois Leisure and Egyptian Media Fantasies" (1999).

What happens when the discourses produced by such intellectuals in the extraordinarily popular medium of the television soap opera enter the social field that is contemporary Egyptian life? In particular, I explore the ambivalences created by their strategies of locating cultural authenticity in the popular (*sha'bi*) classes in a context in which the state and elites have long promoted a developmentalist ideology. Even more problematic is the way this cultural identity is made insistently national, severed from other affiliations and "diacritics" that have had and still have great resonance.

The specific case of these rocky attempts to make cultural identity through television drama in Egypt in the 1990s holds some larger lessons for those of us who would like to think about such broad matters as the relationship between the global and the local. If indeed this case supports the increasingly common recognition of culture as something consciously fashioned and disseminated and as something linked to mobilizing identities in a complex world of nations and transnations, it also reminds us of the impossibilities of closure for such cultural projects that inevitably work upon shifting sociopolitical landscapes, against competing constructions, and within history. In the conclusion, I consider why such efforts have developed in this period in Egypt and what they might tell us about the relationship between nations, states, and globalization.

Serializing Identity in the 1990s

Two major television serials of the mid-1990s, starring popular actors, crystallized the concern with Egyptian identity and authenticity. Both were brought to my attention by the strong responses they generated among the two kinds of communities for which television is produced—"ordinary viewers" and the intelligentsia. I was made aware of the serial *Arabesque* because a friend from Cairo sent a fat packet of press clippings about it to me. It was the most-discussed Ramadan serial of 1994, written by Egypt's best television writer, Usama Anwar 'Ukasha, whose popularity had just peaked with the brilliant multipart historical drama *Hilmiyya Nights,* which had filled the coveted Ramadan slot for four years.[5] The articles in major newspapers and periodicals focused on the central character, Hasan (played by Salah Sa'dani),

5. For a discussion of this serial, see Abu-Lughod 1995.

an artisan who carries on from his grandfathers the art of wood carving—arabesque—in one of Cairo's traditional or popular neighborhoods.

It is the story of Hasan's struggle with himself and for his country. The plot involves the theft of a valuable old chair carved by his grandfather, the service to his country in the 1973 war, the trauma of the earthquake in 1992, the dangers of fundamentalism, the brain drain, and the importance of commitment to community. The protagonist is meant to be an updated version of the prototypical *ibn al-balad* (literally, "son of the country")—the local guy, the salt of the earth, the poor but authentic Egyptian—who has long stood for a set of admired values in drama and everyday life.

The other serial is called, literally, *I Won't Live in My Father's Shadow* or *Lan a'ish fi gilbab abi,* a saying whose idiomatic equivalent in English might be "I won't follow in my father's footsteps" or "I won't live my father's way." It is the rags-to-riches story of 'Abd al-Ghafur al-Bur'i (played by veteran star Nur al-Sharif), who comes to Cairo looking for work (even though the short story on which the serial was based and whose name it took had 'Abd al-Ghafur's son as the central character).[6] He is taken under the wing of a successful scrap-metal merchant in the popular quarter of Bulaq (*wikalat al-balah*), for whom he initially works as a porter. Through his sincerity, hard work, and cleverness (as well as his employer and guardian's generosity), 'Abd al-Ghafur eventually becomes one of the richest and most powerful scrap-metal merchants in the market, going on to develop factories and other enterprises.

As important as this rise to wealth is his family life. He falls in love with and marries a young woman ('Abla Kamil) who, with her brother, has a food cart from which they sell a quintessentially Egyptian poor person's food, *kushari*. They have a loving—and very touching—relationship into old age. Many of the subplots of the serial revolve around the experiences of their four daughters in different types of marriages and of their son, who confusedly struggles to find an independent life through religiosity, study abroad, and a short-lived marriage to an American.

6. The scriptwriter Mustafa Muharram said that although the serial was based on a short story by the writer Ihsan 'Abd al-Quddus, he had invented the whole rags-to-riches story of 'Abdel Ghafur, whom he had asked Nur al-Sharif to play. He picked up the short story's actual theme—of a young man and his marriage to a foreigner who converts to Islam—only in episode twenty-one. Telephone interview by the author, May 1997.

Both serials are about roots, authenticity, and the values of the true Egyptian. Both, in other words, are about cultural identity, using the figure of the *ibn al-balad*—someone of modest or poor background and rooted in what are known as the popular neighborhoods, the crowded urban "traditional" neighborhoods where the rich do not live.[7] Yet the strategies by which the serials seek to construct Egyptian cultural identity differ.

The Nostalgic Register

I Won't Live in My Father's Shadow is in a nostalgic register. Through its subplots and characters, it plays out central themes about cultural identity and authenticity. For example, the protagonist, Abdu (as his wife calls him), is a man of many virtues meant to exemplify the best of Egypt. He is honest, dedicated, and willing to work hard at anything, no matter how menial, to earn a living and work his way up. Once he is wealthy, he does not renounce his origins or community but gives it dignity. He is not, however, humorless or heavy-handed. Along with guts, he has a twinkle in his eye and a clever intelligence. But he is, above all, a man guided by old-fashioned principles (*usul*).

In a 1997 interview, the scriptwriter Mustafa Muharram described to me the protagonists of the serial as people who hold onto their traditions and customs. Money does not change their essences. His fear was that those who have become rich too quickly are "in danger of forgetting their values: fraternity, honesty, and family values." The "simple" Abdu, he said, is meant to stand for the authentic Egyptian who is finding the right way to live in the present age of radical economic and political transformation. Abdu is deliberately positioned between the excesses of Islamism in the popular classes and the rootlessness of the Westernized cosmopolitan upper classes. Abdu's simple religiosity is a component of his authenticity. Unlike that of the Islamists who befriend his son in the mosque and end up trying to kill him for his refusal to join them, his piety is genuine. As a young man, he is humble

---

7. There is a good literature on the subject of *ibn al-balad*. The classic work is Sawsan El-Messiri's *Ibn al-Balad: A Concept of Egyptian Identity* (1978). Armbrust has explored the use of this figure in mass culture, especially in cinema, in *Mass Culture and Modernism in Egypt* (1996). For ethnographic works focusing on *baladi* women, see Early 1997 and Hoodfar 1997.

and grateful for his daily bread. He respects and listens to the advice of his religious sheikh; he and his wife go on the pilgrimage to Mecca as soon as he has "made it"; he deals honorably and honestly with others; and he is scrupulous and generous in giving alms.

Abdu's traditionalism also emerges in his role as wise paterfamilias. He is represented as a benign patriarch. Many viewers I talked to likened Abdu to "Si Sayyid," as they called him, the patriarch of Naguib Mahfouz's Cairo trilogy. (It should be noted that the connection they made was not to the novel but to the popular television serial or films based on it.) Immediately after mentioning this character, however, people would deny the similarities. Clearly, the figure of Abdu evoked the memory of this early patriarch, although and no doubt because he differs from him in significant ways.

One of the most obvious points of contrast—and comparison—is their strictness toward the women in their families. Abdu is not stern; he is merely firm in his principles and values. Although he objects to many "modern" ways—ways of people of other classes or those who have renounced their roots—he is shown not to be harsh and authoritarian, but correct. His strictness with his son, though it causes the boy unhappiness and a long road to self-discovery and reconciliation, is intended to make him a man, able to stand on his own. Like Al-Sayyid Ahmad, the protagonist of Naguib Mahfouz's *Palace Walk* (1989), Abdu also punishes his wife once for allowing her daughters, against his wishes and without permission, to attend a mixed-sex birthday party at their upper-class neighbors' home. But he does not cruelly banish her from the house, as Mahfouz's character does to his wife. The trouble with Al-Sayyid's patriarchy is that it is so unfair, his wife's breaking of seclusion having been so innocent (to visit a holy place) while he himself leads a double life (frequenting prostitutes and dancers). In contrast, Abdu's adherence to old-fashioned principles regarding women is shown to be consistent and wise. He is right, it turns out in the end, to suspect the neighbor's son of bad intentions toward his daughter (discussed further in the next section). He is right in thinking that his family has no business mixing with theirs; it eventuates in grief and humiliation for his naïve daughter. His strictness with his daughters, who are not allowed to go out or join clubs (as others of their level of wealth do), is shown to be for their protection and honor (another value Abdu cherishes).

More interesting is Abdu's marriage, presented as extraordinarily loving and, for many viewers, the heart of the serial. This marital relationship might be classified as neotraditional in the way it combines stereotypical "traditional" elements, such as a sexual division of labor, with what I would argue are quite "modern" and middle-class elements—companionate marriage and the nuclear family—but here displaced onto and confused with "traditional values." The portrayal of this marriage thus represents exquisitely the problems educated professionals such as television writers face when they attempt to depict authenticity through the more "traditional" lower classes. In particular, we see how they must impose their own values on or at least mix them with those of the group they are depicting to make them palatable to a broad middle class. In Fatma and Abdu's marriage is a nostalgia for something that never was and a compression of contemporary romantic middle-class ideals for marriage (choice, true love, mutuality) and fatherhood (loving concern) with some older ideals and elements that also might never have been practices of the lower classes (women's confinement to the domestic).

The Problem Is Class: *Awlad al-balad* versus *Awlad al-zawat*

Despite this romantic vision of a selectively modernized *ibn al-balad* with an amalgam of appealing qualities, *I Won't Live in My Father's Shadow* ran into some difficulties of reception, which, I show, arose from the problem of associating the authentic Egyptian of traditions and values with those who are uneducated and from poor backgrounds.

The most compelling and dramatic subplot of the serial involves a government minister who rents an apartment in the fancy new building the protagonist bought and moved into in Zamalek, an old elite neighborhood of Cairo across the river from the scrap-metal market. Many viewers spontaneously mentioned the government minister (*wazir*) when I raised the topic of this serial, recounting one or another aspect of his relationship to the protagonist: either his son's greedy and immoral pursuit of and marriage to Abdu's oldest daughter or the fundamental differences in lifestyle and values between his family and Abdu's. The relationship between the two men occasions some of the most powerful moments in the serial, moments in which the protagonist's attachment to traditional principles are exonerated and his moral superiority over a supposed social superior is grandly revealed.

For a widow who worked as a house cleaner and had raised four children on her own, the negative depiction of the minister happened to fit perfectly with one of her obsessions: government negligence of the poor and wealth unfairly concentrated in the hands of politicians. When I asked her about the serial, her first response, like so many, was to name the main actor (Nur al-Sharif) and actress ('Abla Kamil) and to sigh affectionately. But then immediately she brought up the government minister. She said, "If anyone's eaten the country's wealth, it is the politicians. There was the earthquake [in 1992] that knocked down these buildings. I don't know who it was, whether it was the American government or what that had sent us lots of things, mattresses and things. I swear to God they kept saying they were going to distribute them, but no one saw any of it. The ministers are the ones who take it. They divide it amongst themselves. They say, let's give some to one or two families and then enjoy the rest. It is incredible. But what really makes me mad is the Parliament."

She had brought up the topic of Parliament earlier, when talking about the difficulties her children were having finding work or being paid enough to live: "In the Parliament each day, they talk and talk, and I'm there watching the ministers. I watch on television. Every minister in Parliament gets a fat salary. Why do they need to meet this way every day? How about meeting once a month instead of every day?" She assumed that they work for a daily wage as she did. Rather than taking this money for themselves, she believed that they should create projects in poor neighborhoods to employ people.

The reactions of others of her background who themselves similarly worked in domestic service were more ambiguous, suggesting the ambivalence at the heart of depictions of *baladi* people. One educated woman had fallen on hard times after her foreign husband abandoned her and now supported herself through home daycare for European expatriates. She surprised me by sympathizing with the government minister's family position, despite the clearly negative portrayal. She recounted, "The minister's son wanted to marry the daughter of the man who owned the building. His father was a minister but didn't have much because he was retired. The boy divorced her. He didn't love her. Yes, how could he, the son of a minister, marry the daughter of someone from this [poor] section of town? The father wore a *gallabiyya*. And you saw how they ate, the day of the invitation. They were tearing the chicken with their hands. There is a big difference between a government minister and someone like this."

The disgust she expressed about these *baladi* people who had money but were boors revealed her identification with the minister's family, despite the serial's intention. There is no ambiguity in the serial's depiction of the son's self-interested greed, the pretentious and manipulative mother's contemptuous superiority, and the initially arrogant minister's weakness, which in the end brought him down.

But shame or simply the keen awareness of one's own status group made many *baladi* people draw lessons the serial had not intended. The reactions of one semi-educated mother of four who worked as a cleaner because her husband was old and housebound are indicative of the power of this awareness to shape interpretation. She talked about Abdu's daughters and how all were good except the one who looked to marry above her station. As she put it, "This wasn't good. She should have married someone from her own level; that would have been better. All she cared about was that he was the son of a government minister. This was wrong. They didn't know the family and hadn't shared a life. She is the one who lost out because he married her out of greed. And his mother's greed. Oh, they [the minister's family] looked down on them. That wasn't nice." This woman concluded that the serial was useful because it taught girls not to look above their social level.

This woman's concerns with issues of social class also emerged in other thoughts she had about what the serial taught parents. Discussing the key incidents in Abdu's son's boyhood that created a rift between father and son—the humiliations of being in a private school and yet not having the spending money or privileges of his peers, with his father refusing to drive him to school and, on principle, to contribute a requested donation to the school—she said, "If his father had been educated, he wouldn't have misunderstood in this way. He would have realized that the school was like that and that all the children's parents contributed. If you send your son to a private school, you have to pay what's needed. We should treat our kids at the level of those around them. Send your children to the school you can afford, so they will be like their peers. Every person should be at his own rank."

Another domestic servant, someone who had come from the countryside to Cairo as a young girl, described how she had watched the serial with her employer, a woman of Syrian origins who was from an important family. She laughed and repeated what her employer had said: "She used to sit there laughing at them and telling me, '*Baladi* people. Look at them eating that way with their hands. Disgusting. What is this? There is no proper order and they talk in a *baladi* way.' " This servant likened her employer to the government minister's wife, who "sat there saying to her son, '*Baladi!* What are these people you have gotten to know? I don't know how you can stand them!' " Her employer would sit there complaining about the things the characters did. "She didn't like the way they ate. She didn't like the way they talked. She didn't like the serial; she didn't like the things they did in it, these *baladi* things. She preferred the things she was used to, the ways of the aristocrats of long ago. She used to tell me, 'I don't know why you like to watch this.' "

When I asked the domestic worker how she had felt about the serial, she said, "I really liked it, to tell you the truth." Yet there were signs that she felt a certain shame or discomfort, given her own position as a similarly uneducated and ordinary person, in her manners and dress far closer to the protagonists of the serial than to her aristocratic employer. Her ambivalence toward such people and thus toward herself was revealed in her reflections on the gender roles of the serial's main family. She viewed Abdu's family as "the family of long ago. When the father came home, everyone would gather and eat together." When I asked if it was really meant to represent the family of the past, she corrected herself and said it was meant to be between past and present. Then she, like so many others, brought up Si Sayyid, the protagonist of the Mahfouz novel, as an example of what happened long ago. Abdu she described as both *baladi* and "moderne."

What did "moderne" mean to her? She first described the past as a time before there was television or radio. The main difference seemed to be in the behavior of girls and women. As she said, "In the days of Si Sayyid, there was no looking out of windows. Girls wouldn't go out by themselves, and women wouldn't go out at all." When I confronted her with the fact that Fatma, Abdu's wife, also does not go out, she made an important point about choice. "No, she didn't go out. But he didn't tell her, 'Don't go out.' She's the one who preferred to be a housewife." Yet she did not agree with me that the emotional and indulgent Fatma is a model mother and wife. She admired Fatma's devotion to husband and family but felt that her lack of education and her seclusion are faults. She said, "Women are supposed to go out—because when a person goes out, she learns a lot of things. The more one goes out, the more one learns. I see things and learn. But she just stayed at home with her housework and the kitchen and food, wondering what to cook today. There are a lot of things one can learn about besides food. For example, organizing the house. Knowing how to rearrange the house. And how to arrange flowers. She didn't have any idea. The house had been set up, and that was that. It was like a house in the old days. You put something in one place, and it never moves from its place until the owner dies."

I was intrigued by redecorating as a sign of modernity and pursued it. The domestic servant gave examples of employers to whose homes she had returned only to find redone kitchens and rearranged furniture. Yet, to her, being "moderne" was more than redecorating. It was being educated and leading a complex life. The negative contrast she drew between Fatma and her own former employer highlighted the busy life and worldliness of the latter. Although educated, the employer liked housework and was always busy at home, yet also went to the clubs and to parties and met with her friends and her daughter. As the servant put it, "Fatma was nice. And she understood some things. But she didn't know as much as an educated woman would know." And again she brought up the government minister's wife as a positive example. "Look at the government minister's wife. She talked in a more highfalutin' way and didn't use words like *kidda* [a low-speech form meaning "like this"]. Isn't this the way it should be? A woman living in Zamalek who talks like Fatma? It isn't right. It is too *baladi*. She should have learned some *afrangi* [Western] things. It is better to be more a part of society. Otherwise, a woman will just be sitting in the house with the door shut, not knowing how to talk with anyone or meet people. Sitting in the kitchen wondering what to cook."

For this woman, being a little "moderne" was a positive thing. Yet becoming educated, knowing how to negotiate a social life independently, going out, and being Westernized were all qualities of upper-class women. The only part of this complex with which she could identify, as a woman who had worked most of her life and who had lived independently, was going out and learning from it. So she seemed to look down on Fatma without herself being able to match up to the standards she had internalized or to criticize the minister's wife. Her feelings about herself were echoed in the remark a friend of hers made, someone who also worked as a domestic. As we talked about a television serial we were watching in which the protagonists were educators, the friend said, "Yes, they are good people, educated people." When I protested, "But you're a good person even though you're not educated," she responded, "Sure, but it's better if you're educated. You know things."

It is, in fact, too late to use a *baladi* person to represent all that is good in Egypt. The discourses of development and enlightenment through education are too hegemonic, having more than a century of work behind them. Even *I Won't Live in My Father's Shadow* cannot resist the discourse of progress in the final episodes. If Abdu and his wife Fatma are absolutely loveable characters, fulfilling some nostalgic wish about how good Egyptians were and are, they also are, in the end, representatives of the past. The concluding episodes about the resolution of the son's and youngest daughter's careers and marriages show the correct path for the current generation. The future includes higher education (the son gains his education abroad and the youngest daughter at the American University in Cairo) and a modern way to work hard and be productive, but without, of course, losing one's values and culture. The son eventually follows in his father's footsteps, but he will be more successful because he knows the ways of the world, and he can read and write. He also sees the light and marries his well-behaved cousin, someone therefore of his own station who shares his values. But she, too, has become educated. The youngest of Abdu's daughters, on the other hand, chooses her brother's best friend for a husband. She does what an earlier generation could not: she meets the man without benefit of chaperones, but she has an internal chaperone—her principles—that prevents her from doing anything she should not in these encounters. And it is she who convinces him to become a productive citizen before he can win her hand. Theirs promises to be a loving and companionate marriage between knowledgeable, educated professionals—a model marriage built, as the writer described it, on love and mutual understanding.

It cannot be forgotten that one of the reiterated messages of the serial is the piece of advice Abdu's patron gives to him: "Educate them [your children] so they'll be better than you are." This raises the specter of the intractable problem that has served, as Armbrust (1996) has documented, as a theme for so much Egyptian mass culture: how to become modern without losing one's values and traditions and, it might be added, authenticity. The problem can best be captured by the subtle shifts in connotations between the more negative descriptor *baladi,* which carries meanings of provincialism and lower-class identity, and the positively valued notions of the *ibn al-balad,* the common people (*sha'b*), and even the adjective *sha'bi* ("popular") when applied to alleys and expressive culture—all of which, as Singerman (1995) argues, carry ideas of indigenousness. Based on her work in a popular neighborhood in Cairo, Singerman observes, "As reservoirs of national identity and the Egyptian character, then, the *sha'b* have a sense of their authenticity and believe that they embody the values and beliefs of the nation" (14). The writers who depict these values and beliefs in television drama share her view. But the reactions of many viewers of *I Won't Live in My Father's Shadow* suggest that it is easy to slip from valuing members of this kind of community as repositories of the authenticity of the nation to disdaining their lack of sophistication and modernity as something that contributes to the "backwardness" of Egypt.[8]

Arabesque: A Return to Consciousness?

On a superficial level, *Arabesque,* seems to be about many of the same issues. As a housekeeper summed up the serial for me, it is about a popular (*baladi*) neighborhood and its authenticity and about a kind of craft that no longer exists. The other theme she mentioned was the threat foreigners pose to Egypt. In the serial, foreigners want to steal a treasure that is part of the national heritage (the carved arabesque chair made by our hero's grandfather), and they want to kidnap a U.S.-trained Egyptian scientist who returns to Egypt to contribute his knowledge to his country.

However, a closer look at the serial, written by a major television writer explicitly to address the question of cultural identity, reveals fundamental differences with *I Won't Live in My Father's Shadow.* Some of the ambivalence toward the *ibn al-balad* figure is built into the central character. And though the theme is authenticity, the serial is resolutely nonnostalgic. It is not simply about the importance of holding on to values. Rather, it asks

8. Julie Skursi (1996) explores for Latin America, Venezuela in particular, the ambiguities of using "the people" in nationalist fictions.

what values can sustain people confronted with the present—a present that is national and tied to the contemporary political scene.

The writer, Usama Anwar 'Ukasha, more articulate and political than many of his colleagues in television, explicitly recognizes in the serial that to claim such classes, artisans who live and work in popular neighborhoods, as representing Egyptians is not unproblematic. His protagonist, Hasan, is a confused and contradictory character. It is under the influence of drugs that he carelessly reveals the secret of the carved chair, the treasure that symbolizes his cultural and familial heritage. This revelation leads to the theft of the chair. As Amal Bakir, in an interview of the actor who played the central role, described the character of Hasan, he is "the simple Egyptian citizen who gave to the nation and participated in the war, this informed citizen, artistic, authentic, intelligent, courageous, and giving, who loves his country and protects its authenticity; but on the other hand who is depressed, a hoodlum, lazy, lost, and enmeshed in the world of drugs and other things, as well as having other negative qualities" (1994, 2). The actor explained that he was attracted to the character because of the way he was full of contradictions and mood swings but was an *ibn al-balad*. Both critic and actor recognized that this character represents the *ibn al-balad* who must find his way in the contemporary period, where significant dangers lurk: "a period in which there was a danger that the citizen be transformed into a profiteer at the expense of his art, authenticity, and culture" (2).

Although one journalistic piece drew out the resemblances between this fictional character and a real artisan now working in Khan el-Khalili, painting a glowing portrait of the real artisan as the true *ibn al-balad* (generous, brave, reasonable, and manly, standing by his community, helping anyone in need, and fairly resolving disputes), others found fault with the writer of the serial for this ambivalent depiction of the lower-middle-class artisan who is supposed to represent authentic Egypt (see, for example, al-Sayyid 1994, 74–77). Whereas several writers complimented 'Ukasha on the mixed depiction of the Egyptian mother, who (unlike the indulgent Fatma in *I Won't Live in My Father's Shadow*) is harsh with her children but out of love and fear for them, one journalist complained that it was pessimistic to make Hasan the essence of Egypt because "Hasan Arabesque is an example of a misguided Egyptian, someone with incredible talents and abilities but circumstances that hinder him; who is creative in his art but too weak to deal with his weaknesses; who is capable of acting but doesn't; and who finally expresses a crisis that Egypt is undergoing" (al-Kardusy 1994, 57–60).

'Ukasha's response to this interview question was telling. He defended his depiction of the central character as in crisis. First, he said, it was a means to highlight the very issue of a crisis in Egyptian identity. Second, it was "to confront the strands of fundamentalism in which you will not find 'the nation' but only religion, in which no one should say 'I'm Egyptian,' but rather, 'I'm Muslim' " (al-Kardusy 1994, 58). In 'Ukasha's work, to phrase it differently, the political and the cultural are fused. A sense of nationhood is knotted to a cultural essence—again, the Egyptian character or personality best embodied by the urban *ibn al-balad* living in the traditional neighborhood.[9]

Arabesque, like all of 'Ukasha's serials, links everyday lives with national politics. In a glowing review in the official Egyptian newspaper, *Al-Ahram,* one writer (Hijazi 1994) credited *Arabesque* with awakening Egyptians from their slumber, restoring their memory, and creating a national consciousness (Hijazi 1994). The aims of the serial, he continued, were "to put the issue of a national existence once again into our collective consciousness. . . . We were not merely viewers but a national mass envisioning its essence . . . and thinking of its future, putting forth the questions it had been quiet about for years and confronting facts it had not confronted before. . . . Our memory was returned to us after months or years of amnesia" (1994, 18).[10]

---

9. In contrast, the nostalgic *I Won't Live in My Father's Shadow* scrupulously avoids the political (except to offer the obligatory swipe at Islamic militants). One of the most amusing subplots is one in which Abdu suddenly seems to take an interest in politics—he is very concerned about a hijacked jumbo jet on the ground at Cairo Airport and what the government will do about it. Those around him are surprised at this uncharacteristic concern with national and international politics. But it turns out that behind his interest in the jumbo jet is an amazing business opportunity: he sees the airplane as a potentially profitable hulk of scrap metal for his trade. And when he becomes a national hero for purchasing the plane, he and his wife are only concerned to use the profit to make the pilgrimage to Mecca.

10. For a discussion of this as a common metaphor, see Gabriel Piterburg's "The Tropes of Stagnation and Awakening in Nationalist Historical Consciousness: The Egyptian Case" (1997). In using the imagery of a return to consciousness, the writer also may be invoking the famous book of the Sadat era by Tawfiq al-Hakim, *'Awdat al-wa'i* (Return of consciousness), which sought to explain how Egyptians had fallen under the spell of Nasser and the 1952 revolution. The book's title echoes al-Hakim's own earlier work *'Awdat al-ruh* (Return of the spirit), which asserted a deeply rooted Egyptian identity dating back to the Pharaohs.

Instead of the apolitical nostalgia of *I Won't Live in My Father's Shadow*, we have a politicized opening to the future. The writer of this article in *Al-Ahram* then remarked that the alley or neighborhood (*hara*) stands for Egypt and that, like Egypt, its history began happily but then began to decline "until it came to the miserable present in which events unfolded and in which the future advanced, carrying on its waves the stars of the present— evil doers, the ignorant, thieves, and hypocrites. In response, some of the good turn their dreams and feelings toward the past and become nostalgic" (Hijazi 1994, 18).[11] But he added, "Those who have been crushed by disasters are the very ones who will defend us against the approaching dangers, not because they want to protect their personal interests but because of principles." So the serial invoked a national consciousness and presented hope for the future in the authentic class of Egyptians, those who are neither riding the corrupting wave of the new capitalism that liberalization and the opening to the West have brought to Egypt nor succumbing to the rhetoric of an Islamist xenophobia.

For this depiction, 'Ukasha drew on a rich tradition of representing the Egyptian nation by the figure of the *ibn al-balad*. The term was used in the nineteenth century to designate the indigenous Muslim population as distinct from foreign rulers and elites (be they Ottoman, French, or other Europeans), the minority religious groups (Copts and Jews) associated with the foreign rulers, or groups from other Arab regions such as North Africa (El-Hamamsy 1982), and by at least 1941 the cartoon figure used by a major periodical to represent the average Egyptian was changed from the more educated "al-Misri Effendi" to the *ibn al-balad* because he "represented a more independent and emancipated personality" (Baron 1997, 115–16). The *baladi* figure had come to be associated more exclusively with "traditional" or un-Westernized urban folk of the lower middle and lower classes, those who lived in the popular neighborhoods or alleys (*hara*s).

One small indication of the enduring power of this image—promoted in literature, films, and now television—is apparent in the continuities between

11. The alley is a resonant symbol of community and lower-class life in Egypt. To explain his successful depiction of 'Abd al-Ghafur, the writer of *I Won't Live in My Father's Shadow* pointed to his own upbringing in the alleys in the neighborhood of Sayyida Zaynab in Cairo (Muharram 1997).

the characteristics El-Messiri's (1978) wide study sample in the early 1970s attributed to the *ibn al-balad* (who follows the old ways, doesn't use foreign words, and is religious, less educated, gallant, generous, funny, loyal to kin and neighbors, and ready to help) and contemporary discussions on the pages of the *Radio and Television Magazine* (Hamdi 1997). In a variety of responses to the question of how realistic were screen representations of the *ibn al-balad* and the Egyptian alley, the idealization of this figure is clear. One actor who had played the role of an *ibn al-balad* noted not only that this character was not affected by social and economic changes but that the "*ibn al-balad* holds onto principles and values, heritage, and religious up-bringing." A set designer likewise argued that what was so distinctive about the people of these popular quarters was that, like the protagonist 'Abd al-Ghafur of *I Won't Live in My Father's Shadow,* the times did not change them. Dr. Ahmad Al-Majdub, the director of the National Center for Socio-logical and Criminological Research, berated television drama for misrepre-senting the popular neighborhood, arguing that in fact the people of these areas "preserve old Egyptian customs" such as friendship, solidarity, and sac-rifice, because of constant face-to-face relations (Hamdi 1997, 46–47).

In *Arabesque,* 'Ukasha has made this figure of authentic and old-fashioned Egyptian culture stand for the nation. As the scriptwriter ex-plained in response to an interviewer who compared his earlier serial *Hilmiyya Nights* to Naguib Mahfouz's trilogy, "Perhaps every writer of my generation graduated from Mahfouz's trilogy, as did a generation of Russian writers from Gogol. Mahfouz's imprint is on all our choices: in the atmos-phere we prefer; in the popular alley/neighborhood where the Egyptian personality/character is to be found; especially in the search for authenticity; and in the fear that Egyptian identity will dissipate" ('Ukasha 1992, 29).[12]

"We Have Always Been Transnational"

The writer of the serial *Arabesque* now links political hope explicitly with a commitment to an Egyptian cultural identity. Although he was in the past an Arab nationalist, he now believes that the solution to national despair and

12. Naguib Mahfouz himself wrote many scripts for cinema and has had many novels adapted for film. See Shafiq 1998, 133.

disintegration lies in the answer to the question of identity: "Who are we?" In *Arabesque* and in interviews, he explored a series of possible answers. "Are we Pharaonic?" Here he cited Arnold Toynbee and then quoted Jamal Hamdan, the author of a major tome on Egyptian civilization, to the effect that "there are remains and material remnants that continue in the fabric of contemporary Egyptian civilization" (al-Kardusy 1994, 59). To the question "Are we Copts?" he answered that Copts have been a minority but that their art is the only true Egyptian art. In response to the next question, "Are we Mediterranean?" he rejected earlier intellectuals' assertions of Mediterranean unity, seeing such discourse as serving European cultural power and interests. Finally, to the question "Are we Arab Muslims?" he answered, "Not really." He admitted a continuous interaction and influence and a hybridization. But he asserted finally that the Arab Bedouin "were only an igniting force in the pre-existing essence of Egyptian civilization; they did not alter the essence itself" (al-Kardusy 1994, 59).

'Ukasha denied the viability of Islamic or Arab nationalism saying, "There is only an Egyptian nationalism." But what this consists in is the power of assimilation and hybridization. In the 1994 interview by Mahmud al-Kardusy for *Nusf al-Dunya*, he insisted that "the only identity—if we must have one—is related to how we absorb or appropriate other cultures, whether brought in by occupation, colonization, or the new open door policies. There is always a process of Egyptianization . . . which derives from the Egyptian's pride and respect for his Egyptianness" (60).

'Ukasha's conclusion was that Egyptianness lies in the ability to Egyptianize "the other." This is the subject he was exploring in the major three-part serial that he was writing when I interviewed him in 1997 and that first aired during Ramadan, January 1998. Called *Zizinya*, it is set in a couple of neighborhoods of Alexandria, including Zizinya, during the decades of the 1940s and 1950s, before the exodus of foreigners following Nasser's nationalization of the Suez Canal. As 'Ukasha said in the interview, it was a time when "the other" lived side by side with the Egyptian and shared his or her everyday life. There were Greeks, Armenians, and Italians. The serial includes even a Jewish family. The question for this serial is, according to 'Ukasha, "Who affected whom? Which culture dominated?" And again, in another 1997 interview I conducted, he reiterated his admiration for Jamal Hamdan's theories about Egypt being a large stomach whose enzymes digest foreign cultures, creating the unique hybrid "the Egyptian personality/character."

Both *I Won't Live in My Father's Shadow* and *Arabesque* trafficked in images of foreigners at the time they were aired, as did many television serials of the 1990s, to make their points about cultural identity. *I Won't Live in My Father's Shadow,* appealing to the sensibilities of many ordinary people, presented the American Rosalind as utterly different and, in the end, "not one of us." Her improbable character is an excuse to praise Egypt; she wants to live in Egypt, where, she says, families are close and there is no fear on the streets; she also converts to Islam to marry Abdu's son, a young man whose stay in Europe has made him want to "marry someone who has the attributes of a European woman—her power, her education, her acceptance of responsibility"—but who is Egyptian and pious because, he adds, "piety [*iman*] is the foundation of a good character/personality." Rosalind has some admirable qualities, despite her atrocious Arabic. She works hard and takes charge of life, unlike Abdu's more passive daughters. But she puts money first and does not bring happiness to her husband. Their marriage fails, much to her mother-in-law's relief.

Arabesque is more complex. Foreigners figure in the serial as villains, but the real question regarding transnational exchange is whether or not there is an Egyptian essence that will emerge victorious despite would-be conquerors. *Arabesque*'s answer is that, indeed, the real victory of Egyptians will come with their loyalty to the community along with some preservation of past values.

What kind of response does this sort of construction of "the Egyptian character" produce in the public? I would argue again that, like the figure of the *ibn al-balad,* who shades into the uneducated *baladi* person, it can produce only ambivalence for viewers, for two main reasons: first, because of the complicated class assumptions of an association between authenticity and the "simple" class, already noted in this essay and explored more fully later; second, because of its denial of the importance of Islam and even of Arabness to identity.

The issue of class can be drawn out through an examination of the key symbol of Egyptian authenticity in the serial—the form of intricate wood carving called arabesque. For one actress interviewed, the highly respected

Huda Sultan, the symbol of handmade arabesque is linked to lasting value—the authentic is priceless (al-Sa'dani 1994, 44–45). But what kind of authenticity is arabesque? First, for many viewers of the serial, the term *arabesque* itself might have been puzzling because it is not an Arabic word; they would have been more comfortable describing this form of wood carving as *mashrabiyya* instead. And instead of being part of the present, it was a craft of the past, as described by the working woman who first told me about the serial. *Mashrabiyya* is found in the grand old houses of the old city, many now museums; it is found in the Islamic Museum. Not insignificantly, arabesque is today sold to two kinds of buyers: tourists and antique connoisseurs wanting a distinctly Middle Eastern look and Egyptian and Arab elites seeking to express their Arab heritage against Western styles. The appreciation of arabesque is thus an elite taste, not shared by the poor or lower middle class in Egypt even if the product might be manufactured in their alleys. In fact, the largest factory for the revival of the production of high-quality *mashrabiyya* was started by As'ad Nadim, an Indiana University-trained folklorist hoping to keep the craft alive. It now sells to wealthy customers all over the Arab world. Thus, it is an odd symbol of authenticity, one that excludes the very classes that are supposed to symbolize this Egyptian essence.

Second, as one journalist pointed out in his questions to 'Ukasha, why use an Arabo-Islamic art form to symbolize Egyptian identity? 'Ukasha's response shows how problematic, from the very angle of identity, his position is. Saying that "there is nothing more expressive of a people's identity than their art," he simply denied conventional understandings of arabesque as Arabo-Islamic, either Mamluk or Fatimid. Instead, he opined, woodworking resembling arabesque was found in the Coptic churches at the time that Arabs entered Egypt in the seventh century (al-Kardusy 1994, 59). This downplaying of the Arab and Islamic character of Egyptian authenticity is a tricky strategy for someone who cares so much about moving his public. *Arabesque* was watched by people whose family members died in wars with Israel and who still express great sympathy for Palestinians, a sentiment given support, even now, by official government rhetoric despite widespread disillusionment with the notion of Arab nationalism. Long decades of education since the 1952 revolution have stressed the Arab character of Egyptian identity, with Arabic language, literature, and folklore being given pride of place; the heroes of Arab-Islamic history being glorified; and, as El-Hamamsy notes, mass media "helping to diffuse ideas and to standardize taste" such that a great degree of "cultural consanguinity" has been created (1982, 304). This general sense of Egyptian culture as Arab (despite increasing hostility and distance from the wealthy Gulf Arabs and the policies for reviving the Pharaonic heritage of Egypt pursued by President Sadat from the 1970s) as well as proud feelings among many segments of the rural population from Upper Egypt to the northwest coast about being themselves of Arab stock (with origins in the Arabian Peninsula) make it awkward for a serial to return to the ideas of a cultural elite in the 1920s, 1930s, and beyond, who argued for a purely (even if digestive) Egyptian national identity.

More problematic is that the majority of people who watched *Arabesque* felt and continue to feel rather strongly that being Muslim is quite central to defining who they are and how to be a good and moral person. There is a growing popularity of serials about religion and about medieval Arab history. Even 'Ukasha granted that "the Egyptian people are the most pious of all Muslim peoples" while condemning "extremism" ('Ukasha 1992, 27–29). Yet he expressed his concern about television officials' strategies during the 1990s—"waving Qur'ans," eagerly claiming to be good Muslims by programming religious shows, proudly interrupting programs for the call to prayer, and submitting more and more scripts to the censorship of Al-Azhar, the major religious establishment ('Ukasha 1993, 68). He declared in interviews with me ('Ukasha 1997) that he is "antitheocratic" and believes in the civil nation, citing the importance of the fall of the church to the development of European civilization. But this strong secularism is a minority position in Egypt, linked with an increasingly small part of the intelligentsia who defend the "Enlightenment" values of modernist reform or some version of leftism. If during the Nasser era Egyptian patriotism and Arabism eclipsed religious identity in rhetoric and policy, the current government does not even endorse secularism, despite its negative treatment of "extremists."[13] How can millions of viewers of a range of classes who are themselves pious and who increasingly vocalize that being Muslim is a key

13. On the government position as expressed in the campaign to fight "extremism" with media, see Abu-Lughod 1997a and 1997b.

part of their social identity accept the absence of religion as a major diacritic of identity, "the Egyptian character" as secular or as simply religiously observant in a quiet and private way?

The response to the first segment of *Zizinya,* aired during Ramadan 1998, seems to have been lukewarm, even though it was reported to have been the biggest production of the year, costing six million Egyptian pounds and involving most of Egypt's favorite actors. The serial's explicit treatment of identity—through the main protagonist, who moves between the worlds of his patriarchal and traditional Egyptian Muslim father and his elegant Italian mother and uncle—received less attention in the press than the general matter of the value of historical serials (which glutted that Ramadan season) and the specific politics of the serial. In particular, those sympathetic to the Wafd Party (the "liberal" party that was active at the time) were incensed that the Wafd Party was portrayed as less than militant in its opposition to the British. One columnist charged that in the thirty-fourth episode 'Ukasha "devalues the role of the Wafd as a popular party that led the struggle against the English. Every nationalist in Egypt has been educated and inspired by the nationalist school of the Wafd. This is a truism for every historian and observer, except for the author of *Zizinya*" (Muhanna 1998, 9).

Again, it is not clear how a serial that treats explicitly the theme of Egyptians, linked to soil and location and able to absorb all others, could be received unambivalently by people whose prerevolution (1952) memories of foreigners (*khawagas*) are tied to class difference and whose current sensibilities have been forged during a long period of nationalistic antiforeign politics, bolstered by the construction of an Egyptian history that tells the story of the territorial nation-state's throwing off the yoke of foreign rule (Piterburg 1997). This nationalism recently has been revived and glorified for the benefit of the younger generation in the wildly popular made-for-television film *Nasser '56* (which was shown in movie theaters instead), about the nationalization of the Suez Canal.[14] This was a film intended, according to its director Mohammad Fadil (who had collaborated with 'Ukasha often in the past), to combat what he saw as a collective depression in Egypt. He wanted to give hope by showing that "as Egyptians we are ca-

---

14. For a marvelous discussion of this film and its impact, based mostly on discussions with the scriptwriter, Mahfuz 'Abd al-Rahman, see Gordon 2000.

pable of accomplishing things, in contrast to the current portrayal of us as economically impoverished and insecure, faced with the sole option of submitting to the New World Order" (Fadil 1993).

But even without that nostalgic throwback, the general rhetoric of the Islamism that has appealed to more and more people since the 1967 defeat, although Sadat and Mubarak pursued "globalization" through the "open-door" policies, has pushed anti-Western sentiment. Could viewers really embrace the protagonist of 'Ukasha's *Zizinya,* who shifts back and forth between heavy drinking, flirting, and European clothing, on the one hand, and the fez and robes of his father and half-brothers as well as friendship with a religious cleric who has been anointed head of a religious brotherhood, on the other? Even more problematic, how were they to respond to the Greek grocer with accented Arabic who not only defends his decision to keep his shop in the popular alley because the people there are good people, people with *shahama* (the attributes stereotypically associated with the *ibn al-balad:* nobility, gallantry, friendship, and generosity), but also declares that he is an Egyptian Greek, and this is his country, too, a country whose occupation (by the British) he must help fight?

I have been trying to show in this essay on television drama in Egypt that the culture industry seems to be in the business of producing not just art or entertainment, but also cultural identity itself, as shown especially in the serials of the 1990s. This work, specifically that which appears on state-controlled television, is tied up inevitably with the nation-state, which—despite pronouncements in the Western academy about its demise and about the very real economic and political forces threatening its sovereignty, integrity, and legitimacy—is still a dominant matrix of social and political life for most individuals and communities and is certainly the dominant context of cultural production (and of political activism, as Basu makes clear in chapter 5 of this volume), especially in those countries that call themselves part of the "underdeveloped" world.[15]

What I also have argued is that a close examination of the strategies writers and others pursue to construct national identities through constructing

15. I argued this point earlier in Abu-Lughod 1993.

cultural essences reveals that because their efforts are tied so closely to contemporary national debates and dilemmas, they are likely to be undermined by conflicting ideologies and the actual social experiences of the people to whom they are directed. If writers represent the Egyptian cultural essence as lying in the "simple" classes, those of modest means who live in the old neighborhoods and who preserve old values, these constructions will encounter ambivalence, even when doctored to suit newer tastes. The backwardness and ignorance associated with such classes—imprinted by the hegemonic rhetoric of developmentalism, where modernity and education are the keys to national and individual advancement—haunt their value. To represent the nation by one local segment and lifestyle is always tricky, too, because of all the other territorial "locals" it excludes: regional, ethnic, rural, and the middle and upper classes.

And if, as in *Arabesque*, television writers represent the Egyptian cultural essence as in crisis but also present the resolution as lying in an appreciation of national heritage and an assimilative identity rooted in the ancient soil of Egypt, they may well provoke unease at their silences on other crucial "diacritics of group identity" that link people imaginatively to wider worlds: Islam and Arabness, in this case. They also may not be able to shake some common ways of marking such identity—as in opposition to Europeans as the colonizing "Other."

A close look at the case of Egypt suggests the sorts of political situations that inspire efforts, however problematic, of national culturing. The urgency with which television serials are trying to shore up a national identity is surely related to the weakening of that strong sense of the nation produced a few decades ago by wars and by the rhetoric and policies of nation building. If Egypt is one of the places where, as Hannerz puts it, "the national may have become more hollow than it was" (1996, 89), it is also the place where the political regime in power and the mass-media instruments at its disposal are working quite hard to fill in that hollowness.

What seems confusing is that television writers such as 'Ukasha and other members of the intelligentsia who work through mass media perceive themselves as critics of the system or the regime in power. They counter accusations of toeing government lines (such as those leveled against 'Ukasha when he wrote a serial with a family-planning message) with arguments such as, "I do not support the government because the government does not sympathize with the people." 'Ukasha is also particularly outspoken against censorship. He interprets the considerable freedom he has been given in recent years as a product of the current regime's belief that "no television drama can incite people to speak up about their problems or make their demands in demonstrations" ('Ukasha 1997).

The strong point of contact and common cause, however, in this cultural support of the nation is the opposition to Islamism. 'Ukasha has described himself as secularist and antitheocratic. This means that despite his tough criticisms of economic liberalization policies and his message that individualism and profit seeking are leading Egypt astray, he is, in the end, less fearful of the state's close involvement with transnational corporations and foreigners than of militant Islamist demands for purity. Perhaps the first to explore the character of an extremist in his *Hilmiyya Nights*, 'Ukasha joined in willingly when the minister of information declared in 1993 the new policy of combating extremism with media. He integrated, as have so many television writers since then, a succession of violent Islamic terrorists into his plots.[16] His reassuring message in *Zizinya*, following thinkers from the 1920s, is that Egyptians need not fear contact with Europeans or the West more generally. The genius of Egypt is that it can absorb and make all these outside influences its own. The current flirtation with global capital, he thus implies, is no more dangerous than were earlier contacts with foreigners or the West. This is a message that is sure to sit well with a state regime whose fortunes now depend so intimately on intercourse with Western and especially American-dominated global elements—the interlocutors who speak the language of privatization, capitalism, globalization, and free markets. Yet many Egyptians' ambivalent responses to such constructions of Egyptian cultural identity as found in *Arabesque* and *I Won't Live in My Father's Shadow*, not to mention in *Zizinya*, suggest the uncertainties of any straightforward success for this national media effort, even if this ambivalence does not dampen the pleasures of watching such television serials and may even keep "the Egyptian character" in emotional focus.

16. Gordon (2000) similarly argues that the resuscitation not only of Nasser but of the pre-Nasser aristocracy and royalty in films and historical serials is part of a strategy for countering Islamism.

 PART TWO

In a World of Uncertain Places, Where Are Area Studies?

7 Why Area Studies?

DAVID LUDDEN

Since the European Enlightenment, two complementary ways to study modern human subjects have developed in the universities. Universal principles have been used to explore human psychology, rationality, evolution, and culture. Data and theory also have been used to show how these features of humanity combine to form distinctive human realities. Two ways of knowing—universal and contextual—underpin all the social sciences and humanities. These are modernity's Adam and Eve, or, better yet, its original twins: one asserts that humanity must be understood by using universally valid, scientific principles, and the other proclaims that human groups and contexts are so fundamentally different that they demand separate study and representation.

Even the most universal of the social sciences and the most particularistic of the humanities disciplines depend on both twins. Economics might be universal, but economies are not. The market economy is a theoretical construct whose substance can be found only in real, live market economies, which are distinctive and contextually defined. Scholars of literature might study texts written by specific authors in particular places, times, and idioms, but toward that end they must deploy universal principles to comprehend the individuality of the author, the coherence of culture, and the meanings of language and symbolism.

Area studies began to evolve with an accumulation of universal and contextual knowledge from various disciplines as part of a broad effort to make university education commensurate with the expansion of European power. The birth of area studies can be seen in Enlightenment efforts to support theories of human progress by comparing Europe to other regions of the world, and this tradition of universal comparison and ranking is being carried into the twenty-first century by theorists of modernity and development for whom Marx and Weber set the tone. During the Enlightenment, encyclopedists argued that the world could be known only by gathering and organizing data from all its specific human contexts, a tradition of universal particularism that many academic enthusiasts of the World Wide Web follow today.

Universal theories about humanity—from sociobiology to rational choice, cognitive psychology, game theory, and neoclassical economics—gain force by being applied in different human contexts. The contemporary world of globalization is certainly forming a single, unified environment for intellectual ambition and science, but global networks also have differentiated the contexts of human activity, experience, and knowing. Globalization and diversification—universality and contextuality—move together, historically and intellectually. The insistent demarcation of boundaries and difference among human groups and contexts seems to be as logical as our division of knowledge among academic disciplines.

Our twin modalities for studying humanity certainly have not been rendered archaic by globalization, even less so by the mere ending of the Cold War, which triggered a critical attack on area studies. The latest historical surge of global interconnectedness may have tossed aside one set of ideas about the contexts of human politics, culture, and history, but compiling reliable data on all the world's distinctive cultural areas remains fundamental for knowing the world (and even for understanding globalization itself).

All disciplines depend on the compilation and analysis of good data about diverse parts of the world because these data provide necessary material for testing theory and for mapping abstractions onto reality. Economics must confront real economies, and political science must analyze real politics. Every scholar will not use empirical data, and pure theoreticians may form the intellectual elite, but disciplines and universities progress when creative practitioners mix universality and contextuality. Grant writers and program developers know this. For disciplines to thrive in the world of globalization, and for the university to produce knowledge commensurate with the scope and needs of globalization, academic institutions need to gather, organize, analyze, and regenerate data on all the contexts that form the real world.

But today academic institutions are questioning the need to sustain programs for the study of specific world areas. The Enlightenment's twins are fighting bitterly. Universalists argue that globalization is defining a single world zone for the application of universal theory, which makes area studies irrelevant. Global business, media, and marketing activities support this argument, but world order is elusive, and world regions still command public attention. Contextualists have created subdisciplines that bridge theory and empiricism. Fifty years of area studies institutions have influenced many disciplines deeply, strengthening contextualism and increasing the power of comparisons across a widening range of cases. As a result, area studies scholarship is a very different academic endeavor than it was fifty years ago. Debates about its future need to consider its evolution in a changing world.

Investments in area studies began in Europe inside the ramparts of French and British imperialism and of German and Russian Orientalism. After 1950, area studies became more systematic in the university as it developed new national orientations in the United States, Japan, Australia, India, China, and Japan. Universities combined knowledge from various disciplines to study human contextuality in modern world regions, as national governments and foundations combined forces with international organizations, under the umbrella of the United Nations, to build area studies programs that took each national culture to be a distinctive context for the study of universal humanity.

Developing at the intersection of disciplines, area studies expanded on the idea that cultural areas are enclosed within national territories and form contours of human contextuality. The "cultural area" became fundamental. It derives from empirical and theoretical work going back to the Enlightenment, to the time when Europe first came into focus as a region of the world by contrast to India, Africa, China, and America. The ideas of "Europe" and of "Western Civilization" underlie area studies and the disciplines alike, which today divide the world into regions along basically the same cultural lines that guided European thought from the Enlightenment onward. China and India are as much Enlightenment ideas as Europe, and they likewise figure centrally in the work of Hegel, Mill, Marx, and Weber. Area studies thus fostered one tenet that united the disciplines by elaborating the contrast between Europe and other areas.

In the past twenty years, area studies have changed drastically along with the disciplines and the world environment. The rapid increase of new data and technology demand more sophisticated ways to describe human contexts. Ideas about the world are in flux. Territoriality is more fluid. Cultural boundaries are moving. Disciplines are shifting. Intricately interconnected crises implicate area studies and the disciplines at the same time. Their shared intellectual environment includes the following new features:

1. An idea is spreading that globalization constitutes a single, universal context for all humanity. This idea negates the salience of cultural areas and the need for area-based knowledge. A global present is being seen as distinctively new, as a rupture with history, which is erasing all the old constraints of contextuality that limited the practical scope of universal theory. More social science is now being done using the image of an integrated global reality to substantiate universal theory. An image of global economy supports universal economic theory. Global culture is superseding cultural areas, regions, and territoriality in theories of cultural change.

2. Cultural change and differentiation are spilling out of boundaries that seemed eternal. Now cultural areas do not seem as coherent as they did twenty years ago because their internal differentiation is better understood and the elements of culture have migrated and intermingled in widening spaces that now include countless diasporas and multicultural zones. The changing substance of cultural areas is now more visible than ever before, but scholars are finding such change to have been typical in past centuries as well. The empirical reality of the bounded cultural areas that underpinned area studies is now obviously dubious.

3. Enlightenment thought is also in question, which undermines any claim to universality in the disciplines and in all definitions of cultural context. Are economic theory and human rights universal or merely products of European hegemony? After all, European power covered the globe with the language of science and humanism. Cultural areas also may be little more than constructs of imperialism and nationalism, imagined territories institutionalized by Europe's domineering modernity. Edward Said's critique of Orientalism in 1978 launched an academic industry of deconstructing modernity's tales about cultures, traditions, and civilizations; and since then, poststructuralism, postmodernism, postcolonial criticism, and critiques of development discourse have questioned scientific rationality.

4. Talking back to the Enlightenment has gone beyond critique. Scholars now have substantiated the proposition that multiple sites—not only the

West—produced and theorized modern forms of knowledge and generated the materials that form the modern world. A real world of multiple modernities has complicated the conduct of the human sciences, and the critical question for scholars today is whether this increasing diversity in our knowledge of the world can be accommodated, comprehended, and enhanced within the university.

5. Knowledge for effective education and scholarship today is not being produced within a single epistemology derived from the Enlightenment or within a single, global paradigm. The trajectory of Enlightenment is shattered. Humanity and its world of knowledge simply do not "add up" as scholars imagined they would. Many of the forms of knowledge that drive the world today contradict and contest one another.

6. As a result, knowledge in the world is now global and interactive but also emphatically local and multiple. No single site can control or produce global knowledge because knowledge producers themselves are located in their world by the way they produce their knowledge, as various sites pursue diverging modalities of knowing. No site for knowing the world can be truly global on its own, in only its own terms. Rather, every site—every scholar, department, discipline, program, and university—is located locally and also connected to countless other local sites within global networks of knowledge. Each is like a page on the Web.

What all this means is that area studies no longer can be a motley collection of disciplinary knowledge about fixed territories of area specialization because disciplines are shifting and territories are in question. The challenges facing area studies require concerted attention from the university because area studies are the primary and most productive venue for the systematic study of human contextuality, and universities need area studies to produce contextual knowledge in the world of globalization.

Six practical conclusions are warranted.

1. Area studies must continue to be a venue for compiling knowledge about areas of the world, but scholars need to focus more sharply on the empirical and conceptual problem posed by the area-ness and the territoriality of knowledge. Area studies must revitalize by changing radically the meaning of *cultural area,* using all the technologies and data available, crossing old borders that separate cultural territories in established area studies programs.

2. Area studies must remain a critical venue for the study of the

parochialism of the Enlightenment and all its modes of knowledge. More studies need to focus on the inheritance of the Enlightenment—above all, perhaps, on ideas about civilization and progress, which define Europe against all of the others.

3. Area studies are perhaps also the most creative venue for studies of imperialism and the imperial aspects of globalization, which continue to divide the West and the Rest. Special attention needs to be focused on cultural change in all regions of the world during the rise of modernity and on dichotomies between tradition and modernity in order to formulate a world-cultural history that can accommodate the many modernities we now see alive in our historical present.

4. Area studies programs need to advance the internationalization of U.S. universities. U.S. academic institutions no longer can imagine themselves to be the center of the world, but rather need to join international networks of scholarship and to pursue more vigorously their engagement institutions outside Europe and Anglo-America. Area studies programs can be efficient conduits for the movement of theories, practices, and resources among intellectual sites around the world because of connections they have developed over the years. To improve international collaboration, area studies scholars should develop ways to share academic resources that have accumulated disproportionately in the rich countries—for example, in the U.S. PL480 collections and at the British Library.

5. Area studies are a necessary counterweight to the decontextualizing force of universal globalism. Universities must produce forms of knowledge that comprehend the contextuality of humanity in order to operate in a culturally diverse global environment and to meet demands from constituents who will continue to identify with specific cultural contexts.

6. To move across shifting boundaries in a culturally diverse world of global interaction, students need the languages of knowledge. The more English prevails in the university, the more parochial that university's knowledge. The basic test of a university's power to produce effective knowledge about humanity is its support for language learning that opens up communication among sites of knowledge production around the world. Using language teaching and research to form multilingual modalities of education is the special task of area studies. Multilingual colleges and universities will provide the most effective education for a global future.

8 The Multiple Worlds of African Studies

SANDRA E. GREENE

The 1990s has witnessed a profound sea change in the way areas studies are viewed by nonprofit foundations, government policymakers, and academic departments. As early as 1990, I remember the World Bank embarking on a recruitment drive at Stanford University to increase the number of specialists among its ranks. At that time, they made it very clear that they were *not* interested in hiring scholars grounded in areas studies. Rather, they sought generalists trained in the use of (presumably universal) theoretical models to address specific issues and problems around the world. By 1995, the Social Science Research Council (SSRC) and the American Council of Learned Societies (ACLS) also abandoned the world areas approach. They disbanded the Joint Committees organized by world area and in doing so took a very deliberate step away from a past that "fostered a vision of International Studies based on . . . geographically organized research and training activities . . . [a vision] that [had] influenced intellectual agendas [since the early 1960s], rewarded training in non-traditional languages and shaped opportunity structures by dispensing dissertation and post-doctoral research fellowships" (Robinson 1997, 171).[1]

Explaining the rationale for the new approach, Kenneth Prewitt, president of the SSRC, described areas studies as "enclaves," separate and separated from other academic fields; he also argued that conventional notions of world areas are wholly inadequate as models for understanding the world given the movement of ideas, peoples, and commodities across such boundaries (1995, 31–40; see also Heilbrunn 1996). By 1997, the Ford Founda-

1. For a useful history of area studies scholarship and its origin in the Cold War, see Wallerstein 1997.

tion and the Mellon Foundation also had embarked on this new but now familiar path (Volkman 1998, 28–29). Similar shifts have occurred in the academy as well. In 1997, for example, Robert Bates (1997b)—an Africanist and a political scientist—published a number of articles in which he argued that area studies have failed to generate scientific knowledge and that abandonment of the singular commitment to a deep understanding of area history, languages, and cultures is necessary for political scientists if those who specialize in areas studies are to be taken seriously by their colleagues.[2] The response by Africanists to these changes and challenges has been both swift and varied. In 1997, the journal *Africa Today* devoted both its April-June and July-September issues to the question of "the future of regional studies." In that same year, the African Studies Association (ASA) posted on its Web page Jane Guyer's 1996 report to the Ford Foundation, *African Studies in the United States: A Perspective*. In this report, Guyer argued for the need to reshape and reconfigure scholarship on Africa but also sounded a cautionary note by stating that we should not abandon the accomplishments of the field. In a 1997 presidential address, Iris Berger, exhorted the members of the ASA not to lose confidence in what African studies had accomplished and to resist ceding ground (2). Others have focused less on defending the accomplishments of area studies and of African studies in particular, emphasizing instead the notion that increased dialogue across traditional boundaries is indeed necessary in a world where there is "an unprecedented volume of flows of capital, people, commodities, microbes, cultural images, technologies, religious and political ideologies, weapons, drugs and pollution—all cutting across political and cultural borders" (Kassimir 1997, 155; see also Guyer 1996 and Harbeson 1997). In the words of Pearl Robinson, "whatever the virtues of the old model of African Studies (and they are many) an increasingly vast realm of research, training, policy analysis, and institution building is falling outside the traditional Area Studies agenda. . . . [A]s we in the African Studies Community contemplate the road ahead, we should think expansively and avoid becoming sidetracked by the impulse to reproduce the past" (1997, 176).

Almost a decade has elapsed since the SSRC and the ACLS sent shock

2. Also see responses to the Bates article and to the debate about the future of area studies more generally in *Africa Today* 44, nos. 2, 3, and 4, as well as in Martin 1996.

waves through the area studies community in 1995 by disbanding their area studies advisory committees. Yet it is clear that the field has already begun to adjust, especially with regard to the new agendas formulated by the non-profit foundations. For example, many of the area studies organizations—including the ASA—already have begun to extend themselves beyond the boundaries of their traditional foci by working collectively for the first time. In 1998, a number of area studies associations began working with the American Historical Association and the World History Association to formulate a proposal to fund a project that would facilitate greater dialogue between area studies scholars (with their deep knowledge of particular world regions) and world history scholars (whose principal interests involve the development of theoretical models to make sense of both historical and contemporary global trends). Similarly, the ASA is currently exploring ways of working with while also influencing the National Summit on Africa, a massive effort to establish cooperative links among governmental, nongovernmental, nonprofit, and for-profit organizations in order to extend to the vast majority of Americans more accurate information about Africa. Within the larger academy itself, new fields of inquiry are emerging that emphasize the need to examine the relationships that exist between the local and the global as well as among world areas. A much older academic interest dating from the 1960s that explored the linkages that existed around the Indian Ocean between India, the Persian Gulf, the Swahili city-states of East Africa, and China has now been joined by a proliferation of conferences and publications on Atlantic studies or on the Black Atlantic. This latter set of interests explores the dynamic relations that existed and continues to exist around issues of race and culture among the countries that border the Atlantic Ocean.[3]

3. Such conferences as well as workshops include the Rutgers Center for Historical Analysis 1997–99 project "The Black Atlantic: Race, Nation, and Gender"; Harvard University's "International Seminar on the History of the Atlantic World"; the September 1998 conference "Transatlantic Slaving and the African Diaspora: Using the W. E. B. Du Bois Dataset of Slaving Voyages," sponsored by the Omohundro Institute of Early American History and Culture; and the United Nations Educational, Scientific, and Cultural Organization (UNESCO) series of conferences on the slave route, held in Canada, the United States, Scotland, and Angola. Other related events and activities include John Hunwick's Northwestern University-based research network "The African Diaspora in the Lands of the Mediterranean"; the

We also have seen this particular academic focus become the basis for defining new professorial positions within the academy. Early Americanists are regularly exhorted to realize that it is no longer sufficient to proclaim publicly and proudly their ignorance of African history at the same time that they are also emphasizing the continent's importance for understanding early American history.[4] We have seen as well an explosion of publications on the theme of the local and the global, emphasizing the extent to which understanding the one is impossible without reference to the other.[5] Equally important are the increasingly common news accounts about U.S. government policymakers who are being forced to realize—in light of policy fiascoes in Iran, Iraq, Indonesia, Pakistan, and the former Yugoslavia—that they must reassess their assumptions about what is indeed universally known and accepted and therefore useful as a basis for policy formulation and implementation.

Area studies specialists, of course, will have to continue to point out the fact that reliance on "universal facts and values" is insufficient if not wholly inadequate when trying to comprehend different world areas and cultures. And area specialists also will have to continue to insist that their voices be heard, with all the multiplicities and contradictions that exist therein. Nevertheless, this assessment suggests that area studies and African studies in particular can adjust, will adjust, and will survive, albeit with fewer resources.

Of greater concern to me is that the effort to maintain a voice in the agendas of the nonprofit foundations, government policy agencies, and the academy may be rendered insignificant by the global capitalist marketplace.

1992 Virgin Islands workshop on the Danish slave trade, including both Americanists and Africanists; and the recent *Radical History Review* call for papers on Africans and the roots of early American culture. The connections between East African coastal cities and the non-African societies on the Indian Ocean also have been explored with greater or lesser interest since the 1960s.

4. Oral presentation by Professor Colin Palmer (City University of New York, Graduate Center) at the Omohundro Institute of Early American History and Culture September 1998 conference "Transatlantic Slaving and the African Diaspora: Using the W. E. B. Du Bois Dataset of Slaving Voyages," held in Williamsberg, Virginia.

5. See, for example, the section entitled "From the Local to the Global and Back" in Grosz-Ngaté 1997, 3–6, for an excellent discussion of and bibliography on this topic.

We are entering a world where the academy itself is urged increasingly to become more businesslike, to be more closely tied to the interests and needs of the business world, and to view as seamless the needs of business and the educational production of students for a global work place (Slaughter and Leslie 1997). Yet this "global workplace" exists only where multinational businesses can maximize its profits and thus satisfy its shareholders. What of those disciplines—the majority in the humanities (history, literature, languages, music, the arts)—that are largely peripheral to the central concerns of the business world? What of those areas of the world—many countries in Africa, Oceania, and the Pacific—that are of little interest to corporate capitalism? Are these fields and these areas of the world to be marginalized further than they already are?

A second concern involves the continuing gap that exists between Africanists in the United States and our colleagues in Africa. At the 1996 annual meeting of the ASA, Thandika Mkandawire, the then president of the Africa-based (in Dakar) Council for the Development of Economic and Social Research in Africa (CODESRIA), voiced perhaps the most eloquent analysis of the long-standing gulf that has existed between these two communities:

> [One of the realities we in Africa] have to contend with . . . is an international division of labor in African Studies. In field research, this has essentially meant that the "North" [in a continuing colonial mode] carries out the conceptual work, designs the fieldwork programs for African researchers who conduct the interviews, fill in the forms, etc. The more frequent form that such a division of labor appears in is that of consultancies. . . . The research carried out by the African counterparts is often . . . intellectually unrewarding and at times downright humiliating. But in our circumstances of penury, it is irresistibly lucrative. The fees received in such consultancies dwarf the official remuneration of the researchers within their respective institutions. And in the dire financial straits in which most of us find ourselves, it is difficult to be selective about one's sources of income. . . .
>
> One effect of this division of labor is that it pushes African scholars towards local minutiae. This might seem a commendable antidote to the extroverted [i.e., lofty theoretical and even other worldly] discourses on Africa, but as Hountoundji observes, even this focus on the local is exter-

nally driven, shaped by the needs of the "North" and ends up reducing African researchers into "knowledgeable informants." (1997, 29–30)[6]

For many Africanists in the United States—and I would even dare say for the majority of U.S.-based Africanists—Mkandawire's analysis was not unfamiliar, yet it was profoundly disturbing because of the difficult questions it raised. How do scholars of Africa in the United States contend with the contradictory character of their own positions? Yes, we are indeed beneficiaries of U.S. power and influence, yet we also are tied to an academic establishment where there is increasing competition for decreasing numbers of positions; where it is more and more difficult to obtain the funds to conduct research overseas; where faculty are pushed to focus more and more on theory and model building rather than on field-based research; where there is growing pressure to be ever more involved with students, to produce ever more publications, and to engage in ever more service activities as well as demonstrations of one's success in the field.

These pressures, in turn, compel some scholars of Africa to focus less on developing ties of cooperation between themselves and scholars in Africa and more on getting as much accomplished as possible in order to secure their own positions within the U.S. academy. Many U.S. scholars of Africa, of course, resist these pressures and use whatever means are available to forge cooperative and collegial ties with their African colleagues, but all of us nevertheless acknowledge the problems Mkandawire outlined. We are even aware of how Mkandawire's points do not tell the whole story, given his emphasis on the social sciences in Africa. Those of us in the humanities are all too cognizant of the fact that not only are so many of our colleagues in Africa forced to become the research assistants of their colleagues from the "North," but some are so marginalized that they are not warranted even this form of humiliating exploitation.

In 1996, when I spent a year as a Fulbright scholar teaching in the his-

---

6. I must remark here that although Mkandawire is correct in some instances, he also homogenizes African studies, which in turn leads to inaccuracies and misrepresentations of large aspects of the field. This is especially true of the remark about the failure of the research community in the West to cite African scholarship. Such failure may be true in some fields, but it is certainly not true in others, such as history.

tory department at my alma mater, the University of Ghana at Legon, I was saddened and shocked that out of approximately fifteen full-time positions allotted to the department, only six of those slots actually were filled. And of the six professors in the department, four had retired and were working on contracts that ended after only five years. Of those four on contract, one retired again that year; two were scheduled to retire again in the next two to three years. Of the two younger faculty members, one had obtained by necessity a law degree and therefore spent quite a bit of time using his legal skills in town away from the university to sustain himself and his family financially. The second of the two junior faculty members was forced to chair the department while trying to complete her Ph.D. Prospects were dim for recruiting new members to the department in order to maintain a Ghanaian presence in the teaching of students and in conducting research activity in Ghana. Library facilities, bookstores, and publishing efforts were languishing despite valiant efforts to cope. Based on international advisors' recommendations, university authorities also expressed no interest in salvaging a department and a discipline that was seen as of limited importance to national economic development.

I know of no Africanist in the United States who would say that we can cope with only our own challenges—those generated by changes in the priorities of nonprofit foundations, government policy, and the academy. Yet for area studies and African studies, we must ask the question: How do we address all of these issues? To address one but ignore the other is either to condemn the field to complicity in maintaining the legacy of colonialism or to skew the field terribly where the research, publishing, and teaching on Africa is dominated by those of us Americans, Europeans, and Africans who live and work in the United States or Europe and who are responding in our research and teaching to issues more of interest to scholars in North America and Europe.

A third concern involves an often neglected area: the world of race. At the very heart of how the field of African studies defines itself is the issue of race. It is a field primarily concerned with Africa south of the Sahara—that is, "black" Africa—which continues to be the case despite some scholars' ever-present challenges to bring North Africa into the continent. This racialized definition of the field has created unease for many in the field. Some scholars, for example, wonder if they can continue to define themselves as Africanists when studying white residents of Rhodesia (now Zimbabwe) and

South Africa. Others grapple with the desire to embrace North Africa despite the racial attitudes found in that region. Still others include extensive discussions of Ancient Egypt in their history courses while simultaneously trying to wean their students of defining the population of Ancient Egypt according to contemporary definitions of race.

Africanists also have been forced to confront the racism that taints virtually every popular image and understanding of Africa, Africans, and African Americans in the United States. As the founder of the first African studies program in this country, Melville Herskovits (1958a, 1958b) of Northwestern University consciously used both his studies on the early state of Dahomey and his study of the African roots of African American culture to attack racist notions about Africa and African Americans. Yet he, like so many others, was not able to escape completely the pervasive tendency to define Africans, those of African descent, and African culture as that against which everything else is defined. Thus, in 1958, when Herskovits was publishing his cultural Pan-Africanist volume *The Myth of the Negro Past,* he also supposedly "boasted of his role in helping deny funding to 'negrophile' W. E. B. Du Bois' Encyclopedia Africana" (West and Martin 1997, 313). In 1969, racial tensions erupted at the annual ASA meeting when the vast majority of Africans and African Americans walked out to protest what they identified as their continued exclusion from the field because of their "racial" identities. Sentiments founded on fears of having to compete with Africans and African Americans were voiced more recently in 1995 by Philip Curtin, a major figure not only in African history but in the entire historical field. In his 3 March 1995 editorial published in the *Chronicle of Higher Education,* Curtin stated baldly that institutions of higher learning in the United States, especially the most prestigious ones, should not make concerted efforts to diversify their faculties by hiring African American and African scholars to teach courses and conduct research on Africa-related topics, especially African history. According to Curtin, white scholars, American and European, have had a more long-standing association with the field and therefore were more qualified and in a better position to maintain the high level of academic research and publishing associated with the field.[7]

7. Response to the Curtin opinion piece included letters by Keletso Atkins, John Higginson, Atieno Odhiambo and colleagues, Thomas Spear, Christopher Lowe, and Joseph E.

The racial definition of the African continent and of African studies as a field, racist sentiments expressed by Africanist scholars (prompted in part by the greater competitiveness within the academy for limited positions and resources), and the responses to these sentiments have presented a continuous challenge to African studies. Especially destructive, however, are those sentiments that have the potential to split the community of scholars interested in Africa, for such sentiments (those expressed by Curtin, for example) erode our ability to forge a common agenda and to work together to tackle common concerns. Such attitudes also negatively impact the field's ability to grow because they (when consciously or unconsciously expressed) discourage African Americans from entering the profession. By not encouraging a serious scholarly interest in Africa among the sector of the American population that historically has had the strongest and most long-standing interest in the continent, and by refusing to confront racism within ourselves and within the larger society, we not only weaken the field as a whole, but also undermine our own efforts to convince others of the importance of Africa and African studies.

Many rightly attribute the failure of the United States and of the United Nations to intervene in Rwanda to avert the 1994 genocide of the Tutsi, in part, to the racist images of Africa prevalent in the West. In February 2000, when the National Summit on Africa held its national convention to rally support for and to begin the process of developing grassroots interest in U.S. policy initiatives focused on Africa, the delegates were reminded continually that this effort was absolutely necessary because up to that point no serious constituency for Africa existed outside the scholarly community. When congressional representatives returned to their home districts to hear the concerns of those who had elected them, Polish Americans expressed concerns about Poland, Irish Americans about Ireland, but very few Americans (of African descent or otherwise) expressed concern about or interest in Africa. Only by putting aside our unease with confronting issues of race can scholars of Africa begin to work with African Americans (who do indeed have the greatest untapped interest in Africa in

Harris and Robert J. Cummings, published in the "Letter to the Editor" section of the 14 April 1995 *Chronicle of Higher Education*.

the United States) to give greater prominence to Africa and African studies, a prominence that may have profoundly positive consequences for both.[8]

What then are the challenges facing area studies and African studies in particular? In recent years, these challenges are defined most often as those presented by the changed funding (and hiring) priorities of nonprofit foundations, government agencies, and the academy; the pressures of globalization; and the need to reconfigure areas studies in light of the increasing emphasis on transnational realities. It is indeed important and even critical that area studies and African studies meet these challenges. And, in many ways, African studies programs already have begun to face those challenges, as indicated earlier. In addressing this new agenda, however, we must not forget to address those questions that have been begging for answers for decades if not centuries. African studies scholarship, in particular, must address the past—its own history of race and racism, its own complicity with colonialism—at the same time that it faces the challenges of the present and future. In some instances, it already has begun to do so. Many institution-based African studies programs regularly apply to and receive funding from private foundations as well as from the federal government to establish mutually beneficial linkages with African universities. The ASA has put in place new procedures to facilitate association journal publication of work by African scholars based in Africa. Both African and African American members of the association, male and female, now are nominated and elected regularly to positions on the board and as officers of the association. In the last three years, the ASA also has sought to establish collaborative projects with CODESRIA and UBUNTU 2000,[9] as well as with discipline-based

8. In emphasizing race divisions within African studies, I am fully cognizant of other divisions within the field: gender and disciplinary divides. I believe, however, that race has been and continues to be the single issue studiously avoided both by Africanists and by American society. Although numerous studies indicate that white women in particular have benefited perhaps the most from affirmative action, and although the very existence of area studies indicates the extent to which disciplinary boundaries have been forged, race continues to be the one uncomfortable subject yet to be addressed directly among Africanists and within American society more generally.

9. UBUNTU 2000 is a quite recent African organization, based in South Africa and devoted to promoting the arts, arts education, and the analysis of African arts.

Africa-wide organizations on the continent. But far more is needed, especially in establishing linkages and in defining cooperative projects with African American organizations. Virtually nothing on a collective or organizational basis has been done by the field on that front to date. In pursuing all of these projects, the African studies field not only can redefine itself in terms of new funding priorities, but also can reposition itself as a field that deliberately and consciously exists at the intersection of multiple worlds (the world of funding, of international relations, and of race), offering new approaches and solutions to age-old dilemmas and challenges.

9 Deterritorialization and the Crisis of Social Science

TIMOTHY MITCHELL

As commodities, finance, cultural forms, and information move more quickly around the globe, the characteristic way of organizing expert knowledge about the rest of the world in U.S. universities appears to be in trouble. Area studies, as this form of intellectual organizing is known, are said to have been created in response to World War II and the Cold War. With the passing of that compartmentalized world, the compartments of area studies must give way to more global forms of expertise. As our intellectual horizons become more global, the questions then follow: What kind of place can we find for the local, and how might we now imagine the relationship between the local and the global?

I approach these questions first by asking how the relationship between the local and global was imagined earlier. How did the old world of area studies portray what was local, and how was the local brought into relation with things global or universal? In answering this question, I propose a different history of area studies. This history finds the origins of area studies not in the Cold War or in World War II, but in developments beginning in the 1930s. And it finds them not only in changes occurring in international politics, but in what happened to the social sciences in the prewar period. These changes, I argue, shaped a particular set of assumptions about the local and the global and built them into the departmental structure of U.S. universities and into the pattern of academic careers. To rethink the local and the global today, it is not enough to tinker around with area studies programs. It is a question that must be addressed, as it was in the 1930s, to this larger academic structure.

World War II and the ensuing crises of the Cold War did not give birth to area studies. One can argue on the contrary that they may have postponed the development of area studies.[1] In the first place, as Barbara Clowse has shown, the passage of the National Defense Education Act in 1958—the most important event in the organization of postwar U.S. area studies—was related more to domestic ideology than to Cold War politics. The significance of the Sputnik crisis and its attendant hysteria, according to Clowse, "was not that it produced initial interest in such bills but that it disarmed opposition to federal aid" (1981, 49; see also Rafael 1994). The opposition reflected two domestic concerns: the possibility that unrestricted federal aid to states might be used for sectarian schools and breach the First Amendment separation of church and state; and the fear that, following the 1954 *Brown v. Board of Education* decision, federal aid would be used to enforce the racial integration of schools (Clowse 1981, 42–43). These domestic battles delayed the funding of area studies programs in the United States, setting back developments that were already under way.

In the second place, the concerns of area studies first emerged in the interwar period and were related to developments that were simultaneously political and intellectual. As Edward Said argues, the period between the wars was characterized by a civilizational anxiety, especially in Europe, which turned to the study of Oriental civilizations. Borrowing new ideas of total humanistic knowledge fostered by classical studies and histories of civilizations, scholars began to see in the idea of another "civilization" a way of exploring the contemporary challenges to the self-assurance of the West, "to the West's spirit, knowledge, and imperium" (Said 1978, 248). In the United States, where Oriental studies had developed out of biblical studies and previously had been devoted largely to Semitic philology, the new approach to Oriental civilization was pioneered by the Egyptologist James Henry Breasted. In 1919, Breasted founded the Oriental Institute of the University of Chicago, with funding from John D. Rockefeller Jr. and the Rockefeller-funded General Education Board. Breasted's vision for the de-

1. Rafael (1994) makes a related argument, drawing on Robert Hall's 1947 influential report *Area Studies, with Special Reference to Their Implications for Research in the Social Sciences.* On the prewar development of studies of the non-West, see Cooper 1997.

velopment of Oriental studies in America was a transformation from a philological concern to a historical discipline "in which art, archaeology, political science, language, literature and sociology, in short all the categories of civilization shall be represented and correlated" (qtd. in McCaughey 1984, 101).

The other major U.S. university that developed a new approach to the study of Oriental civilization was Princeton, where there was a history of connections with the Arab world through Protestant missions, in particular with the American University of Beirut (AUB, formerly the Syrian Protestant College of Beirut)(Winder 1987, 43–44). In 1927, Princeton established the country's first department devoted to modern Oriental studies and brought the historian Philip Hitti (1886–1979) from AUB to teach modern Arab history. Hitti chaired the department from 1941 until his retirement in 1954. In 1947, he founded the Program in Near Eastern Studies, the first U.S. program to integrate the study of Arabic language and culture with studies of modern history, politics, and society (Kritzeck and Winder 1960). In this chapter, I focus on the history of Near Eastern studies—or Middle Eastern studies, the name used for the field after World War II—as a major case through which to discuss the development of area studies. My general argument about area studies and the social sciences applies to all the regions of area studies, albeit with important differences of detail in the formation of one field or another. However, I am not able in the space of this chapter to explore the significance of these differences.

These prewar developments in the United States should not be separated from the more influential changes taking place in the regions whose history and culture were being studied; in the case of the Middle East, cities such as Beirut itself, where Philip Hitti had taught from 1908, as well as Cairo, Tangier, and Istanbul saw the establishment and growth of research centers devoted to the study of modern history and society during the first half of the twentieth century.[2] Also important were the interwar develop-

2. At AUB in this period, there was a great expansion of research on the contemporary region. For example, see the bibliographies of literature dealing with the Mandate territories since 1919 published in the 1930s under the auspices of the AUB (Social Science Series). In Tangier, the Mission scientifique au Maroc was established by the French in 1904 and began publishing the *Revue du Monde Musulman* in 1906. In Cairo, the Société d'économie poli-

ments in Europe. In London, the Royal Institute of International Affairs in the 1930s commissioned a comprehensive survey of the Western impact on the Arab world and Turkey since 1800. The authors drew up a plan for "an organic study of the life of the Moslem societies, and the force, ideals, and tendencies at work within them" (Gibb and Bowen 1950; see also Gibb 1932). This plan of research and publication was a blueprint for the development of what would come to be called *area studies*. The overall project of "the tracing of social evolution and the bearing of this process upon present conditions"—or what would later be termed *modernization*—was divided horizontally into three time periods, reflecting the assumption that the region's history should be written in terms of its relation to the West: (1) a survey of the social institutions of Islamic society in the eighteenth century, "prior to the introduction of western influences"; (2) an examination of the Western impact since 1800; and (3) an investigation of present-day "conditions and forces in play" (Gibb and Bowen 1950, 3).

The research program further proposed twelve "vertical divisions" to break the field into manageable components, while stressing in the language of British social anthropology that "the interrelations of the various social functions" made rigid boundaries impossible. The vertical components were: the family, the village (including nomads), industry, commerce, the city, the army, government and administration, religion, education, law, slavery, and non-Muslim minorities (Gibb and Bowen 1950, 4–14). The authors, H. A. R. Gibb and Harold Bowen, hoped eventually to produce a "synthetic study of the problems [of social evolution] as a whole, under such general heads as rationalization and the release of individuality," but they pointed out that this project would "occupy a whole staff of research workers for many years" (13, 14). By 1939, they had managed to complete and send to press the first part of volume 1 on the eighteenth century. The outbreak of war, however, that supposed midwife of area studies, postponed its publication until 1950. The second part of volume 1 was delayed even

---

tique was created in 1909 and began publishing research on contemporary Egypt in its review *L'Egypte Contemporaine;* at same time, the government set up a national statistics office and began to publish a statistical annual. Related developments occurred in Turkey, where the new republic, established in 1923, began the publication of a statistical annual. See also Eickelmen 1998, chapter 2, and Mitchell 2002, chapter 3.

longer, until 1957, and the remainder of the project was abandoned (Gibb and Bowen 1957).

Despite these delays, Gibb and Bowen's program shaped the development of Middle Eastern studies in the United States, including the work sponsored by the Social Science Research Council (SSRC) over two decades. In October 1952, a series of papers was presented at a conference at Princeton University, "The Near East: Social Dynamics and the Cultural Setting," sponsored by the SSRC Committee on the Near and Middle East. The titles of the papers read like the table of contents of Gibb and Bowen's study: "the nomads," "the villager," "the industrial worker," "the bazaar merchant," "the entrepreneur class," "economic planners," "the army officer," "the clergy," "intellectuals in the modern development of the Islamic world," and "minorities in the political process."[3] The SSRC subsequently sponsored conferences on topics that began to fill in the Gibb and Bowen framework, including a meeting on minorities in the Middle East and another (at Berkeley in 1966) on Middle Eastern cities (Berger 1967, 8; Sibley 1974).[4]

Prewar proposals for an "organic" and "synthetic" study of the social evolution of the contemporary Middle East could draw on a new generation of scholarship on the area. Besides the work conducted at research institutes in Cairo, Beirut, and other cities of the region, a group of European colonial sociologists and ethnographers was beginning to publish historical-ethnographic studies of the twentieth-century Arab world.[5] And by the end

3. The program included four other topics, "the Israeli farmer," "the immigrant in Israel," "the Palestine Arab refugee," and "the crisis in the Near East." Their addition to the original Gibb and Bowen agenda reflected the events of 1948—49. This willingness to include the study of Israel and the Palestine question as a normal part of an academic conference was soon to disappear. The conference papers were published in S. Fisher 1955.

4. The papers of the 1966 SSRC conference were published in Lapidus 1969; papers from another SSRC conference, held in June 1967, were published in Cook 1970.

5. See Eickelmen 1998, chapter 2. See also Asad 1973; Burke 1979, 1980, 1984; Vatin 1984. The major works for this period include those by Edmond Doutté (1867–1926), Arnold van Gennep (1873–1957), Jacques Berque (1910–95), Robert Montagne (1893–1954), Edward Westermark (1862–1939), and E. E. Evans-Pritchard. See Doutté 1908; van Gennep 1914; Montagne 1986 (originally published in 1931); Westermark 1968 (originally published in 1926); Evans-Pritchard 1937, 1940. Neither of Evans-Pritchard's two books on the Sudan dealt with an Arabic-speaking community. Other notable research of the interwar period includes Ayrout 1938, Blackman 1927, and Heyworth-Dunne 1968

of World War II, a number of important economic and political-historical studies began to appear in Britain, mostly by scholars of Arab background, including Albert Hourani, George Antonius, and Charles Issawi.[6]

To this new body of literature, Orientalists such as Gibb and Bowen brought from Oriental studies the idea that the Islamic world formed a cultural unity, based on a common cultural core that only the Orientalist was equipped to decipher. As Gibb later argued in justifying the Orientalist's role in area studies programs, his function "is to provide that core out of his knowledge and understanding of the invisibles . . . to explain the why, rather than the what and the how, and this precisely because he is or should be able to see the data not simply as isolated facts, explicable in and by themselves, but in the broad context and long perspective of cultural habit and tradition" (qtd. in Johnson and Tucker 1975, 7). It is important to note that this scheme of "organic" knowledge of the Middle East as an interrelated whole did not seem, in the 1930s, to pose a problem regarding the relationship between area studies and the social science disciplines. The elaborate plan of vertical and horizontal divisions of the subject matter was based on a "natural principle" of demarcation according to occupational groups (the village, industry, commerce, the army, religion, and so on—all the way up to government and administration, conceived simply as another occupation). There was no separate analysis of "the state" or of a distinct sphere called "the economy." Correspondingly, there was no theoretical or practical problem of how to relate this analysis to the distinct disciplinary domains of economics, political science, and sociology. At Oxford, where Gibb taught, these disciplines were not yet organized as separate faculties.

When World War II shifted the center of gravity of academic research to the United States, two factors set back the development of Middle Eastern area studies. First, there was a rupture with the centers of research in the Arab world and with the colonial ethnographers and other scholars who moved between Europe and the Middle East. The United States had no

---

(originally published in 1939). Also important was the work of Hans Kohn (1929, 1932) on nationalism.

6. See Antonius 1946; Bonne 1955; Hourani 1946; Issawi 1947; Keen 1946; Khadduri 1951; Tannous 1944.

comparable scholarly base. Although wartime funds had supported crash programs in Middle Eastern languages at several U.S. universities and individual scholars had been introduced to the Middle East through military service, including intelligence work, another decade passed until Sputnik enabled the universities to acquire a new flow of government funds. At the same time, senior Orientalists had to be brought from Europe to lead the new Middle East programs, and this, too, took time.[7]

Second, unlike the situation in prewar Europe, universities in the United States already were divided into separate social science departments. This division of labor could trace its origins back as far as the turn of the century, but in the years either side of World War II it had taken on a new significance. In earlier decades, what distinguished the disciplines were the different kinds of social questions they addressed. Economists were concerned with prices, markets, and business cycles; political scientists with public law, legislatures, and the behavior of parties and voters; and sociologists with the social problems arising from industrialization and the growth of cities. In a process beginning in the 1930s and completed by the 1950s, the social sciences transformed themselves into, as it were, a kind of area studies. Each created an object that marked the exclusive territory of the discipline and defined its boundary with others.

The clearest example of this transformation was provided by economics, which from the late 1930s invented the term *the economy* as the object of its knowledge, a concept that was in general use only by the 1950s (Mitchell 1998). Political science tried to do something similar by reworking the old idea of the state but in the late 1940s and 1950s abandoned the state in favor of the more inclusive and scientific idea of the *political system* (Mitchell 1991b, 77–96, and 1999, 76–97). In sociology, there was a corresponding

7. Gibb moved from Oxford to head the Center for Middle Eastern Studies at Harvard in the mid-1950s; Gustav von Grunebaum, an earlier refugee from Vienna, moved from Chicago to direct the center at UCLA; in 1956, Yale hired Franz Rosenthal, a German Orientalist who had reached the United States in 1940; in 1952, Berkeley hired George Lenczowski, a French-trained Middle East expert who had arrived in the United States in 1945. Several other leading European-trained Oriental studies scholars came to the United States, including scholars of Islamic art (Oleg Grabar and Richard Ettinghausen), Islamic law (Joseph Schacht), Islamic religion (Wilfred Cantwell Smith), and Islamic history (notably the historian Bernard Lewis in the mid-1970s).

shift from the study of discrete social problems and processes to the analysis of society as a whole or, in the more elaborate Parsonian formulation, the social system. In anthropology, the change gathered momentum in the same period, with Franz Boas, Ruth Benedict, Clyde Kluckhohn, A. L. Kroeber, and others reorienting the discipline in the United States around a new, spatialized definition of the term *culture*, meaning the whole way of life of a particular country or people.[8] The word *area* actually was used at the time to refer to these newly mapped theoretical territories.[9]

These changes can be related to the professionalization of the social sciences in the middle third of the twentieth century, including the claims to scientific authority that could be built on exclusive territorial control of new theoretical objects.[10] But they also registered and contributed to a broader political and intellectual change: the nationalization of social knowledge. Histories of nationalism focus on its origins in eighteenth- and nineteenth-century Europe and more recently on its colonial origins.[11] Yet it is easy to forget that the term *nationalism* came into common use only in the twentieth century and that only in the interwar period did official and academic knowledge begin to picture the world as a series of nation-states. With the growing strength of anti-imperialist movements in the colonial world, the weakening and gradual collapse of European empires, and the development by the United States of more effective forms of imperialism (in Central America, the Carribean, the Pacific, and the Persian Gulf) based on nominally sovereign local regimes, the world was now to be pictured not as a network of empires but as a system of presumptively equivalent nation-states. Each geographical unit was imagined, in turn, to possess an economy, portrayed in terms of the novel statistical trope entitled *national income;* a self-contained political system or state; a homogenous body called society; and

8. The new concept of culture opened the way for postwar U.S. anthropology to study complex, literate societies, including those of the Middle East. See Geertz 1995, 99–109.

9. See the Harvard memorandum produced by Talcott Parsons, Clyde Kluckhohn, O. H. Taylor, and others in the 1940s, "Towards a Common Language for the Areas of the Social Sciences," cited in Geertz 1973, 41.

10. The professionalization of the social sciences during the interwar period and the rise of "scientism" are examined in Ross 1991.

11. For a discussion of the literature on nationalism, see "The Stage of Modernity" in Mitchell 2000.

even a distinctive national culture. Each unit also came to have an imagined national history.

As professional, political, and academic knowledge came to see the world as a series of nation-states, it also came to imagine it to consist of a series of discrete national economies, societies, cultures, and histories. The objects that now defined the intellectual territory of the social sciences had borders that coincided with those of the nation-state. In the same decades that the world-encircling networks of commodities, wealth, and power came to be represented in the simplified form of a universal system of sovereign nation-states, the social science disciplines were reorganized around objects that in each case assumed the structure of the nation-state as their universal social template.

Thus, the development of one form of area studies in the United States intersected with another. The attempt to construct the Middle East and other regions as distinct territorial objects defining a legitimate field of study crossed paths with the attempt to create "the economy," "the political system," "culture," and "society" as distinct social spaces, each defining the territory of a self-contained discipline. The so-called crisis of area studies in the late twentieth century, as I argue later, is better understood as a crisis in the ability of both kinds of object to delimit and legitimate a field of scholarship.

After World War II, when the attempt was made to develop the study of non-Western areas in the United States, the division of the academy into territorial disciplines of social science presented both a problem and an opportunity. On the one hand, the division of social analysis into the separate study of the economy, political system, culture, and society, which had seemed more straightforward for the study of the United States, did not always seem appropriate for the study of the backward regions of the non-West. On the other hand, this problem paradoxically revealed the new importance of area studies to the development of the social science. In the postwar period, with each social science devoted to its own area of social reality, it was hoped that the insights of the different disciplines could be combined into what Talcott Parsons called "a total structure of scientific knowledge." Area study was analogous to the study of medicine, the totality of human society corresponding to the total human organism. It was assumed that area studies, by focusing "on a definable context may have a profound effect on social science research." The development of institutional sociology and social anthropology would provide the bridge between economics and political science and psychology, enabling "an integrated treatment of the total social system of an area": "The development of area studies is an important path to the further development of these disciplines [sociology and anthropology]" (qtd. in Wagley 1948, 5–7). Many of the political scientists, sociologists, and others most involved in the construction of area studies shared this agenda. Thus, Gabriel Almond called on political scientists to study the "uncouth and exotic" regions of the world in order to make political science a "total science" (Mitchell 1991b, 85). The development of area specialists would provide the detailed knowledge of exotic regions required to universalize the science of politics. Area studies also would contribute to this universalization by providing the means for the social sciences to cross-fertilize one another while retaining their territorial exclusivity as separate disciplines (something that they would risk losing if the same collaboration occurred in the study of American society).

Another potential contribution of area studies to this project of universalization was the increased recognition of cultural relativity or the acknowledgment of cultural differences in the social sciences. At a national conference on the study of world areas held in November 1947, Pendleton Herring of the Carnegie Corporation argued:

> Many specialists now interested in the study of areas have been trained in subject matter fields that are very much the product of our own Western culture. This holds particularly for economics, sociology, psychology and political science. The conceptual schemes upon which these disciplines are based are, in large measure, the product of Western thought and institutions. . . . Specialists whose training derives from this context are now attempting to apply their methods of analysis to cultures that are very different. . . . If there be a provincialism within these disciplines, it will quickly be revealed when the expert applies his formulations to alien cultures. (qtd. in Wagley 1948, 6–7)

Area studies would serve as a testing ground for the universalization of the social sciences. In the postwar period, the practical relevance of area studies, it was said, would be for international cooperation among people of "diverse values, ideologies and objectives" (Wagley 1948, 8). The assumption was that sound scholarship "is valuable to the nation" and that between academic needs and "national interest" there lay no conflict. Area research was meant to be a part of the disciplines (social sciences, natural sciences, or humanities) to provide "comparative and concrete data to bear on generalization and theory" (Wagley 1948, 8).

What I am proposing, then, is that the new structure of expertise in the U.S. university embodied and represented a particular relationship between the universal and the particular—or, as we would say today, between the global and the local. The social sciences at this time were built around the nation-state as their obvious but untheorized frame of reference. The study of the economy, unless otherwise specified, referred to the national economy (or to "macroeconomics, as it came to be called); political science compared "political systems" whose limits were assumed to correspond with the borders of the nation-state; *society* referred to a system defined by the boundaries of the nation-state; and even *culture* came to refer most often to a national culture. In each case the nation-state was assumed to define the normal location and extension of social phenomena. There was no problem of local versus global, in the sense we speak of today, for "the local" was naturalized by the social sciences to correspond with the boundaries of the nation-state.

At the same time, the new shape of the social sciences provided an unproblematic picture of what today we talk about as "the global." On the one hand, in disciplines such as political science and economics, the global was pictured simply as the international: in place of today's images of unbounded flows of capital, goods, information, and finance, the structure of the social sciences made it possible to imagine the global as simply the international: the exchange of actions or goods between separate nation-states. In fields such as international relations and international economics, these exchanges could be represented and contained within distinct subfields of each social science. The relationship between the local and the global was laid out in a straightforward and self-evident manner in the very structure of one's discipline.

On the other hand, and more significant, what today we call "the global" was invoked and represented in a more general way, in the most characteristic feature of the new U.S. social sciences: their claim to universalism. This claim was based on the belief that the social sciences could uncover a single set of rules and categories governing the development of human society. The rules and categories were to be derived from analyzing the historical development of the West, a history that was by definition global, for there was no history outside the historical time of the West, no development other than the development already enjoyed by the West. The social sciences could become total sciences by extending these principles of historical and social explanation to include the countries beyond the West. This extension, as we have seen, brought the social science disciplines into contact with the new fields of area studies, which were to make available the particularities of the non-West to the global theorizing of the social sciences. The social science disciplines (including history), therefore, occupied the place of what was universal or global, represented as a knowledge of "history" or "development" and its laws or patterns. Area studies occupied the realm of the local. In this way, too, then, the idea of the global versus the local was built into the structure of U.S. academic knowledge.

The crisis of area studies today is usually understood as the problem of how area fields are related to the academic disciplines. Typically, however, only one partner to this relationship is considered the source of the trouble. Area studies scholars are told that their problems will be solved by getting back together with their disciplinary partners and accepting their authority. Reviews of the state of Middle Eastern studies, as of other regions, even—and perhaps especially—those written by the more critical figures in the field, end with appeals for area scholars to return to their disciplinary homes. The disciplines are more serious sites of scholarship, and most of them, it is said, "can claim to be more universal" (Khalidi 1995, 5). Yet it is in fact this claim to represent the universal that is in question in the authority of the disciplines. The future of area studies lies in their ability to refuse the disciplinary claim to universality and the particular place this claim assigns to areas.

The grounds on which the social science disciplines lay claim to their authority have changed from the situation fifty years ago when U.S. area studies first emerged.[12] Since the 1970s, the disciplines gradually have had to abandon the attempt to define themselves by laying claim to academic sovereignty over a particular area of social reality. Some time ago anthropolo-

12. A related argument might be made about the discipline of history.

gists lost their confidence that cultures are something that can be located as distinct, coherent, total ways of life, handily coterminous with a particular nation-state.[13] Political scientists, especially those outside the field of U.S. politics, made an effort in the 1970s and 1980s to reintroduce the idea of the state as the central object of the discipline. The attempt failed, and no other object provided the discipline with a territorial focus (Mitchell 1991b, 85). Economists by the 1970s had abandoned their collective faith in Keynes, who had provided them with a common language for talking about "the economy." There has been no agreement since on whether the economy as a whole or individual rationality is the proper object of economic analysis, and the economy itself has become increasingly difficult to measure or demarcate (Mitchell 1998). Sociology long ago accepted its status as a collection of subfields, many of which share their territories with parts of other disciplines.

The inability of culture, the state, the economy, or society to survive as distinct territories of social scientific investigation—what one might call the deterritorialization of the disciplines—reflects and interacts with another deterritorialization, that of contemporary global history. The confidence of the postwar period that each culture, economy, and social and political system could be the object of a separate social science represented an unexamined confidence in the total, self-enclosed, geographically fixed form of the nation-state as the assumed space of all social scientific inquiry. It was, after all, the nation-state that provided the whole of which economy, culture, state, and society were the components. Many, probably most, of the recent difficulties with the ideas of culture, society, state, and economy relate to processes, identities, and forces that challenge or outreach the nation-state.

There is an irony here. Transnational forces and identities are said to be one of the major factors placing the future of area studies in question. A region such as the Middle East no longer can be assumed to define a legitimate field of study, it is said, because so many of the forces of contemporary globalization transcend or cut at right angles to such a region. However, the same deterritorialization has undermined, in a different way, the ability of the social science disciplines to demarcate distinct territories for inquiry. Yet the SSRC has not called for the dismantling of the disciplines, and very little

13. For recent discussions, see Appadurai 1996 and Geertz 1995.

effort is made to connect the future of area studies to the very real questions about the current crisis and future shape of the social sciences.[14]

Social scientists' response to this experience of deterritorialization was to rely increasingly on another means of defining their distinctiveness. They identified themselves by their method. For anthropologists and economists, culture and economy had from the beginning come to correspond to distinctive methods of research—participant observation in one case, the mathematical representation of individual or collection equilibria in the other. In economics, moreover, field research was left to be conducted outside the academy by statistical agencies of the state. Following deterritorialization, despite frequent disputes about how these methods should be carried out, both fields maintained a consensus that participant observation and equilibrium analysis, respectively, whatever the difficulties, defined the essence of the discipline. Political science and sociology were less fortunate, unable to agree on a method and increasingly divided by certain factions' effort to identify the discipline in terms of one particular method.

The current problems of area studies programs arise to a significant extent from this crisis in the social sciences. They arise particularly from the problems faced by political science. Although the course of every discipline can affect what happens to area studies, anthropology and economics present fewer problems because in anthropology (as in history and literature) everyone is an area expert and in economics no one is. So neither discipline typically presents its practitioners with the choice between being an area expert or a theorist. In economics, you are always the latter (in different degrees of purity); in anthropology, you aspire to be both. Sociology continues to be so focused on North America and western Europe that it remains slightly removed from the debates over area studies, at least as regards a region as neglected as the Middle East. That leaves political science.

Political science is in an unusual position. A dominant coalition within the discipline seeks the intellectual certainty and professional authority of a universal knowledge of politics. Within this coalition, a powerful faction, now controlling many of the leading departments, believes that the formal

14. See Wallerstein's 1996 article "Open the Social Sciences," which summarizes a report on the social science disciplines funded by the Gulbenkian Foundation (Gulbenkian Commission 1995).

methods of microeconomics provide the best or even the only means to this universal knowledge. Unlike economists, however, these political scientists cannot rely on the statistical agencies of the state (the international financial agencies) to carry out their field research for them—in part because such agencies concentrate on collecting economic rather than political facts and in part because the extension of economic methods to the study of political questions very quickly begins to involve those messy local details that economists like to leave aside as so-called externalities. The result is that even the most (self-styled) theoretical political scientists find it difficult to abandon the need for the kind of local political understanding traditionally supplied by area research.

These developments in political science have an implication for area studies. Foreign area studies will not be abandoned but will be encouraged by and incorporated into political science. They will be incorporated, however, only as sites of the local and particular knowledge required for constructing the universal knowledge of the discipline. "We should engage more directly with this work [rational choice theory]," writes David Laitin, a leading scholar of comparative politics, "continually tantalizing theorists with uncomfortable data" and "us[ing] our area knowledge to discover interesting anomalies" (1993, 3). This procedure governs both the terms in which and the extent to which area studies are to be appropriated.

Two kinds of language are common for establishing the particularity of foreign regions in relation to the generality of political science—the new language of "institutional outcomes" and the older one of "culture." The term *institutional outcomes* refers to the assumption that some universal process of change governs the politics and history of non-Western regions, such as development or democratization or the introduction of free markets. The pure logic of these processes is inflected locally, however, by the existence of particular coalitions of interest groups, economic distortions, cultural factors, or other anomalies, which shape what is called the *institutional form* of the universal phenomenon.

The other term commonly used for expressing local difference is the old idea of *culture*. In fact, the term *institutions* is in many uses simply an updated way of talking about cultures, with the advantage that institutions are more compatible with the assumption that individuals act as rational utility maximizers. The two terms refer to those aspects of the social world that cannot be explained as individual rational action and for this reason are often equivalent: "Cultures," Robert Bates explains, "are distinguished by their distinctive institutions" (1996c, 1).

The importance of terms such as *culture* and *institution* is that by locating the sphere of the local, the anomalous, and the contingent, they refer to and guarantee a separate sphere of the universal, which usually requires political scientists to content themselves with an extraordinarily narrow understanding of the term *culture*. Bates, for example, refers to "the political significance of culture and the producers of culture: artists, priests and intellectuals" (1997b, 1).

These considerations also govern the extent to which foreign regions become incorporated into the discipline and the circumstances under which this incorporation occurs. A review of work on Middle East political economy asks about "the mysterious alchemy through which world regions escape the confines of area studies and achieve legitimate status in general debates about development and underdevelopment" (Chaudhry 1994, 42). The alchemy becomes less mysterious once one acknowledges the force of the term *general* in this question. World regions will be incorporated when and to the extent that they can be made part of certain general narratives: a narrative about industrialization, about democratization, about globalization, and so on. This is neatly illustrated in Bates's essay. The problem of studying world regions in political science is the problem of finding a "shared vision," a consensus as to what constitutes meaningful research and normal science in the field. Bates argues that three potential research frameworks exist in the field: first (for studying middle-income countries), democratic theory; second, the political economy of growth; and third, social theory, which examines "contemporary appeals to religion, ethnicity, and identity" (1997c, 2). Each of these frameworks (even the third, as I discuss later) provides a way of incorporating the non-West into a universal story, whose narrative is always that of global history, which means the history of the West.

The consequence of this relationship between discipline and world region, then, is that the object of study remains defined and grasped only in terms of its relationship to the West and only in terms of its place in a narrative defined according to the global history of the West. In this final section,

I explore what this restriction means for the particular case of contemporary Middle Eastern studies by briefly looking at three well-received contributions to the field of research on political economy.

The major synthetic study of the region's political economy, *A Political Economy of the Middle East* (1996) by Alan Richards and John Waterbury, quite plainly states the importance of the universal narrative:

> Europe's structural transformation over a number of centuries from an agrarian to an industrial urban base has shaped our general understanding of the process [of development] but has not provided a model that will be faithfully replicated in developing countries. The latter may skip some stages by importing technology or telescope others. Developing countries will cope with population growth rates that Europe never confronted. So too, the process of class formation in the Middle East and elsewhere has varied considerably from that of Europe. (37)

The standard criticisms of this kind of modernization approach, from the perspective of capitalism as a global structure of accumulation, have been made often enough and do not need repeating. I wish simply to make the following point: the authors claim that they are not taking the West as a model that can be replicated faithfully. Exactly. They are taking it as a model that *cannot* be replicated faithfully. It is the failures, variations, skipped stages, and telescoped histories—all the forms of difference from the West, the "anomalies" to which David Laitin refers in the passage I quoted earlier—that define the understanding of the region's history and politics. Historical itineraries, political forces, and cultural phenomena will be included in the story only in terms of how they cause the Middle East to fit or deviate from the narrative of the West's modernity. This is not simply a question of what is included or omitted. The narrative is a global one of modernization, "a process that has a logic of its own," as Richards and Waterbury affirm (1996, 75). This logic moves the narrative forward, representing the source of historical change and the motor of social transformations. The local variations, distortions, delays, and accelerations receive their meaning and relevance from this singular logic. They may divert or rearrange the movement of history but are not themselves that universal movement.

Conventional political economy of this sort analyzes a region such as the

Middle East in terms of two simple, universal concepts: the state and the economy. In place of the complex workings of political power at different levels and in different social fields, it substitutes the narrow idea of the state and analyzes politics as the formulation and execution of a limited range of economic laws and policies. The narrative assesses the success of these policies by describing changes in the size and structure of "the economy" as represented by conventional measures of gross domestic product, sectoral balance, and so on.

Other more-critical works explore some of the problems with this approach. Simon Bromley (1994) points out that the distinction between state and economy cannot be taken for granted in studying a region such as the Middle East. Following Karl Polanyi (1944), he recalls that establishing this distinction was a central feature of the history of advanced capitalism in the West. The distinction removed the process of appropriating surplus value from the contested sphere of politics and increasingly confined it to the organization of economic life. Yet this critique turns out to have a serious limit. Having reminded us that the separation of the economic and the political is not a universal phenomenon, Bromley assumes that the Middle East nevertheless should be understood in the same terms. The struggle to consolidate the separation of state and market "has been a large part of what the history of these societies has been about," he writes. It remains, however, "unfinished business." The positive step of historicizing categories that social science takes as universal (and as marking even the boundaries between fields of universal social scientific knowledge) is undone by taking the formation of these social categories as the framework in which to understand the history of the non-West. This history then inevitably appears unfinished (Bromley 1994, 186).

Interpreting Middle Eastern histories as incomplete or even simply variant cases of universal processes can produce quite strange readings of political developments. Kirin Chaudhry, my third example, is one of the most persistent advocates of the need to reinsert the study of the Middle East into the general field of political economy, where it might become, she believes, "an important piece of the development puzzle" (1994, 48). In a widely praised book on state formation in Saudi Arabia and Yemen, she, too, follows Polanyi in understanding the creation of the national state as simultaneously the creation of a national economy, a process that matches "the broadest sequencing patterns of state-making in early modern Europe" (1997, 98), with, of course, important local variations. Yet to make the history of the Arabian Peninsula fit the sequences of modern Europe requires a strange reading of that history. As in Europe, Chaudhry argues, state and national economy in the Middle East were built on the development of taxation. In order for this claim to be made, however, as Robert Vitalis (1999) points out, a variety of financial relationships specific to the history of Arabia—pilgrim revenues, British and U.S. subventions, extortions from merchants, advances on petroleum royalties—must be described as taxes. And Chaudhry gives Aramco, the U.S. oil consortium that created large parts of the Saudi state as extensions of its oil business, no more than a passing mention. In the conclusion to her study, she acknowledges, realistically enough, that no general statements about "the development puzzle" can be derived from her cases. Institutional outcomes, she admits, "can co-vary in highly irregular ways that cannot be captured in any formulaic fashion" (1997, 314). The foreign capital that transformed her two cases of state formation following the 1970s oil boom produced "both similarities and differences of institutional outcome" (311). These outcomes "depend on a host of historically constituted relationships" (314).

Such examples can be multiplied. What they show is that, on the evidence available, reinserting Middle East area studies into the generalizing languages of political economy does not produce any increase in a universal knowledge of politics. It may help undermine others' unsupportable generalizations, as Chaudhry shows in the case of the new institutional literature, but such general theories usually are critiqued adequately when they first appear.[15] The generalizations survive simply as unsupported "theories" to be refuted endlessly, long after they are dead, in area studies scholarship.

Writing about the politics of the Middle East as part of a general field of political economy functions largely as a rhetorical device, providing linguistic markers of one's seriousness of purpose and scientific credentials. The phrasing of sentences and the titles of books constantly resituate the historical account as simply a specific instance of a set of vaguely specified universal phenomena. A particular case, it is said, "exposes the importance of domes-

15. As Paul Cammack did with the new institutionalism in his 1990 *Social Register* article, for example.

tic contingencies"; another shows that "Capitalists, disunited, can undo the efforts of nascent state builders"; and so on (Chaudhry 1997, 310).

And there is, as I have been suggesting, a significant loss if one allows the authority of the social science disciplines to persuade us that the only worthwhile way of engaging with the politics and history of other world regions is to the extent that they can be made to appear as particular instances of the universal stories told in and about the West. The languages of political economy and the market now represent, as modernization theory earlier did, the universal truth to which all local experiences must be related and into whose language all local political expression must be translated. Chaudhry, for example, proposes a study of "ideational landscapes of economic deprivation" (1994, 45–48) as a model research project for further development of the field of Middle Eastern political economy. Noting the great number of social movements across the region today involved in different forms of moral protest and struggles over political identity and community, she proposes a comparative study to examine, in these differences, the variety of ways in which "local economic and political interests are expressed in the language of religion and identity" (46). She adds that "These different reactions promise insight into fundamental alterations in the relationship between economic and political organization, between government and citizens" (45). In other words, the diversity of languages in which communities articulate their political demands and identities, their visions and their revulsions, are to be translated into the universal language of political economy. As Dipesh Chakrabarty (1997) points out in a different context, this view basically proposes that one has nothing to learn from what these subaltern groups are actually saying. The languages of political Islam, for example, can appear in Western scholarship only through a process of translation that enables them to speak in terms of the post-Enlightenment discourse of the West. There is no way around this problem of translation. But those anxious to contribute to the universal knowledge of the social sciences do not even recognize it as a problem (Chakrabarty 1997, 37–43).[16]

The local forms of political organization and expression are understood as mere languages, meaning the cultural and "ideational" forms for express-

---

16. See also Asad 1993, in particular the chapter titled "The Limits of Religious Criticism in the Middle East: Notes on Islamic Public Argument."

ing the real interests that shape their world. The language into which these expressions are translated—political economy—is assumed by definition not to be an ideational form, not a cultural practice, but the transparent and global terminology of economic reality. Thus, in discussing the economic crises in terms of which these cultural responses will be analyzed, Chaudhry notes that "Through economic liberalization, domestic constituencies long protected from international prices experienced the *genuine* scarcities of their heretofore protected societies" (1994, 47, italics added). The prices of a protected national market are false, it is implied, whereas those of the international market are genuine. Both markets, both sets of scarcities, however, are political arrangements, reflecting the enforcement of certain constructions and distributions of property, power, monopoly, and social management. Both can exist only, if one wants to use the term, as *ideational landscapes*—that is, as arrangements constructed out of understandings about property, wealth, prices, and so on. Yet because the market, especially the so-called global market, is understood as a universal form, it cannot by definition be something "cultural," something constructed. The cultural refers to the particular and local, the province of area studies, not to the genuine and universal, the province of those other, unexamined area programs, the disciplines.

I have argued that a distinction between the global and the local defined the structure of academic disciplines and university careers over the last two-thirds of the twentieth century in the form of the relationship between the universality of disciplines and the particularity of area studies. There have been, it is true, many imaginative attempts—in fields such as cultural studies, postcolonial theory, gender studies, geography and urban studies, ethnic and diaspora studies, and cultural anthropology—to rethink the relationship between the local and the global or between the particular and the universal. Indeed, one can argue that for the past twenty-five years fields of this sort have taken over much of the role played by area studies programs in the preceding twenty or thirty years: providing a place of intellectual escape from the dominant disciplines, where the boundaries between these disciplines and their claims to universality can be ignored. Nevertheless, these alternative fields have not become major disciplines, with the control over university resources and the shaping of intellectual careers that this designation would bring. And, in this sense, much of the old distinction between local and global or between particular and universal has been reinforced.

Perhaps it is the case, then, that we should stop talking about the world in terms of the local and the global, for it is this very distinction that underlies and reinforces a hegemonic structure of knowledge. So long as we insist on a clear and unquestioned distinction between global and local, a certain kind of social science will continue to talk comfortably about the global, leaving a variety of minor programs and interdisciplinary fields to wonder about the corresponding importance of the local and its relationship to things global.

This is not a suggestion that we suddenly should see everything as local and particular, any more than it is a suggestion that we henceforth should see everything as global. Obviously, whenever we study a set of social forces or relationships, one of the things that may interest us is the extent of their reach from one context to another or the connections they may have with other phenomena. Many relationships and forces have an effective or imaginative reach that is quite global. What I am arguing against is just the distinction we make between local and global and the way in which this distinction awards to some phenomena a universal essence, rationality, and energy but renders others merely static, reactive, or "cultural."

What such a move would require is a new approach to such concepts as the market, modernity, capital, and the West. Even in the more critical forms of political economy, as Ernesto Laclau (1990) has pointed out, we attribute to concepts such as capital or the market a universal force.[17] Most of the talk about globalization does so in one way or another. This universal force reflects the assumption that there is an underlying principle of rationality or historical transformation that gives the market or global capital its force. Different kinds of thinking make this assumption in different ways: the underlying principle may be the ineluctable calculation of individual self-interest or the increasing self-enlightenment and interaction of humankind, or it may be the inevitable development of productive forces or the process of technological innovation or the conquest of the physical boundaries of space and

17. For a further discussion of this question, see "The Stage of Modernity" in Mitchell 2000.

time. Whatever the approach, any reference to "the global" carries with it a reference to some motor or energy that drives history forward and gives it its logic, its principle of expansion, and its trajectory. With such formulations, "the local" comes to stand for everything that does not possess this energy, this principle of movement, this underlying logic. The local is therefore secondary, reactive, and nonoriginal. It resists the global, perhaps distorts or even transforms it into some mutant form but is not itself the source of historical movement or of any kind of universalism. These are the assumptions built into the language of local and global.

An alternative approach would deny to modernity, the market, or global capital not their power, but their singular logic. It would insist on the contingent nature of such phenomena and explore the ways in which their global reach has been achieved only through constant interaction with groups, relations, and social forces that helped to constitute them—and therefore are no more "local" than is capital or modernity itself. Such a view of the phenomena we describe as global would lead us, I think, to abandon the easy use of the terms *local* and *global*.

10 The Middle East as an Area in an Era of Globalization

RASHID I. KHALIDI

What do we call the places we study, those of us who teach about far-away parts of the world, whether in history, anthropology, or other fields? Almost unthinkingly most of us adopt and adapt to terms that on reflection are neither accurate nor fully descriptive. Thus, in the first class in many of my courses, I find myself apologizing for describing the region under consideration with the unsatisfactory term *the Middle East*. And I find myself obliged to utilize this term in this chapter in spite of the conceptual baggage that it carries with it and some of the other problems it raises.

Many scholars' dissatisfaction with the term *Middle East* as a designation for the region lying between the Atlantic Ocean, Central Asia, and India results in part from the fact that in and of itself the phrase is neither self-explanatory nor inherently meaningful: In the middle between what and what? East of what? This designation is in fact one of many relics of an earlier, Eurocentric era, when things were "near" or "far" or in the "middle" in relation to the privileged vantage point of Europe.[1] Although similar names for other regions, such as *the Far East* and *the Indian subcontinent* have been replaced in favor of what are apparently more geographically neutral terms

An earlier version of this essay was delivered at the "Globalization, Cities, and Youth" conference in Cairo in March 1997 and was published under the title "The 'Middle East' as a Framework of Analysis: Re-mapping a Region in the Era of Globalization," *Comparative Studies of South Asia, Africa, and the Middle East* 18, no. 2 (1998): 1–8.

1. The term *Middle East* was invented by an American naval officer, Captain Alfred Thayer Mahan, who used it in his influential book *The Influence of Sea Power upon History, 1660–1783*. It was later popularized by the British liberal imperialist Halford MacKinder. See Adelson 1994.

such as *East Asia* and *South Asia,* this has not happened with regard to the Middle East.

Needless to say, there are many other possible ways to describe this region. One would be strictly in terms of its geography (as West Asia and North Africa or as the land mass between the Atlantic, the Mediterranean, the Indian Ocean, and the Black Sea). Of course, the very continents we take so much for granted are themselves constructs (where does "Europe" end and "Asia" begin?), but they have a certain resonance of scientific objectivity.[2] Another way to describe this region might be in terms of its culture (Islamic or Mediterranean, for example) or its predominant physical characteristics (a generally dry region of river valleys, highlands, and deserts bounded by inland seas).

In most academic units in the United States devoted to the study of this region, this change in description has not happened. Whatever terms were adopted and in general use at the time a unit was established have tended to remain in use since then. Thus, the older language-based departments in most universities generally use the similar but older term *the Near East* (for example, Chicago, Princeton, Cornell, Berkeley), and the more recently established departments and the newer area studies centers tend to use the equally problematic term *the Middle East.*[3]

With very few exceptions, the term *the Middle East* has remained in use in academia and in turn has influenced usage in the public sphere throughout the English-speaking world (and through its analogues in other European languages, even farther afield). Although most people who use the term are undoubtedly unaware of its genesis and derivation, the description of this region in terms of its position vis-à-vis Europe, rather than for some-

2. In *The Myth of Continents: A Critique of Metageography* (1997), Martin W. Lewis and Karen E. Wigen point out, among other things, that Europe, Asia, and Africa are a single land mass and that the Indian "subcontinent" is larger than the "continent" of Europe.

3. In a few cases, an effort to be more geographically accurate has been made: at the State University of New York at Binghampton, the relevant area center is called the South West Asia and North Africa Center. The letterhead of the Center for Middle East Studies at the University of Chicago, which retains the term, describes it as "a center for the study of North Africa, Western Asia, Central Asia, and the Islamic world."

thing intrinsic to it, is archaic and misleading. It also shapes perceptions of the region in terms of the perspectives and concerns of others.

It is perhaps a function of a sort of intellectual colonialism that within the region itself the Arabic, Turkish, and Persian terms most commonly used to describe the region are simply straightforward translations of this archaic term. Use of the term *al-sharq al-awsat* in Arabic and of analogous terms in other regional languages indicates that a description—and therefore an understanding—of this region in terms of the interests of others is quite as prevalent in the countries of the Middle East itself as outside it.

In some Western countries, there is even a perverse sense that the West has a peculiar proprietary interest in this region, perhaps because of the developed world's dependence on Middle Eastern energy resources or perhaps because of the region's vital international strategic importance in terms of air routes, waterways, and propinquity to Europe, Central Asia, South Asia, and Africa. This proprietary sense was indicated clearly during the Gulf War of 1990–91, when American politicians and commentators frequently referred to "our oil," speaking not of the oil fields of Texas and Oklahoma, but rather those of Saudi Arabia and Kuwait.

In the past, the people of this region have had many ways of describing it, representing quite distinct alternative worldviews. In Arabic, the terms *al-ʿalam al-ʿArabi* ("Arab world") and *al-ʿalam al-Islami* ("Islamic world") or the even more heavily weighted terms for the Arab nation and the Islamic community, *al-umma al-ʿArabiyya* and *al-umma al-Islamiyya,* represent powerful competing frameworks for delimiting, describing, and understanding that part of the globe and its population. These terms are in part coterminous with the areas encompassed by the term *Middle East.* Each term is quite clear and quite precisely understood by any Arabic speaker.

One finds these terms most commonly in the political writings of Arab nationalists and Islamists, but they are employed far beyond these circles. They have been used commonly with differing effect (and to describe different things) in public discourse all over the region for much of the past century. In spite of the impact of these powerful trends of thought, it is the imported term *Middle East* in translation that today and for most of the past half-century has seemed to enjoy the greatest currency in the Arab countries and in others in the region.

Among the other problems regarding the designation *Middle East* is the lack of a precise definition of the areas, the countries, cultures, religions, and language groups that are encompassed by it. No consensus exists as to precisely where the Middle East is and specifically what its limits are and therefore what it includes. Some definitions include North Africa, but others do not—the U.S. State Department, for example, for many years considered the Middle East to include the West Asian countries and Egypt, but not the rest of North Africa. By some definitions, countries such as Turkey and Afghanistan are included, but by others they are not, stretching across a very broad range of countries that form a large "periphery" of the "central" countries of the region. About the only areas included in virtually every definition of the Middle East are the Fertile Crescent—another old term to signify geographical Syria and Mesopotamia—and the Arabian Peninsula. Iran and Egypt almost always are included, but even they are left out by a few definitions.

A further problem is that even if there is a general sense of which broad areas are included, there is no clear idea of where the precise limits of the region are. This is true in particular wherever there is no large body of water such as the Atlantic, the Mediterranean, the Black Sea, or the Indian Ocean to provide a clear boundary. A number of questions arise as a result. In western Africa, where in the Sahara does the Middle East end? In eastern Africa, does the Middle East include the Horn of Africa or not? At the region's eastern limits, in West Asia, are Pakistan and Afghanistan part of the Middle East or not? To the northeast, how much, if any, of Central Asia is part of the region? The last question has been reopened by the collapse of the Soviet Union and by the resultant closer involvement of the countries and peoples of Central Asia with Turkey, Iran, Saudi Arabia, and other states to their south, which has renewed historic connections between them. All of these questions underline the limits to the utility of any regional definition, particularly if such a definition restricts the subjects of study and analysis.

Beyond these definitional problems, there are others relating to the confusion widely prevalent in the United States about the identity of the people who live in this region. Students constantly ask whether all the people of the region are Muslims or if they are all Arabs, and if so, does this mean that other peoples living in the Middle East, such as the Turks and Iranians, are also Arabs? Although we might expect that people with even a minimal education would be beyond asking such questions, they in fact commonly are asked by many Americans who are neither ignorant nor poorly educated. However rooted in a deep general lack of knowledge about the rest of the world in this country, this confusion is at least in part a function of the fact that the term used to describe this region confounds many nonexperts or at least fails to enlighten them sufficiently.

For many Westerners, the Middle East is synonymous with Islam. This misconception fails to take into account the many millions of non-Muslims who live there, whether Copts in Egypt, Jews in Israel, or Christians of various Eastern and Western denominations in Palestine, Lebanon, Syria and Iraq, as well as adherents of other faiths, such as Bahais and Yezidis. This misconception furthermore conceals perhaps the most important fact about the demography of the Islamic world today: that the vast majority of Muslims now live outside the Middle East, the area that was the historic core of the Islamic world. Today most Muslims worldwide reside in the countries of South and Central Asia and in Indonesia, Malaysia, and China.[4] The center of gravity of the Islamic world today is thus in these areas, well to the east of the Middle East, where it once used to be located, however that region is defined.

If the Middle East is not synonymous with the Islamic world, what is its central focus? It perhaps can be defined best in terms of the peoples who today speak Arabic, Persian, and Turkish, the three main historic languages of Islam. Even that definition is not without flaws, however, because many millions of people in the region speak other languages, such as the Berbers, Israelis, and Kurds, to name but three; moreover, many people living well outside this region speak these or closely related languages, such as Tajik, which is very close to Persian, or a number of Turkic languages.

Leaving aside the difficulties related to the definition of the Middle East per se, there exist other, broader problems with this term. There are several different regions as well as many institutional processes whereby these re-

---

4. Around the middle of the twentieth century, approximately 220 million Muslims lived in the Arab world, Africa, Iran, Turkey, and the Balkans; more than 300 million lived in the Indian subcontinent, Southeast Asia, the areas that used to be part of the former Soviet Union, and China: see Hodgson 1974, 76–77. The demographic balance has tipped even further in favor of the latter regions since then.

gions are defined, studied, and processed into knowledge in universities and elsewhere. Currently perhaps the most important of these processes is area studies. The entire enterprise of area studies first developed in the U.S. academy with government encouragement at the outset of the Cold War. This approach has left us at the outset of the twenty-first century with a Balkanized set of fields, each one in some measure separated from the others, and all of them suffering from a greater or lesser degree of isolation from much of what is going on in the broader realms of the social sciences and the humanities.

I have argued elsewhere[5] that a variety of complex processes that transcend regions have been given far less attention than they deserve specifically because of the way in which the Middle East has tended to be studied under the rubric of area studies. These processes include the trade, capital, and labor flows between countries all around the rim of the Indian Ocean, which in differing forms appear to have been quite significant for a very long time (and which have received far less attention than a newly discovered "region," the Pacific Rim). This neglect has occurred in part because these processes transcend several fields that have been reified through what is now known and treated as "Middle East studies," "African studies," and "South Asian studies," with each holding its separate conferences and publishing its own scholarly journals.[6]

It is certainly the case that until recently relatively little attention has been paid in the Middle East field to what was happening in other branches of area studies. This was true as regards the South Asian field, where the subaltern school has had a profound influence that has now gone well beyond the history of that region alone, or as regards Latin American studies, where *dependencia* theory for many years was highly influential in analyses not only of Latin America but of development and underdevelopment generally.

It indeed can be argued that in some respects the situation today is

---

5. For details, see Khalidi 1995.

6. There have been many efforts within area studies to transcend the barriers among these fields, via joint meetings of area studies associations (thus, for example, the Middle East Studies Association met in New Orleans one year with the Association of African Studies, and several joint sessions were organized) and via publications such as *Comparative Studies of South Asia, Africa, and the Middle East*.

worse than it was before the modern area studies approach was devised.[7] To explain why this is the case, it is necessary to discuss briefly the genesis of area studies in the United States in the wake of World War II. This approach to understanding the world emerged in a situation where the United States suddenly had become the dominant world power and found itself involved in the politics of a broad range of countries far beyond the limited zones in Latin America, the Caribbean, and the Philippines that previously had been U.S. spheres of influence. It very quickly became clear that—with the exception of a few isolated specialists, including missionaries, businessmen, and diplomats—there was no body of expertise in the United States on the history, politics, culture, and economies of most other regions of the world.

The major European colonial powers had spent decades and sometimes centuries developing a considerable range of academic, scientific, and scholarly expertise and considerable academic resources on many areas of the world, with the greatest effort almost invariably concentrated on those areas where each power had the strongest interests or the most-developed ambitions. Unlike them, the United States had none of these things. In the European academy, beyond the concentration of resources on each imperialist power's sphere of real or projected influence, generally there was a cadre of specialists dedicated to the attempt to apprehend, understand, and master the languages, cultures, and history of the rest of the world. This attempt not only mirrored Europe's mastery over the world but often was the precondition for and the result of that mastery.[8]

As an indication of how extraordinarily limited were the official U.S. resources devoted to the examination of the rest of the world before Pearl Harbor, it suffices to note that there was no U.S. intelligence service with international scope before the establishment of the Central Intelligence

7. These conclusions are not entirely original: there has been an ongoing discussion of the area studies paradigm in the academic disciplines, the foundations, and the area studies groups themselves. See, for example, a variety of articles in *Items,* the bulletin of the Social Science Research Council, notably Heginbotham 1994 and Prewitt 1996, but see also Bates 1996, Globalization Project 1997, Hall and Tarrow 1998, and Khoury 1998.

8. The seminal work on this subject is Edward W. Said's *Orientalism* (1978), which has provoked a rich literature that continues to proliferate. Related works include Amin 1989, Blaut 1993, Cohn 1996, Inden 1990, and Kiernan 1969.

Agency in 1947 as a successor to the Office of Strategic Services, which itself was a World War II creation.[9] Similarly, with a very few isolated exceptions, there were no programs for study of the modern languages, history, society, or culture of most other parts of the world (besides Europe) in U.S. universities or in any other U.S. institutions before World War II. The programs that existed in a few elite universities tended to be focused on ancient history, archaeology, and the philology of dead languages. These programs were clearly not sufficient if the United States were to play a dominant role in the post-World War II world to which its leaders aspired.

Seen in this light, the development of the area studies approach originally was driven by the need to produce a body of knowledge on an interdisciplinary basis that would make up for the almost total absence of detailed, reliable information about the modern world available to American policymakers. This information was suddenly crucial to the management of the world system over which the United States towered at the end of the war.[10] Thereafter, an entirely new set of institutions grew up, such as foreign-language and foreign-area centers, while entirely new fields of academic endeavor emerged, such as Middle East studies, and with them new professional associations, such as the Middle East Studies Association of North America. Only a few decades earlier, none of these institutions had existed in the United States.[11]

Given this background, why is the situation today worse in some ways

9. For an insight into the profound changes taking place in the U.S. state in this period, see Yergin 1977.

10. This effort was rooted deeply in the needs of the new post-World War II U.S. world hegemony and in the related needs of the Cold War, as can be seen from the name of one of the first congressional measures to provide funding for foreign-language instruction, the National Defense Education Act of 1957. Since the early Cold War years, much has changed, with academics, universities, foundations, and professional associations in many fields asserting their own agendas, which were often counter to those of the government (but less frequently counter to the interests of business and finance). This dissent from government policy could be seen during both the Vietnam and Gulf Wars and in the various U.S. interventions in Central America of the Reagan-Bush era, when many and ultimately perhaps most American experts on these three regions opposed the government's policies.

11. By 2000, this organization, founded in 1966, had a roster of members that ran to more than 150 pages. It holds annual conferences that draw as many as two thousand people.

than it was before the area studies approach developed? The answer is that before then such organized knowledge as existed about many of these regions—in particular the Middle East, South Asia, and East Asia—was subsumed under the general rubric of "Oriental studies." This knowledge was organized on the basis of approaches to philology, religion, culture, and history that were generally quite similar. Often antiquarian in their interests and resolutely focused on the premodern, these U.S. branches of the European Orientalist disciplines nevertheless shared their strengths as well as their weaknesses. Among these strengths was an understanding that the ancient civilizations they were concerned with had many things in common and that they thus were best studied in conjunction with one another and in terms of the paradigm of the "civilization."

Thus, to take one example among the small number of U.S. universities with a strong tradition of Oriental studies during the first half of the twentieth century, study of the ancient Near East, South Asia, and East Asia (with gestures toward the "modern" including some emphasis on Islamic studies) at the University of Chicago initially took place within the walls of one institution, the Oriental Institute, founded by the Egyptologist James Breasted in 1919. Even after each of these three regions had acquired its own separate department (the Department of Near East Languages and Civilizations, the Department of South Asian Languages and Civilizations, and the Department of East Asian Languages and Civilizations) and the latter two were relocated outside the Oriental Institute, all three units retained an orientation resolutely on the distant past. Thus, the majority of scholars within the Department of Near East Languages and Civilizations always dealt with the ancient world, and for these scholars—although it might have seemed like a joke to outsiders—modern history started with Alexander the Great.

A few other U.S. academic institutions—such as Princeton, Harvard, Michigan, Columbia, and the University of Pennsylvania—supported a similar range of activities in what was then called Oriental studies. For all the failures of classical Orientalism, well described by Edward Said in his influential book *Orientalism* (1978), it at least managed to avoid the kind of compartmentalization of different areas, in some cases amounting almost to a ghetto mentality, that has afflicted modern area studies.

On the other hand, although the almost exclusive focus on philology, linguistics, archaeology, ancient history, and the history of religion within

Near Eastern, South Asian, and East Asian branches of Oriental studies fostered certain kinds of comparative work, closely linked to one another and to some areas of the humanities as broadly defined, it can be argued that this entire enterprise was cut off from what was going on in the social sciences. It is certainly true that within the context of the development of the paradigm for the organization of knowledge in the academy in Europe and the United States around the turn of the twentieth century, the study of these ancient civilizations was considered to fit most appropriately within the discipline of Oriental studies, rather than within the social sciences.

In a penetrating study of the genesis of the structure of modern Western forms of knowledge, entitled "Open the Social Sciences" (1996), Immanuel Wallerstein has analyzed this compartmentalization.[12] He shows that during this formative period for the core disciplines of the social sciences, only the "advanced" countries of the West were seen as having politics, societies, and economies worthy of study. The non-West was perceived as devoid of such things because it was "timeless," stagnant," and "backward" and therefore incapable of the social and economic evolution that occurred in the West. Thus, the social sciences established to study these realms of human endeavor—notably economics, political science, and sociology—hardly extended their scope beyond Europe and its most important colonies, notably the United States. As for these "other" regions, there was either anthropology, if they were "primitive" societies, or Oriental studies, if they were "ancient" ones.

The new enterprise of area studies did not suffer from these old prejudices about the non-Western world (whatever new prejudices may have affected it) or from a lack of attention to the social sciences, at least at the outset. Indeed, a number of prominent social scientists, among them the anthropologists Milton Singer and Jamie Redfield at the University of Chicago, were among the pioneers and most important propagators of the new area studies approach. Much later, however, after the passing of the glory days of area studies—lasting from the 1950s to the 1980s—several of the U.S. social science disciplines increasingly rejected involvement with any

---

12. This article was Wallerstein's summary of a recent survey of the social sciences by a panel of eminent academics sponsored by the Mellon Foundation (Gulbenkian Commission 1995).

form of area knowledge.[13] At one major U.S. research university, for example, graduate students in a social science department stated that members of the faculty had told them unequivocally that there was no point to their learning foreign languages.[14]

Many of the social science disciplines have become increasingly resistant to any connections to area studies and increasingly reluctant to make appointments of area specialists in their disciplines. The exceptions to this trend include anthropology and history, both of which coexist uneasily with the "harder," more quantitative fields within the rubric of the social sciences. The situation at the University of Chicago, where area studies may be said to have begun and where social scientists were instrumental in the elaboration of the area studies paradigm, can serve to illustrate this point. With two new junior appointments in early 1997, this university ended a period of five years during which there was not one regularly appointed Middle East specialist in the anthropology, economics, political science, psychology, and sociology departments. Even worse, for more than a dozen years, there has not been one tenured faculty member specializing in the Middle East in any of these departments. The University of Chicago situation concerning faculty specialists on other regions—such as Africa, East Asia, and eastern Europe—was only slightly better.

At other U.S. universities, although conditions were occasionally better in certain departments or with regard to specific regions, by and large they were generally quite similar to the situation at Chicago and for similar reasons. As the social sciences generally became more quantitative as well as more self-consciously theoretical, the linguistic, cultural, and historic concerns of many area specialists have come to seem quaint and retrograde. Thus, the president of the Comparative Politics Section of the American Political Science Association argued in a letter to members of the association that many scholars in political science viewed area studies as opposed to the newest trends in political science, as a drag on the profession, and as defec-

13. *Items* is full of analyses of why and how this trend has developed. See the articles cited in fn. 7. The vice president of the Mellon Foundation noted that foundations are moving away from support of "area studies, as they are traditionally defined" (see letter cited in Khalidi 1995, 2).

14. They were political science students at Indiana University.

tors from the so-called quantitative side of the division in the academy to the so-called qualitative side (Bates 1966, 1).

It thus can be concluded that study of many other parts of the world is in profound trouble in the United States. As we have seen, area studies no longer has the prestige it once did in some of the most important disciplines of the social sciences. Meanwhile, the situation is no better for Oriental studies or for the language and literature departments derived from it, which already were isolated historically from the social sciences. They suffer both from the disdain of scholars influenced by Said's critique of them and from budget cuts because many administrators believe that the arcane and difficult practices fostered by Oriental studies draw few students (and especially few of those all-important undergraduates, whose tuition is increasingly vital to the financial well-being of U.S. universities today).

This trouble has been compounded by the end of the Cold War, which once made available generous funding for Russian and Chinese studies in particular and for area studies generally. Expensive government support of the intensive study of the languages, cultures, societies, politics, and history of distant parts of the world was once defended in Congress on the grounds that it was necessary for waging the struggle against the Soviet Union and its proxies in these regions. Now that the USSR has disappeared and the United States appears to be triumphant throughout the world, some members of Congress—which is notably parsimonious where anything international, let alone international education, is concerned—see such study as an unnecessary luxury. In consequence, this support has begun to dry up or at least to diminish. For some on Capitol Hill, if the expertise derived from area studies cannot be shown to be essential for explicit foreign-policy purposes (or as an adjunct to the expansion of U.S. business interests throughout the world), it is not necessary and certainly does not merit support with tax dollars.

Following the proclamation of a U.S. victory in the Cold War, there has been a resurgence of the idea that "the business of America is business," as well as a triumphalist vision of capitalism that sees it as the height of human social evolution and the measure of all things, past and present. This atmosphere has reinforced the tendency to see international studies as having utility primarily insofar as they serve to expand the international reach of U.S.

business. This attitude recently led Congress to authorize the establishment of Centers for International Business Education and Research at a number of U.S. universities.

The common belief that globalization at base means that the world is becoming more like the United States causes other problems for area studies and related fields. In public-policy circles and in some other forums of public discourse in the United States, this belief leads to the idea that in this homogenized and Americanized brave new world there is less rather than more need for local knowledge of other parts of the world. Thus, a crude form of the argument goes that in dealing with the teeming masses of the rest of the world, there is no need to read their exotic languages or learn their strange customs in order to deal with them because they all will be speaking English and eating Big Macs soon, if they are not doing so already. And if for some perverse reason they do not accept these values, we have no need or desire to communicate with or understand them in any case.

This chauvinistic and crassly commercial triumphalism finds another, ostensibly more sophisticated form in expression of the opinion that the end of the Cold War means the final validation of the capitalist system and of Western liberal democracy as the height of historical development of the human race—the "end of history" in Francis Fukuyama's (1992) memorably imbecilic phrase.

However this potent disdain may be expressed, it translates into a belief that there is little sense in studying the rest of the world. Such ideas have increasing power in some sectors of American society and could be heard notably in congressional discussions in 1996 and 1997 regarding the cutting of funding for federally supported foreign-language training (fortunately, these cuts ultimately did not occur, thanks to the efforts of a few defenders of international education and some enlightened members of Congress). These ideas nevertheless are being powerfully contested in the academy and elsewhere. They certainly are not accepted by a growing number of American students in high school, college, and graduate and professional schools, who seem to understand intuitively that globalization means that they will have to learn more rather than less about the cultures of other parts of the world, which are considerably nearer than ever before, whether because of the increasingly multicultural nature of American society or because of the greater accessibility of other parts of the world in this era of cheap, quick, easy travel and instantaneous communication.[15]

A concluding example of the disdain some Americans hold for the rest of the world and for the Middle East in particular can be found in the profoundly obtuse but nevertheless superficially compelling argument put forward by Harvard political scientist Samuel P. Huntington in his influential 1993 *Foreign Affairs* article, "The Clash of Civilizations?"—which was followed three years later by a book of the same title (Huntington 1996). Under the veneer of the ostensibly equal treatment Huntington accords to each of the seven or eight civilizations he describes (he is not sure whether there is an entity such as the "African civilization"), his argument boils down to "the West against the Rest" in the broadest terms and to the West (including the other civilizations he lists) against Islam in more immediate terms.

Not surprisingly, the clash between civilizations that Huntington sees as the most likely in the future and as the most intractable is that which will take place between the West and Islam. Also not suprisingly, the authority on whom Huntington relies for his portrayal of Islam is none other than Bernard Lewis, whose offensive 1992 article "The Roots of Muslim Rage" in the *Atlantic Monthly* was instrumental in setting the parameters for a discussion of Islam in the U.S. media and among the punditocracy in terms of social pathology.[16] Huntington essentially adopts Lewis's biased outlook, spending the better part of four pages of his essay on the subject, concluding with the words, "Islam has bloody borders" (1993, 35).

Huntington's denigration of Islam is embodied in his depiction of both its religion and culture as profoundly alien and as monolithic and unchanging, as well as in his portrayal of an uninterrupted history of conflict between the Islamic world and all its neighbors. This is an ahistorical and reduction-

---

15. These students may search for knowledge about the world in the departments that are the heirs of Orientalism—the language and culture and language and civilizations departments—or that are in other parts of area studies or elsewhere, whether within the social science disciplines, in business or law, or in the growing field of globalization studies. The point is that their numbers are clearly growing.

16. For a harshly critical perspective on Lewis's anti-Islamic prejudices, see Edward Said's *Orientalism* (1978) and *Covering Islam* (1997), xxix-xxxiii.

ist portrayal, as is obvious to anyone with the slightest knowledge of the rel-evant history, but it is nevertheless one that finds a wide resonance in Amer-ican culture. It would appear that such a representation also finds resonance in some quarters of a number of European societies. According to a report in the *New York Times*, European Christian Democratic parties meeting in Brussels in 1997 denied Turkey membership in the European Union in part (it can be suspected in large part) because of their deep reservations about whether "a Muslim country should be included" in the European Union, in the words of one unnamed source (Kinzer 1997, A7).

Huntington's work thus makes him the latest of a series of writers with wide audiences in the U.S. academy and outside it to demonstrate a particu-lar animus toward Islam, the Arab world, and the Middle East generally. Among the most important of these writers have been two experts in the field, Bernard Lewis, on whom Huntington relies, and Daniel Pipes.[17] The work of such academics, with its scholarly veneer, is complemented by that of journalists who have specialized in the links between the Middle East and terrorism.[18] The existence of such a trend has been best analyzed by Edward Said in his works *Orientalism* and *Observing Islam* and is in fact an enduring feature of modern American and European political culture.

Evidence of the pervasiveness of this trend can be found in historian John Woods's (1996) comprehensive study of the blatant stereotyping of Muslims, Arabs, and Middle Easterners in the U.S. mass media and, in par-ticular, in political cartoons in the daily press. Employing dozens of images, mainly cartoons, Woods shows clearly that it is possible for these media to use crude racist images about these groups almost with impunity—which is

17. Pipes has published a number of works that display such an animus, occasionally thinly veiled, notably *Slave Soldiers and Islam: The Genesis of a Military System* (1981) and *Greater Syria: The History of an Ambition* (1990). More important in this respect has been his work as director of the Foreign Policy Research Institute in Philadelphia, a think tank whose primary task appears to be to denigrate opponents of Israel, perceived and real, whether in the United States or in the Middle East.

18. Among the journalists who most influence American public perceptions on these top-ics are *New York Times* correspondent Judith Miller, author of most of a series of articles on Muslim terrorism entitled "Holy Warriors," 14–16 January 2001, and "terrorism expert" Steve Emerson, whose ubiquitous appearances on television contributed considerably to the anti-Muslim and anti-Arab public hysteria of the past few years.

in clear distinction to treatment of almost every other major national, ethnic, or religious group in the United States, even those who in the past have been the objects of fierce racial or religious prejudice in the United States or elsewhere, such as people of African descent and Jews.

In summary, we have seen that there are serious problems with the definition of the Middle East as a region and as a field of inquiry; there are problems with Middle East studies in particular, with area studies, and with the study of the rest of the world in general; there is a distancing from important segments of the world that influential elements of the American and European elite (but not all of American or European culture) see as unworthy of interest or as threatening; and there is a particular hostility toward Islam, Arabs, and the Middle East in some of these same quarters. In view of all these disturbing trends, what is to be done?

It is probably preferable to focus on the first three sets of problems rather than the fourth, for the hostility in the United States and in the West toward Islam has deep and quite specific roots, a serious discussion that would take us far from our subject. It is worth noting parenthetically, however, that this hostility is bound up with issues beyond the broader problems affecting area studies. Indeed, it probably can be addressed effectively only as part of the resolution of other issues—notably the Arab-Israeli conflict and the two-decade rupture in U.S.-Iran relations. Much of this hostility is grounded in a carefully cultivated ignorance and fear of the Middle East, Islam, and the Arabs, both of which appear to be necessary for mobilizing support for specific approaches in U.S. foreign policy among segments of the American public.[19]

19. An important element of coordination in this campaign grows out of lobbying in support of Israel on Capitol Hill, led by the American Israel Public Affairs Committee (AIPAC), publisher of the widely distributed and influential newsletter *Near East Report,* which cultivates hostility toward and fear of various forms of what it calls Islamic, Arab, and Middle Eastern "radicalism," fundamentalism, and terrorism. AIPAC had a staff of 115 and a published budget of $15 million in 1997. It is only one part, albeit a key one, of a network of allied lobbies, think tanks, and other bodies that engage in extensive public disinformation regarding the Middle East as part of their championing of their vision of Israel's interests. Another crucial part of this network is the Washington Institute for Near East Policy, whose founder and former director, Martin Indyk, served as assistant secretary of state for the Middle East and ambassador to Israel under the Clinton administration and authored that administration's "dual containment" policy directed against Iran and Iraq. The Washington Institute issues

Leaving aside these vexed questions relating to the Middle East (which nevertheless have some lessons and implications for other areas of the world), we should consider carefully the question of the degree to which utilizing regions as our overall unit of analysis obscures some of the phenomena that we study or should be studying. Perhaps it is time for us to give greater attention to the many important processes and trends that transcend regions and that thus must be addressed on an extraregional basis. This change in attention may be on a disciplinary basis, within sociology or anthropology or history. It may involve bringing together more than one region and discipline in an ad hoc fashion or even redefining regions, or it may involve studying new phenomena on an entirely new basis—for example, on the basis of the paradigms of globalization or human rights. In any case, it is clear at least that we must expect solutions from directions different from the "traditional" areas into which area studies are divided.

Moreover, most of the existing fields grounded in Orientalism—for all their value in other respects, notably rigorous language training and a bringing together of history and archaeology—are singularly ill adapted to deal with these processes. As a rule, we have seen that university departments of Near East or South Asian or East Asian languages and civilizations or languages and literatures place a heavy emphasis on philology, archaeology, and ancient history and are resolutely backward looking. They are thus generally not appropriate venues for the study of subjects such as globalization, urbanization, and the environment or of much else that is even less novel than these topics. Nevertheless, it is essential to any prospect of understanding other parts of the world that the valuable work such departments engage in, especially training in languages and in ancient history and archaeology, be protected assiduously from the current anti-intellectual, bottom-line trends in academic administration.

Similarly, area studies, dominated as they are by federally funded National Resource Centers, are by their mandate rooted in Title VI legislation and regulations that generally confine them to study of a single region rather than allow them to use processes that transcend regions.[20] Ultimately, perhaps the organization of both the language, literature, culture, and civiliza-

---

recommendations for Middle East policy at the outset of every new administration, recommendations that often serve as a blueprint for the policy that is actually followed.

20. There are in fact also Title VI-funded international studies centers.

tion departments and the area centers should be rethought in a radical and fundamental way. This reorganization might end many area studies scholars' isolation from the broader social science and humanities disciplines, thereby bringing together with others those historians, literature specialists, linguists, and archaeologists who work on the regions covered by area studies and Orientalism.

If this happens, it is crucial that the most valuable elements of traditional Oriental and area studies be recuperated and recycled—in particular the essential language training that they foster and the forum they provide for scholars studying a particular region to work together. It remains to be seen how much good might be lost with the bad if such a transformation were to occur, how much is irremediably mired in the historical and institutional contexts out of which these scholarly forms emerged, and how much would necessarily disappear as these contexts change.

Outside the Western context, there is an obsession with each country's and each region's history and development, an obsession that tends to preclude research that cuts across regions. But perhaps it is here, in the rest of the world outside the United States and Europe, with their heavy institutional investments in both conservative Oriental studies and region-bound area studies, that an open-minded attitude to these processes that transcend specific areas of the world can be found most easily. Perhaps the right environment for work that transcends traditional regional and disciplinary boundaries can be found in areas such as the Middle East, where there is an acute consciousness of the ties of the countries and peoples of the region to adjacent parts of the Eurasian-African land mass and of its intimate integration historically and currently in numerous global processes.

If so, there is every reason to encourage such a development, for through it scholars and intellectuals in such countries will be able to begin work in fields where the developed countries do not have the advantage of a head start and where institutional inertia and natural conservatism hinder many universities and scholars in Western and developed countries from moving in new directions. With regard to these new approaches and new fields, scholars from the non-Western world at the very least have certain advantages that Western scholars do not have, although the latter of course retain the advantages of their comparatively lavish funding and the relative stability of their working conditions by comparison with colleagues elsewhere.

In any case, it is necessary to devise new paradigms that can help us to see new connections and new combinations. One example is the long-standing linkages between the countries of the Indian Ocean Rim, a vast region that encompasses many cultures and countries with a history of extensive connections with one another, but which too often are studied as separate components. Another example is the integral relations in the present and the past between Central Asia, the Caucasus and Black Sea regions, the Middle East, and South Asia, relations that temporarily were obscured first by Russian and British colonialism and later during the Soviet period. There are many more such sets of linkages—some regional, such as the two just mentioned, and some truly global in nature: Islamic banking and finance, for example; or the impact of satellite television, cassettes, videos, e-mail, cell phones, faxes, and Web sites on politics, notably in the activities of radical transnational religious and political movements; or the long history of extraordinary capital, labor, and population flows within, through, and out of South Asia and the Middle East.

In the Middle East in particular, there are many specific incentives to think about these issues, for they are central both to many of the region's problems (including its problems with the developed world) and perhaps to the solutions to these problems. It would help if some of these problems were seen as shared across the region and across regions and if solutions that transcend the region thus might be devised. This wish may sound almost trite, but it is one of the key realizations that taking a nonregional perspective makes possible: although Middle Easterners and others may see the problems of their societies as unique and specific, many such problems are far from being so, whether they involve external dependency, autocratic government, pollution, urban crowding, overpopulation, food dependency, corruption, or something else.

Of course, this region has specific languages and cultures. The latter are shared in some measure with other regions but are different in some important respects, including the impact of Islam, which, in spite of its many universal aspects, is practiced differently in different regions and often produces different social and political results in each case. We must study and understand both what is shared and what is unique if we are to understand why some global phenomena appear in quite a similar fashion all over the world but have completely disparate effects in others. If anything justifies aspects of the Oriental studies and area studies paradigms, it is these specificities of language and culture that we must understand and respect but also must transcend on occasion.

I hope these observations on the Middle East in an era of globalization will contribute to the rethinking that will be necessary if we are to remap not only the Middle East but other regions and if we are to understand how to preserve a comprehension of their specificities while being open to the broader trends that are becoming increasingly important in the postmodern world in which we live.

There can be little question that this process will benefit greatly from significant input from those who come from regions outside of Europe and North America and thus are less weighted by the heavy intellectual and institutional baggage of rigid disciplines, inflexibly defined areas, and conservative departments that many of us located in the developed world carry. Although these non-Western scholars generally do not enjoy the support of well-funded institutions and may operate in circumstances that are less than ideal for scholarly endeavor, they are often in immediate touch with many of the phenomena that we study from afar and thus benefit greatly from involvement in the lively debates within their societies. In order for the process of remapping regions and rethinking the organization of the scholarly project we are engaged in to be successful, it must be a collaborative project involving both those within and those without the regions being remapped.

 PART THREE

Globalization and the Area Studies Debate

11 Culture Against History?

The Politics of East Asian Identity

ARIF DIRLIK

In this chapter, I take up some problems that pertain to the question of an East Asian identity in its relationship to the idea of "the West." I do so by making a brief detour through changes over the past three decades in attitudes toward culture in the definition of identity. Because the problems I raise are by now familiar ones, my goal here is primarily to draw attention to the contrast between contemporary approaches to the question and those that prevailed only a few decades ago, to offer some thoughts on change in the world situation that may account for the transformation, and to conclude with a few comments on the possibilities offered by a historical perspective to comprehend contemporary problems better as well as to overcome some of the dilemmas that they present. One of my basic concerns in the discussion is the difference in the perception of "areas" of scholarship among U.S. scholars of Asia and "Asian" scholars who find a different meaning in the undertaking that we call "Asian studies." The questions I consider, therefore, are not just temporal but spatial as well.

The Past and the West, Then and Now

In a book written more than two decades ago, *The Crisis of the Arab Intellectual* (1976), the Moroccan intellectual Abdallah Laroui took up a question that he believed to be fundamental to non-Western intellectuals' confrontation with the West: the question of historical or cultural "retardation." The ascription of native cultural backwardness as an explanation of Western domination presented the native intellectual with a seemingly insuperable dilemma: to escape the past by Westernization, in which case the native intellectual could no longer claim a historical identity of any kind, or to reaffirm the past as the source of identity in resignation to perpetual retardation. Laroui located the crisis to which the title of the book referred in this entrapment between "the West" and the "past." Whatever the solution chosen, the choice itself condemned the intellectual to alienation from his or her present, as he put it.

Now, there are two types of alienation: the one is visible and openly criticized, the other all the more insidious because it is denied on principle. Westernization indeed signifies an alienation, a way of becoming other, an avenue to self-division (though one's estimation of this transformation may be positive or negative, according to one's ideology). But there exists another form of alienation in modern Arab society, one that is previewent but veiled: this is the exaggerated medireviewization obtained through quasi-magical identification with the great period of classical Arab culture (Laroui 1976, 121).

We may observe, further, with the hindsight of Edward Said's *Orientalism*, published two years later (1978), that these two "alienations" (the liberal and the fundamentalist, respectively) were entangled, moreover, in Western hegemony insofar as they were premised on representations of Arab culture in Western Orientalism; whether rejected or reaffirmed, the past referred to was a product of Orientalism, now internalized by the Orientals themselves—what I have described elsewhere as "self-Orientalization," and others as "Orientalism in reverse" (Said 1978).[1] Laroui's own answer to the dilemma was a radical Marxist historicism that would reconnect the individual with the concrete present of his or her society:

> The historicism we are leading up to, one that is in many respects instrumental, is not the passive acceptance of any past whatsoever and above all not the acceptance of one's own national past; rather, it is the voluntary choice of realizing the unity of historical meaning by the reappropriation of a selective past. This choice is motivated by pragmatic considerations, perhaps, by modesty, above all by nationalism in the most natural sense of the

---

1. I referred to the situation Laroui described as "self-Orientalization" in an essay written in response to *The Crisis of the Arab Intellectual*. See Dirlik 1987, reprinted in my book *The Postcolonial Aura* (Dirlik 1997c, 23–51). Further elaboration is presented in Dirlik 1996, also reprinted in *The Postcolonial Aura*, 105–28. Chatterjee (1986) has underlined the importance of self-Orientalization to understanding certain types of nationalism in the Third World.

word; the will to gain the respect of others by the shortest possible route. In this perspective, we see clearly that it is not the moderate liberal who is being realistic, for he chooses to believe in the improbable equality of nations. Rather, it is the radical nationalist who is the realist; provided that he affirms his existence, he cares little if he loses his essence (his authenticity). (1976, 99–100)

The voluntarism suggested by the phrase "the reappropriation of a selective past" is somewhat misleading because Laroui's argument in its main thrust suggests that the reappropriation of the past will be part of a process of struggle for existence in the present, a process that involves not just a struggle for national liberation but also a class struggle to overcome alienation within the nation; "praxis," he notes on the same page, "is historicism in action." What he had to say concerning the creation of a new culture through revolutionary praxis had a parallel a decade earlier in Franz Fanon's (1968) statement that a national culture is not a folklore or an abstract populism that believes it can discover the people's true nature. It is not made up of the inert dregs of gratuitous actions—that is to say, actions that are less and less attached to the ever-present reality of the people. A national culture is the whole body of efforts made by a people in the sphere of thought to describe, justify, and praise the action through which the people has created itself and keeps itself in existence. A national culture in underdeveloped countries therefore should take its place at the very heart of the struggle for freedom that these countries are carrying on (Fanon 1968, 188). These were attitudes, I have suggested elsewhere, that were common to the understanding of culture in most national liberation struggles of the late colonial period, from Morocco and Algeria to Cuba and China. They represented a notion of cultural creation that sought to transcend entrapment in the oppositions of "the West" and "the past" or of "modernity" and "tradition" by taking their point of departure in a situation where both "the past" and "the West" were inextricable constituents of the ever-present reality of the people. And what they sought to create was not *just* a national culture, but a national culture that was part of a greater struggle for freedom and justice (Dirlik 1997c, 43–44).

National liberation movements are now of the past, and so apparently are the solutions to the question of cultural identity offered by national liberation leaders and theorists from Frantz Fanon to Abdallah Laroui, Ernesto

Che Guevara to Mao Zedong. But the question of cultural identity is still very much there; indeed, it has come to the foreground insistently as it has been divorced from its ties to questions of political economy, however inseparable the two seemed to be in earlier, primarily Marxist conceptualizations. It is also rephrased now in the language of globalization that has replaced modernization as a paradigm of change, but without providing any solutions to either the problems inherited from the past or the proliferation of cultural conflict under its regime. Although these conflicts endow the question with a new urgency, there are no new answers perceptible on the global cultural horizon. If anything, a cynicism toward the claims of all-universalizing solutions has replaced the utopianism of an earlier period, which had been sparked by the end of colonialism and fueled by hopes that postcolonial regimes (the Third World) could regenerate a universalism that had been betrayed by both capitalism and Soviet-style socialism. The failure of national liberation regimes—a consequence in part of their own failings, including the exaggerated utopian hopes they invested in themselves, but also a consequence in no small measure of the engineering of global policies designed to guarantee their failure—has resulted in a worldwide retreat from imagining alternatives to the present, while the so-called globalization itself has added new dimensions to the question of cultural identity.

Traditions once condemned to the past have made a comeback with a vengeance. The critique of liberal scholarship beginning in the 1970s repudiated the modernity-tradition distinction as an issue of Eurocentrism, and such critique lives on in contemporary cultural studies, which is even more adamant in repudiating the distinction. But such critiques seem to be irrelevant to what goes on in the world, where the erstwhile colonized peoples insist on their traditions, this time not as remnants of the past but with their own claims to modernity. Surely, one of the crucial questions that we must ask is why, in the midst of globalization, the world is being fragmented in so many ways that few dare to speak of universalism these days; particularisms of all kinds, including some that previously were unimagined, have assumed such pervasiveness as to define existence universally.

China, Globalization, and the Disavowal of History

Laroui acknowledged the direct inspiration in his analysis of the work of Joseph Levenson on the fate of Confucianism in modern China. Levenson argued, in his seminal work *Confucian China and Its Modern Fate* (1968), that Marxist historicism had resolved a problem that had plagued Chinese intellectuals ever since the encounter with the modern West had forced a parochialization of Confucian values from their universalistic status into the circumscribed endowment of a national past that was inconsistent with the struggle for modernity—a problem he described in terms of a tension between value and history.[2] Although not a Marxist himself and not particularly sympathetic to the Chinese Revolution, Levenson nevertheless recognized the Communist Revolution in its own right as a historical phenomenon and understood the source of the appeals of Marxist historicism, in which he found the ability to resolve this fundamental tension in Chinese intellectual life by relegating Confucianism into the museum, salvaging Confucius for the nation but also rendering him irrelevant to the living present. As he put it,

> Confucius . . . redeemed from both the class aberration (feudal) of idolization and the class aberration (bourgeois) of destruction, might be kept as a national monument, unworshipped, yet also unshattered. In effect, the disdain of a modern pro-Western *bourgeoisie* for Confucius cancelled out, for the dialecticians, a feudal class's pre-modern devotion. The Communists, driving history to a classless synthetic fulfillment, retired Confucius honorably into the silence of the museum. (1968, 79)

It may be one of the profound ironies of our time that this situation has been reversed since Levenson wrote his analysis: Confucius has been brought out of the museum once again, whereas it is the revolution that is on its way to being museumified, not by feudal worshipers of Confucius, moreover, but by the bourgeoisie who once disdained Confucius. And it is not just the revolution that is at issue. Levenson's analysis and his evaluation of what the revolution had achieved in resolving the tension between the past and the present were informed by a teleology of modernity—that with the victory of modernity, the claims of the values of ancient civilizations inevitably must be relegated to the past. If the pasts of those civilizations have been resurrected once again, it is not only because of the passing of revolu-

2. Levenson's work, we might note, was a direct inspiration for Laroui's *Crisis of the Arab Intellectual* (1976).

tions, but, more important, because of the questioning of this teleology that has come to the fore as globalization has replaced modernization as a paradigm of contemporary change.

The passing of the Chinese Revolution and of socialist revolutions in general may be attributed to their particular failings. Similarly, advocates of the Confucian revival may attribute the revival to the particular virtues inherent in Confucianism. Although there may be something to be said for such views, I think they suffer from a debilitating parochialism that fails to account for a larger historical context where it is not just socialist revolutions that are relegated to the past, but also the very idea of revolution, and it is not just the Confucian tradition that is at issue, but the return of traditions in general. Nor do such views explain attempts to articulate Confucianism to the values of entire regions, such as East and Southeast Asia, or to those of an entire continent, such as Asia.

Further complicating the situation are conflicts that attend these efforts. For all the talk about Asia and Asian values over the past few years, the idea of Asia remains quite problematic, and so do the ideological and cultural sources from which Asian values are to be derived. The most visible competitor to the Confucian revival may be the Islamic revival that has become visible during this same period, but the period also has witnessed a Hindu revival in India as well, and right-wing nationalists in Turkey, echoing East Asian nationalists and their Euro-American cheerleaders, have resurrected earlier Pan-Turanian utopias to assert that the twenty-first century will be a Turkish century. In other societies in Asia, Buddhism continues to hold sway. It is difficult to avoid an inference that all these revivals, coinciding temporally, are products of the same world situation, though they obviously have local inflections depending on social context and ideological claims. On the other hand, their differences from one another are quite significant and feed intra-Asian conflicts that have a variety of sources. In some cases, most notably in the case of Islam but also to some extent in the Confucian revival, which involves diasporic East Asians (especially Chinese) living outside of Asia, the ideological movements at issue extend beyond continental boundaries, calling into question, this time from a global perspective, anything that we might describe as "Asia" with any sense of concrete referentiality.

A rapidly changing world situation rules out any confident analysis of these developments, but it is still worth thinking through some of the phe-

nomena that have attended their emergence and speculating on their implications for contemporary ideas of East and West. Somehow all this has to do
with what is called *globalization*. But globalization as a paradigm is itself still
very much uncertain in its implications. It is at once a description of certain
changes at work in reshaping world and a new discourse that seeks to perpetuate older hegemonies—U.S. imperialism, as some would have it—in
new guise. Whatever its eventual outcome may be, however, it parts ways
with the earlier modernization discourse in raising questions about a teleology of modernity that pointed to Euro-America as the end of history and in
assaulting the nation as the principal unit of political organization. From different directions, each of these departures from the regime of modernity
may contribute to the emergence of cultural forces that counteract cultural
globalization. The dislodging of Euro-America from the center of history
enables the reemergence of national traditions that were suppressed under
the regimes of modernity.[3] The reassertion of national traditions derives additional force from the need to fend off attacks on the nation, which in fact
may serve the purposes of the powerful, who stand to benefit the most from
globalization—not just powerful nations such as the United States, but
transnational corporate forces of one kind or another. The culture industry
that for the most part is based in what used to be called the First World but
seeks to recruit consumers from around the world contributes in the name
of globalization to the reification of national traditions, which are commod-
ified and relayed back to the people who claim them, further sharpening
boundaries between such traditions. The seemingly benign policies of multiculturalism in the First World, in particular in the United States, owe their
origins to transnational corporations' efforts to accommodate the diversification of producers and consumers that has accompanied the process of
transnationalization.[4] Although few can object to cultural tolerance, multiculturalism, too, reifies cultural divisions and translates, under adverse situa-

3. Akbar S. Ahmed (1992), for example, argues that the postmodernist repudiation of
Eurocentric teleology has enabled the resurfacing of non-Euro-American traditions (referring, in this case, to Islam) that had been suppressed under the regime of modernity.
4. See "The Postmodernization of Production and Its Organization: Flexible Production, Work, and Culture" in Dirlik 1997c, 186–219, for the origins of multiculturalist policies
in corporate rethinking of management that dates back to the 1960s.

tions, into deadly cultural conflict. The shift in concern to ethnic, national, racial, and cultural difference also has relegated to the background important questions of class and gender that cut across the boundaries of groups so defined. This shift has much to do with the retreat from revolutionary or radical social imagination that coincides with globalization and is in some ways a product of the latter.

It seems to me that the search for an Asian or East Asian identity or for a national identity within an Asian or an East Asian context is entangled in this new situation and is illustrative of its problems, if only because East and Southeast Asian societies in their economic success have contributed more than any other region of the world to the ascendancy of the new paradigm of globalization. I do not mean to imply here that the question of these identities is itself new. The question of national identity has been a perpetual question in East Asia since the beginnings of "Western" domination in the eighteenth century, a domination that was to compel a quest for nationhood and with it the definition of national identity. In the case of Japan, it might even be suggested that the problem of national identity predated contact with the "West," as Japanese thinkers in the eighteenth century began to raise questions concerning the relationship of Japanese identity to the Confucian ingredients in Japanese culture.[5] An East Asian identity was bound to present itself as a problem when the China-centered world system in East and Southeast Asia broke down politically in the second half of the nineteenth century. The effects of this breakdown were felt deeply in Qing China, which now found itself relocated from the center of a world long assumed to be *the* world to the margins of a greater world and marginalized even in its own world by the rapidly ascendant Japan. The relationship of national identity to not just the "West" but to the preceding Confucian world order was to emerge during this period as a problem in both Korea and Vietnam, mainstays of "the Chinese world order." The question of identity nevertheless has a history that has been occluded in much of the recent discussion of East Asian or Asian identities.

I have argued elsewhere that although the Confucian revival may express long-standing grievances against the Eurocentric suppression of East

---

5. Harry Harootunian has examined the emergence of "nativism" in Japan in many works. For an extensive discussion, see Harootunian 1970.

Asian pasts, it has been empowered in its most recent manifestation by the economic success of East Asian societies that were able, therefore, to assert their own cultural prerogatives against Europe and North America (Dirlik 1995, 1997a).[6] I use the past tense ("were able") because the resurrection of Confucius coincided with a moment of crisis in the global capitalist economy of the late 1970s and the 1980s, but it may be in jeopardy now that the European and U.S. economies have recovered, and it is the Asian economies that find themselves in trouble, calling into question the whole project of globalization and once again turning miraculous Confucian capitalisms into historically condemned "crony capitalism." Be that as it may, in its heyday Confucian capitalism served not only to fuel the argument for globalization but was endowed with the task of salvaging a faltering capitalism. Involved in the promotion of the idea were not just intellectuals from East Asian societies, but, perhaps more important, American intellectuals of East Asian origin as well as American intellectuals whose relationship to East Asia was exclusively ideological. Needless to say, for some East Asian intellectuals, Confucianism had never been dead, but it was a global investment of faith in East and Southeast Asian economies that endowed them with a new voice. It was the same faith that encouraged others to rediscover their Confucianism and even their Asian-ness, as in the case, for example, of many Americans of Chinese descent. It was this same faith that played a part in the projection of the newfound success within global capitalism upon Asia as a whole or upon the imaginary region of Asia Pacific, leading to brave assertions of a forthcoming Chinese, Asian, or Pacific century. How this drama will play out remains to be seen. For the time being, Asia as the motor force of the world

6. The observations here derive mostly from Dirlik 1995 and 1997a, which also provide documentation. Similar arguments to mine, that the Confucian revival involves issues that are quite contemporary, are to be found in William A. Callahan 's unpublished paper "Negotiating Cultural Boundaries: Confucianism and Trans/national identity in Korea." I am grateful to Dr. Callahan for sharing his paper with me. Other similar arguments, with reference to Southeast Asia, can be found in C. J. W-L. Wee's essay "Framing the 'New' East Asia: Anti-Imperialist Discourse and Global Capitalism" in Rashid 1997. The same volume includes an interesting article by Chaibong Hahm, "The Clash of Civilizations Revisited: A Confucian Perspective," which argues against the deployment of Confucianism in cultural identity politics on the grounds that, as a set of practices rather than as a body of doctrine, Confucianism is nonexclusivist and porous in its boundaries.

economy has turned once again into an Asia that requires Western guidance to save it from itself or even an Asia that may be a threat to global order.

All this suggests one thing: that even at the moment of a seeming assertion of an autonomous self against the West, the West has been very much part of an Asian self-discovery either as an active or an absent presence. U.S. policy theorizers from Herman Kahn to John Berger to Samuel Huntington played a direct part in the theorization of Confucian or neo-Confucian culture as a dynamic force in the emergence of East and Southeast Asian economic vitality. They also provided theorists of East Asian origin with theoretical legitimacy. At the same time, the West and an urge to overcome a century of humiliation at Western hands have been very much on the minds of advocates of an East Asian or Asian revival among those intellectuals who themselves hail from those regions. Most important, the geography of Asian revival has been informed very much by the geography of Orientalism. It is no coincidence that the revival has expressed itself in terms of geographical regions that were in the first place products of Euro-American spatializations of Asia in Orientalist scholarship and subsequently in the area studies of post-World War II vintage that were informed by the global strategic interests of the United States.

Beyond Orientalism

It may be possible to suggest that East Asia and perhaps parts of Southeast Asia have a cultural reality beyond the constructs of Orientalism. In their enthusiasm to deconstruct the legacies of Orientalism and area studies, scholars of Asia and East Asia, especially in the United States, have been too quick to reject as mere hegemonic "inventions" earlier mappings of those areas—which contrasts with the continued preoccupation of those who inhabit Asia or East Asia with their own separate identities. It is also arguable, as in the case of the nation, that U.S. scholars' attacks on these earlier mappings serve certain interests better than others and render it impossible for those who inhabit those regions to assert autonomous identities against a hegemonic globalization driven by U.S. power, an assertion that might offer cultural alternatives to the Euro-American modernity (or postmodernity) that continues to inform prevailing visions of globality.[7]

7. I have argued this point at greater length in Dirlik 1997b.

Inventions or not, these areas are products of legacies that endow them at the least with a *historical* reality. That the relationships between societies in Asia or East Asia have produced as much difference as commonality or have been marked by intra-Asian conflict and colonialism does not render these areas into any less of a culture area. After all, deadly conflicts between European societies have not prevented Europeans from claiming a common heritage based on origins in classical civilizations or on the legacy of the Enlightenment. We may note that some scholars have called into question the idea of Europe, too (not to speak of a unitary entity called "the West," which lumps together Europe and North America or the Americas in general).[8] But it is nevertheless remarkable that questionings of the "West" or of Europe do not seem to attract the same intensity of attention as the deconstruction of other culture areas—possibly because of the immense influence of postcolonial criticism.

The problem may not be whether or not there are culture areas in Asia or East Asia, but, more important, that these areas have been defined from the outside, in accordance with Euro-American interests and perceptions rather than in accordance with the historical logic embedded in local interactions and cultural formations. Distinctions between East, Northeast, or Southeast Asia as well as any clear delineations of those areas and of their relationships to the rest of Asia may represent above all the realities of Euro-American power and imagination, but that does not mean that the regions cannot be defined differently, with due attention to the porosity of the boundaries that divide one region from another.[9] In terms of long-standing historical exchanges as well as common textual traditions, it is possible to speak of a region that encompasses both East and Southeast Asia, linked in turn to other parts of Asia through commercial and intellectual exchanges. After all, elites in China, Vietnam, Korea, and Japan did draw on the same classical and sacred texts and the institutions they implied, even though those texts were articulated to local circumstances to produce different his-

8. For an interesting discussion of "deconstructing Europe" by a distinguished historian, see Pocock 1994.

9. Hence, it is arguable in terms of the "areas" of area studies scholarship that the inhabitants of these regions at all times belonged to more than one area—in other words, that the very notion of "area" is overdetermined. I owe this insight to Professor Paik Nak-chung's comments on an earlier version of this chapter.

torical trajectories. It is important to remember also that until approximately a century ago these texts were perceived not so much as the products of one national entity (China), but as sacred texts of universal relevance—much the same as the Greek and Roman classics or the Bible might have been perceived by Europeans.

Equally important are relationships of economic exchange, especially the motions of populations, that would contribute to the formation of East and Southeast Asia as a world system unto itself but also as a culture area as well. Once again, it was populations from the country we now know as China that played a strategic part in these relationships, but it was not until the twentieth century that these populations thought of themselves as being "Chinese" rather than as descendants from some locality within that political ecumene.[10] Migrants from China themselves assimilated to local conditions, but in the process they also played a part in the diffusion both of social and economic practices and of ideas throughout the whole region (Salmon 1987). It is important to remember also that these exchanges and motions of populations took place increasingly within the context of an expanding European world system and cut across regional boundaries within Asia, connecting East Asia with places as far as Africa, Australia, and the Pacific.

Asian modernities were to contribute further to the growth of regional consciousness and to endow it with new meanings. This contribution was readily visible in the appearance of Pan-Asian ideologies in the twentieth century. The ideology of an Asian identity, Pan-Asianism, dates back to the late nineteenth century and coincided, ironically, with the emergence of national consciousness in one Asian society after another during the same period. East Asians did not realize that they lived in Asia until they saw themselves so located in maps from Europe; the term *Asia* was introduced into Chinese by Jesuits in the seventeenth century, but there is little indication that it made much of an impression on the Chinese until the nineteenth century, when world geography acquired an urgent importance in efforts to understand the new world into which China and East Asia in general were drawn inexorably. The geography of imperialism, ironically, also shaped the geography of resistance to it. Radical nationalists from various societies—

10. I use the term *ecumene* here advisedly in order to avoid projecting onto the past the nationalist claims of the present.

circulating around Asia in search of ideas, funds, and constituents for their nation-building efforts—became aware, through their encounters, both of the common plight of their societies and of their "Asian-ness," which would produce a common radical discourse around the idea of Asia.

Around the turn of the twentieth century, Tokyo, in many ways comparable to London for radical European intellectuals, was a magnet for radical Asian intellectuals from India to Vietnam, China, Korea, and the Phillippines in search of modernity.[11] Guangzhou (Canton) served in the 1920s as the capital of Asian radicalism (known by the mid-1920s as the "Paris Commune of Asia"), and in the Guangzhou Uprising of 1927 radicals from Vietnam, Korea, and Japan fought side by side for the revolutionary transformation of Asia. In the 1920s and 1930s, the practices and ideas of Kemal Ataturk in Turkey and of Mohandas Gandhi in India left a deep impression on both radicals and conservatives in China and Japan. Japanese imperialism in the 1930s found legitimation among many Asians in its claims to defend Asia against "Western" imperialism, bourgeois or communist. The same quest goes on in our day in the appeals to "Asian" or "East Asian" values against Euro-American domination.

If there is a historical reality to Asia or East Asia, however, claims to East Asian identity call for strategies of analysis different from those that have been employed in discussions accompanying the Confucian revival—strategies of analysis that factor in not only historical conflicts, modern nationalisms that expressed themselves in renunciation of this common legacy, and intra-East Asian imperialism, but also the existence of intellectual and popular traditions that provided alternatives to the so-called Confucian tradition and also divided these societies from one another. Where does Confucianism stop and Daoism and Buddhism begin? How does Shinto play into Japanese Confucianism or Shamanic practices into Korean Confucianism? How do popular traditions come into a definition of these societies in terms of Confucian culture? To illustrate that Confucianism by no means suffices in the cultural definition of China—much less of East Asia—but is on the contrary bound up with state and class interests against other possible cultural definitions of China, we may have no farther to go than the current

11. For an examination of these encounters around the turn of the twentieth century, see Karl 1995.

popularity in China of the Falun Gong against a regime that seeks to bolster its faltering socialist legacy with Confucian homilies. These complexities have been absent from discussions of Confucian China or a Confucian East Asia, which have engaged instead in a cultural reification not only of entire societies but of an entire region that coincides suspiciously to Orientalist cultural geography.

Claims to Asia and Asian values provide even more egregious illustration of the legacy of Eurocentric Orientalism in their suppression not only of regional differences but also of class and gender differences. Such claims often betray a preference for Asia's past over its present, drawing on supposed cultural legacies that distinguish "Asia" from "Europe." In such cases, "Asia" has been interpreted to confirm the prejudices of the most confirmed Euro-American Orientalists—as the location that is the "Other" of Europe. The "otherness" has resorted to different kinds of vocabulary depending on historical circumstances, but what most appeals to Asian-ness share in common is a reification of Asia, which is often accompanied by an Occidentalism that is hardly distinguishable from Orientalism. A prominent representative of this position in the early part of the twentieth century was the Indian poet and thinker Rabindranath Tagore (1861–1941), who drew on a distinction in European Orientalism to promote the idea of a spiritual Asia against a materialistic West.[12]

Tagore's ideas were echoed in China in the 1920s by those who contrasted the "spiritual" civilization of the East against the "material" civilization of the West. Such distinctions live on in the present in claims to "Confucian" and "Islamic" Asian civilizations that apparently retain their spirituality in spite of all signs of success in capitalist economies. Asians with their "spiritual" legacies, it seems, conquer all odds in order to preserve their "culture" against the onslaught of the "West." That such a position denies history to Asia, much in the Orientalist mode, goes without saying. But it also disguises immense differences in ethnic, class, and gender experiences of modernity, and in the process of asserting an Asian identity against an imag-

12. Tagore's influence in East Asia and the problematic of Pan-Asianism have been examined in Hay 1970. In Dirlik 1996, 13, I discuss the circulation in Asia of European Orientalists' ideas of Asia.

ined "West," it has oppressive implications of its own where differences within "Asia" are concerned.[13]

There has been a predicament built into Pan-Asianism all along that has derived from a confounding of national aspirations with continental ascriptions, appropriating supposedly continental characteristics for national ends while also projecting on the continent what were taken to be national characteristics. In the course of the twentieth century, the instability of the idea was manifested in the diametrically opposed uses to which it was put. Pan-Asian solidarity could motivate common revolutionary struggles, as it did in China in the 1920s and 1930s, when Japanese, Korean, and Vietnamese radicals fought side-by-side with the Chinese in a revolutionary struggle that would not only liberate China, but also launch the liberation of Asia as a whole. Pan-Asianism also could justify and even legitimize intra-Asian imperialism where one society could take it upon itself to liberate all of Asia from Western (and communist) imperialism, in the process subjecting other Asian societies to its domination—as in the case of Japanese imperialism in the 1930s and 1940s.[14]

If Europeans created the idea of Asia, they served also as midwives to the birth of Pan-Asianism, a connection that has been an added source of instability in the comprehension and uses of Pan-Asianism. Changing relationship to the "West," the context for both Asia and Pan-Asianism, has played a part in shaping the relationship of societies in Asia to one another and to the idea of Asia. Having created the notion of Asia in the first place, Euro-American involvement in Asia repeatedly has exposed the illusoriness of pretensions to continental consciousness. It is important to remember here that the first "Asian" nations to qualify for admission into modernity according to its gate-keepers, Turkey and Japan, at the two extremities of Asia, quali-

13. For further discussion in reference to a radical "asian" rejection of "history," see my essay "Reading Ashis Nandy: The Return of the Past or Modernity with a Vengeance" (Dirlik 2000). Nandy's radical rejection is based on the fact that "the West" is an intimate part of Asian consciousness and is not to be repudiated, therefore, except through a "decolonization" of consciousness.

14. For a recent study of the part played by Pan-Asianism in Chinese nationalists' compromise with Japanese imperialism during World War II, see Dongyoun 1999.

fied for the admission to the new world order by "escaping from Asia," Japan after the late nineteenth century and Turkey subsequent to the Ataturk reforms after 1923. It is equally instructive to remember that "escaping Asia," although qualifying these societies for candidacy for this new world order, has not meant actual admission into the ranks per se because their "Asian-ness" still handicaps them, for all their efforts, from becoming "Western." And that in spite of the facts that Japan proved itself as capable of imperialism against its Asian neighbors as any power from the "West" and that Turkey enthusiastically entered the war in Korea to prove that it was on the side of the good guys against bad Asians!

The very idea of "Asia," then, has the West as an inextricable constituent. In the words of the prominent Indian thinker Ashis Nandy, whose influential works consistently have drawn attention to the fact that the West is no longer an outsider to Asia and Asians but is very much internalized in the Asian self-consciousness,

> Asia is a geographical, not cultural entity. Though many Asians have defined their continent culturally during the last 150 years, that definition can be read as an artifact of Asian reactions to Western colonialism rather than as a search for larger cultural similarities. . . . [C]ultural definitions of Asia have been mainly a psychological defense against the internalized imperial fantasy of the continent as a location of ancient civilizations that had once been great and were now decadent, decrepit and senile. (1998, 142–49)

The search for East Asian or Asian identity as exemplified by the Confucian revival is not the only response to Eurocentrism or the only search for alternatives to it. Postcolonial discourse in our day, in contrast to earlier days of national liberation, would seem to be obsessed with the problem of exorcizing the Euro-American ghost that has become part of a global legacy. The exorcism seems to take different forms according to political and cultural disposition. The search for an East Asian or Asian identity would seem to be most favored by those who have never given up on those traditions, but also by states and capital, who perceive in those traditions both a means to identify the self and a means to keep in check the disorganizing effects of success in the capitalist economy without questioning capitalism as such. Their orientation coincides with the urgent need felt by large sectors of the population (as in the case of China, for example) for some sense of national identity in the face of cultural globalization—that is, the invasion of local cultures by the technology of global consumption culture. The latter, in turn, plays up local cultures and traditions as part of global marketing strategies, producing ethnic and national cultures even as it draws all societies into the seemingly irresistible and inexhaustible vortex of a market culture.

Others—mostly cosmopolitan intellectuals of a critical bent who are quite aware not only that national cultures themselves are products of the history of Euro-American modernity but also that the reification of national culture itself provides occasion for oppression within and aggression without—point to ambivalence and ambiguity, if not as a solution to anything, then at least as a way of avoiding the harm done by cultural reification at the national, regional, or global level. As one such intellectual writes with reference to a text produced by a Korean American, "I believe that the ambivalence in this text is irreducible. This is because, on the one hand, the need to fight against imperialist oppression—which may well require manufacture in the future of the national community as the subject of resistance—is far from diminished in the world today and, on the other hand, the homogenization of the national community could too often lead to the tremendous victimization of those who are culturally and linguistically heterogeneous. However unbearable it may be, the text seems to say, we have to live with this ambivalence" (Sakai 1997, 39). Ambivalence here arises from a recognition of the aporia presented by cultural choice or even from the definition of culture as such. The very notion of "ambivalence" has acquired currency in recent years as an antidote to cultural reification and bigotry. On the other hand, there is no way of avoiding a sense that it is also a statement of hopelessness and, even more seriously, that it betrays an obliviousness to a historical situation in which the ambiguity of texts and the ambivalence of intellectuals may be out of step with proliferating demands for identity.

A third option, perhaps most appealing to activist intellectuals who continue to believe in the possibility of radical transformation, is the option of dialogue from the bottom up—dialogue among Asian intellectuals from different locations within Asia that seeks nevertheless to avoid national, regional, or continental reifications of culture. In some ways, this option represents the transportation to Asian locations of what has been called "globalization from below." It is nonexclusive in the sense both of refusing to draw a wedge between "East" and "West" and of recognizing common problems that unite many in Asia with populations elsewhere, from Africa to Latin America to Europe and North America. A representative sampling of this position is to be found in the volume *Trajectories: Inter-Asia Cultural Studies* (Kuan-hsing 1998), wherein the editor and the various contributors self-consciously take up positions that acknowledge the legacy of earlier radicalisms without trying to avoid the recognition of new problems that have emerged with changing times. What may be most important in the undertaking, as one of the contributors (Nandy) argues, is a recognition of the pathologies both of a Eurocentric domination of the world and of Asian societies themselves, which have become inextricable from one another over the history of modernity (Nandy 1998, 142–49). The point is how to overcome these pathologies without entrapment in oppositions that are no longer relevant. Overcoming the colonial legacy of modernity as well as the destructive consequences of globality requires attention to life at the everyday level, where the various strands of the past and the West are intertwined to form many local cultures that are rendered invisible in notions of culture that are incapable of looking past continent, region, or nation.

Globalization and the Conquest of the Third World

Globalization discourse has revealed contradictions within Eurocentrism more explicitly than ever before and has allowed for the resurfacing of traditionalist discourses that question Euro-American claims to modernity. But this does not mean the end of Eurocentrism. In a recent article, Ien Ang (1998) argues cogently that Europe's continued assumptions of European superiority are expressed in a persistent self-image of Europe as the savior of the world. I already have noted that globalization itself is in many ways a rephrasing of U.S. economic and cultural hegemony and serves as an excuse for exporting worldwide American economic, political, and cultural practices. Even multiculturalism serves to contain cultural difference in a manner consistent with those practices.

I am more interested here, however, in the more insidious persistence of Eurocentrism even in the rejection of Eurocentrism. This is what I argued earlier with regard to the Confucian revival of the past two decades and with regard to the quest for East Asian or Asian values, which, for all their efforts to assert autonomous values against the hegemony of Eurocentrism, are marked nevertheless by the temporalities and spatialities of a Eurocentric conceptualization of the world. This is evident also in the reinterpretation of so-called Confucian or Asian values to accord with the demands of capitalism, with all its developmentalist premises, which goes unquestioned in much of the discussion. In fact, some critics of Eurocentrism in Europe and North America have sought in recent years to divorce capitalism from Euro-American modernity, making it into an endowment of Asian societies as well, which raises questions concerning Euro-American claims to modernity and may be complimentary to non-European societies that are now demonstrated to have had the same potential for development as modern Europe. What is less noticed is that this kind of revisionism rewrites the history of the world after the model of Euro-American capitalist modernity, in the process making capitalism into a fate of humankind globally and thus erasing alternatives to Euro-American capitalist modernity to be found in these different historical traditions. It is in many ways a Eurocentrism with a vengeance (Frank 1998).[15] Eurocentrism casts its shadow even on those attempts to escape its legacy, as in the radical efforts to overcome both Eurocentrism and Asiacentrism to which I referred earlier. Euro-American institutions are quick to insinuate themselves into any dialogue, even into those between

15. An earlier Eurocentrism thrived by denying the part others had played in European development. Gundar Frank does succeed in overcoming this denial; where he errs is in failing to distinguish other economies' contributions to European development from a global economic trajectory. The result is to project on a global past the teleology of modern capitalist development. We might suggest that a similar problem dogs efforts to assert an Asian mode of development, which takes modern capitalism for granted, while insisting on the role "Asian values" have played in shaping it. Not only do such views take for granted a teleology of modern capitalism, but they also resonate with an earlier Eurocentrism's disavowal of history, this time by taking the "West" out of the historical picture. What we seem to have presently is a current replay of old ideas about diffusionism (by land or by sea) versus an immanent universalism that is reminiscent of a Stalinist Marxism, according to which each society in its own way moves along a path that is predetermined by the natural progression of human societies. What has been lost in the process is the other, more historically informed Marxist attention to contradictions, the possibility of alternative paths, and how teleologies are constructed by suppression of alternatives. I have discussed the issues raised here at far greater length in "History Without A Center? Reflections on Eurocentrism" (Dirlik in press).

non-Western radicals, as in the case of a conference intended to discuss "Asian" paradigms in the study of Asian societies, which was funded, according to the announcement, by the Ford Foundation!

Does this mean that Eurocentrism is a historical prison house from which there is no exit? This may be a self-defeating way of posing a question that might be phrased differently: Does the repudiation of Eurocentrism require a denial of the historical role played by European and American societies, which in many ways also constitutes a denial of history to the society of the self? It is this denial that issues either in unconscious slippage into Eurocentrism by writing world history along the paradigms and problems that are products of the Euro-American organization of the world in the first place or in escapes into traditions that became conscious of themselves as traditions in the face of Euro-American cultural negation of alternative pasts. It makes much more sense, under the circumstances, to historicize both Europe and societies of the self, to recognize that although Euro-American modernity may have been a product of a particular conjuncture in history, the forces unleashed by this modernity—from capitalism to the Enlightenment, from the nation-state to colonialism—nevertheless had a transformative role globally. This transformative role needs to be distinguished from global homogenization because it was articulated at all times through a dialectic of the global and the local but was transformative nevertheless. Any consideration of alternative futures, therefore, needs to take its point of departure not in some premodern past, which may be unknowable except through its textual traces, but through present realities, in which, to recall Laroui, pasts and Wests are ever copresent in constantly shifting configurations. To take recourse to the past or to the West as if they were entities frozen forever in time is to refuse the dialectic that endows the terms with their historical meanings, perhaps even to freeze them so as to acquire some control over the direction of history. But, if I may recall a fundamental insight of Marxism, any effort to act in history in order to have some say over the future requires not the denial but the recognition of historicity—in Laroui's words, "praxis as historicism in action." We need not subscribe to any Marxist or modernist teleologies to acknowledge the importance of recognizing not only the historicity of the past and the present, but also the historicity of our own efforts to intervene in the process or even to write about it, which may be a different form of intervention. The idea of Asia or East Asia seems to provide the location for such intervention presently, if only because this idea is open to egregious misinterpretation and abuse.

East Asian Alternatives?

The question presently is not whether or not there is an Asia or East Asia, but more who is to define what Asia or East Asia may represent. It is a question that involves not only Euro-American perceptions of Asia, but also, and even more important, intra-Asian approaches to the question. Young-seo Baik (1999) describes "Asia" or "East Asia" as an "intellectual praxis."[16] Asia, the place that we assume to be there when we speak or write of it, is indeed a product of our imaginings, which we produce even as we take it as the point of departure for the production. It makes equal sense to speak of "Asia" or "East Asia" as a discourse that produces its objects not out of thin air but in endowing those terms with different historical meanings. Asia or East Asia, in other words, is not merely a geographical entity that provides us with stable objects of research or politics, but projects to be realized that may offer alternatives to Euro-American modernity as we have known it. The confusion of East Asia as legacy and project lies at the basis of much misrepresentation in contemporary discussions of "Asian values," which render into legacies of the past what are but mostly conservative responses to contemporary cultural transformations. There is a glaring contradiction between such cultural claims that reproduce Orientalist readings of Asia and East Asia (what I described earlier as "self-Orientalization") and the evidence of daily cultural transformation. East Asia as legacy imprisons the in-

16. There is a glaring contradiction between such cultural claims that reproduce Orientalist readings of Asia and East Asia (what I described earlier as "self-Orientalization") and the evidence of daily cultural transformation. East Asia as legacy imprisons the inhabitants of the region in an imagined cultural endowment. Recognizing East Asia as a project (or as "intellectual praxis" or discourse) offers possibilities not only for distinguishing the political agenda that inform different readings of Asia, but also for redefining the region so as to account for it as a historical rather than an unchanging cultural entity.

habitants of the region in an imagined cultural endowment. Recognizing East Asia as a project (or as "intellectual praxis" or discourse) offers possibilities not only of distinguishing the political agenda that inform different readings of Asia, but also of redefining the region so as to account for it as a historical rather than an unchanging cultural entity.

It seems to me that this project, if it is to be meaningful in a contemporary sense, has to address not just problems of the region, but contemporary problems in general. It is especially important in this regard to keep in mind both the arbitrariness of regional or national divisions and the social divisions and complexities that are disguised in appeals to cultural difference. The idea of East Asia may be meaningful only if it is articulated to contemporary problems of globality and if it offers solutions to problems of economic and political justice that have their point of departure in a present reality, a reality that is a product both of the "past" and the "West." Thus conceived, East Asia as a project also calls for a rewriting of the past, not as it has been rewritten in nationalist historiographies, but with an eye to what East Asian historical experiences of culture and politics may have to reveal by way of alternatives to contemporary norms of national and international organization. Merely to claim a cultural identity against the "West" is no longer sufficient, not only because the "West" is already an inextricable part of East Asia, but also because such claims may serve only to perpetuate social injustices and oppressions in a new cultural guise.

A radical vision of East Asia needs to recognize that the modernity to be transcended is no longer just a "Western" modernity but an East Asian modernity. Indispensable to such a vision is the repudiation of the region as defined top down in the interests of power, not just of Euro-American power but also of the structures of national and social power internal to the region. If the idea of East Asia or, for that matter, of any other region is to be meaningful in a transformative sense, it needs to be grounded in a reconceptualization of the very notion of regional formations—from the bottom up in accordance with everyday needs and interactions that point to diverse historical experiences and trajectories, which have been rendered invisible in both Orientalist and nationalist mappings of the world. Modernity's historiography has organized the past around imagined culture areas, civilizations, or nations, which upon closer examination turn out to be products of the prerogatives of power of one kind or another. It is about time that we rethought regions in their historicity because they are produced in translocal and transnational alliances of everyday struggles for survival and meaning, which may or may not coincide with the geographies of colonialism or with its localized statements in coercive nationalisms.[17]

17. I suggested earlier that claims to regional culture (be it Asia or East Asia) often serve nationalist yearnings, where supposed national characteristics are projected on entire regions and continents. Interestingly, the opposite also can be the case because there are built-in contradictions between regionalism and nationalism. Europe offers instructive examples. As the European Union has taken shape, there have been proliferating assertions of local cultural identities against nation-states, as in the case of Catalonian identity or as in the demands of Corsicans for linguistic independence from France—which the French minister of culture described in a recent interview as the "Balkanization" of France (*CNN Report,* Seoul, Korea, 29 September 1999). A regional perspective, in other words, may empower the statement of local cultural differences against nationalist homogenization, just as globalization on a world scale empowers the "return" of "forgotten" traditions. I venture to suggest here that similar results would ensue were there to be an "East or Southeast Asian Union" or both, which would offer a different frame of reference (and legitimacy) than that of the nation-state.

12 Knowledge, Place, and Power
A Critique of Globalization

EQBAL AHMAD

I want to begin by saying that I'm honored that Ali Mirsepassi asked me to give the last talk here. It was really a gesture of good will by a gracious Iranian to an aging man. I am very grateful. I have really enjoyed the talks, nearly all of which were very interesting, and some of which were quite brilliant. If you hear some dissonant notes from me, it is by no means a criticism of any one person, but just a case of an old Marxist not having grown up enough into the new world. First of all, I have a certain discomfort with the very word *globalization*. I am very uncertain whether it is a project or a fact. And I have an increasing suspicion that it is more a project than a reality. As an analytical category, it may even be less useful than the modernization framework, which became so popular in the 1950s and the 1960s and which has proven to be so barren to understanding the world that we were trying to understand. The problems I see with the framework of globalization are several, and I will tick them off fairly quickly.

One is that it is an old phenomenon being viewed as a new one. To be sure, we all know the jet engine, the Internet, and the entire gamut of information technology have shrunk the world in ways that it was not in the sixteenth, seventeenth, eighteenth, nineteenth, or first half of the twentieth century; there's no question about it.

But what we call globalization began much earlier and came to a climax much earlier and, worse, did more damage, great damage, much earlier. We

This chapter is a transcription of the talk by Eqbal Ahmad that concluded the Five Colleges Faculty Symposium "Global-Local: Revisioning the Area Studies Debate," 16–18 October 1998, at Hampshire College, Amherst, Massachusetts. Frederick Weaver edited the transcript.

216

should remind ourselves that we are living and talking in a hemisphere where white men were not at all here and brown men are barely present now. The color of entire continents have changed from one continent to another. The entire Caribbean has gone black. Great civilizations—the Mayas, the Incas, the Aztecs—have been destroyed, and they were all victims of globalization. They were victims, in other words, of a certain world system in which some powers or a group of powers dominated the world at the expense of the rest of the world, and that particular reality has not changed. That pre-World War II equilibrium is now returning with vengeance to the world, and that's the situation that we are beginning to describe as globalization.

What has happened, then? What we mean by globalization is that the intensity of communications, contact, migrations, and so on has increased with the new technologies and political mechanisms—compared to the past forty years. And only compared to the past forty years because the interregnum produced after World War II—i.e., the interregnum of decolonization—threatened new kinds of uncertain relationships between the West and the Rest. After 1953, the capitalist market had problems expanding into certain areas of Africa, the Middle East, and South Asia. These are areas where newly independent regimes had gone into a period of economic nationalism, including a wave of nationalizations and efforts, successful and unsuccessful, to cut themselves off from the international market. That pre-World War II equilibrium is now returning with vengeance to the world, and that's the situation that we are beginning to describe as globalization. It also means that the communist regimes have collapsed, and their collapse has involved a massive expansion of the capitalist market into areas where it had previously had to retreat after the October Revolution of 1917 and then after the Soviet expansions of the post-World War II period.

Those situations have now changed, and capital is king. It is this kingship or empireship of capital that our friend Francis Fukuyama hailed as the end of history. You all recall that. My main argument, therefore, is that the world system that had emerged some time ago, dominated by a certain number of Western metropolises or capitalist metropolises and their corporation, is still there; only its intensity and its scope have changed.

May I tell you a short story that actually occurred in my presence only a year ago? In a small town called Fan-u-al, Mr. Nawaz Sharif, the prime minister of Pakistan, stood and started telling the people that he had inherited a very bad economy from Benazir Bhutto, but soon after he had come into power, Burma Shell Corporation began coming into Pakistan, and Mobile Oil Company had arrived in Pakistan, and IBM was negotiating to enter Pakistan. Just as he was leaving, I heard an old man ask, in Urdu: "Tell us, is the company Bahadur coming back?" Company Bahadur is the old Urdu name for the East India Company that colonized India, and it struck me that the peasant understood something that Mr. Nawaz Sharif had not understood. The collapse of nationalism and things like the *infitah* (open-door policy) in Egypt have significantly added to the expansion of the market.

My second problem with globalization is that the word (but not your talks) suggests an equitable and just balance of knowledge and power that is entirely absent from the world. This is not a world of globalization. It's a world of inequalities. Changing the word is not going to help analysis. It will not change that reality.

If *globalization* refers to anything, it signals a shifting of intensity and scope, as I said earlier. But there is a need to be clear about what is globalized and what is not globalized. Capital is successfully globalizing, and, with it, consumption patterns are globalizing. And services to a certain extent are globalizing. Labor or people, however, suggest a different rhythm. In the wake of decolonization, capital had fled from Asia, Africa, and the Middle East or from certain countries in them. This retreat of capital, which occurred because of the uncertainties of decolonization, caused labor to follow capital. And throughout the 1950s and 1960s, we witnessed a massive migration of African, Middle Eastern, and South Asian labor to Europe to the point that nearly 12 percent of the total labor force of Europe became non-European during these two decades. Now in this current period, which we call globalization, capital is again reassured of its place in the world, and therefore capital is returning to labor. Labor is not needed anymore in the metropolitan nations, and, therefore, in the age of globalization you have extremely strict controls on labor migration.

It is impossible today to be a Pakistani. It is literally impossible. I'll give you an example. The year before last, BBC was doing a profile of me. When they were finishing with the profile, they asked me to come and be there for the editing, which we had to do in the studio. I have a Pakistani passport, and I went to the British embassy in Islamabad and applied for a visa. In order to apply for the visa, I was told to bring not merely my passport, but also a statement from the bank, a statement signed by the bank manager (just a copy of the thing wouldn't do), a statement from my employer (which was still Hampshire College), a statement from two persons in Pakistan who would act as guaranty for me, and a round-trip ticket. So I came back and told the BBC producer, "Get out of here; I'm not coming." I've stopped going to Europe. I have literally stopped going to Europe. In this age of globalization, my movements are more restricted than they were ten or twenty years ago because there are more suspicions about me as labor, brown labor, crossing the boundaries of Europe. Ironically, the film profile was entitled *Crossing Boundaries.*

Returning to the issue of inequitable balances in the time of globalization, there has occurred in the last twenty to thirty years an extraordinary concentration of knowledge, technology, and science in the industrialized capitalist countries. We cannot deny the fact. When talking at Hampshire College two weeks ago, Kofi Annan accurately and eloquently described how everything was becoming globalized except knowledge itself. And knowledge is capital in this age of globalization.

The situation is dire; I have never before seen the university and higher-education sector in Third World countries so badly gutted. I don't know about Latin America; that's not my beat. But in Africa, in the Middle East, and in South Asia, higher education is being murdered, and in the murderous process the three great globalizing institutions have been actively engaged for twenty years. They are the World Bank, the International Monetary Fund [IMF], and the United States Agency of International Development [USAID]. All three have said, " 'Third World' countries do not need higher education; you have too many college graduates. What you need is primary education, adult literacy. And you have created a situation in which this entire region of the world is being turned into a pool of, at best, skilled wanderers."

I made a massive stink about it in Pakistan and India last year. Now partly in response to that stink we have made, the World Bank has set up a study group to report on the needs of higher education in Third World countries. Whether that report will produce anything or not, I do not know, but to date the record of the World Bank and the IMF is that they do not give any money, any loan, any credit for the development of higher education, except for business schools. The only schools that have emerged have been the schools of business management. Period.

Globalization means inequality. In general as well as here in the last two days, I have noticed an avoidance of the issue of class relations and of inequality in the discourse of globalization. I was struck by the fact that I don't think class has been mentioned at this conference more than twice. It just didn't come up as a subject. The fact remains that class differentiations have massively widened in most of the world, including this world, including right here where we are speaking. Inequality has grown to an enormous scale, even in this country where prosperity reigns; distances between rich and poor have widened. And yet we have ignored the issue of class because this new vocabulary doesn't quite accommodate it.

A host of questions—questions of culture, questions of national identity, of convergences between local and global, of transnationalization of feminist consciousness, even of place as a center of attachment—have been discussed here and all without reference to class. And each of these issues has a massive class component, a massive class component. We have to avoid such avoidance.

At the nexus of globalization and its consequences are two sets of social entities on which we need to focus. The first set is the state and corporation—more specifically, the dependent state and the corporation. And elites, both local and metropolitan, comprise the second set. There are organic linkages between these two sets of entities, and these linkages leave out large majorities of people, thus marginalizing them. This process of marginalization requires not only a look at the nature of the state but also at its behavior because the interests, the outlook, and increasingly the cultures of the metropolitan state and the dependent state, the metropolitan elite and the dependent elite, are currently converging in ways that they had not done before.

A few days ago the *New York Times* published some figures on foreign undergraduates in America. They numbered 500,000, of which 375,000 are from what we call Third World countries. Who are they? Whose children are they? What kind of money can they afford? I'll give you one figure: 15,000 of these are Pakistani, and if we assume that each one of our 15,000 Pakistani undergraduates in the United States has half financial aid, then Pakistan's foreign-exchange expenditure is $150 million. But you certainly can't assume that they are all on half financial aid.

This is one of the reasons that I have been trying for six years to set up a private university in Pakistan and cannot get the licensing done. Someone comes in and obstructs it. During these last twenty years, only one new institution has been supported by multinational aid agencies and by the Pakistan government, and that has been the Lahore University of Management Scientists, period. Business school. Why should they promote this university I'm trying to do? Their children have been taken care of. The World Bank is not going to put the money in it. The IMF is not going to give me the loan. Why should they do it? Move on.

There was always a nexus between the metropolitan elite and the local elite. The native elite by and large always collaborated with the colonizer. Today that collaboration has taken a completely new dimension. Benazir Bhutto stole $2.3 billion in three years. You see, this is globalization because before World War II, or even as late as 1970—before the Internet, before new information technology—it would have been impossible in such a short period of time for her to siphon off and launder so much money from Pakistan.

Now she can do it. And you remember, Suharto is estimated at $4 billion. Suharto, Marcos, and others are kleptomaniacs. And their numbers are growing. Or take a look at another consequence of it: Third World cities—literally every one of them that depends on a globalized commitment is developing an apartheid system. In some cities of India and Pakistan, you can draw an unambiguous line. On this side of the town lives the English-speaking elite with connections to the metropolis, and on this side of the line you have the non-English-speaking people, a few middle class, some rich, more poor—the natives, in other words. The decolonized postcolonial societies are developing a much greater system of apartheid today than what Franz Fanon had described to you in the divide between the Casbah and the European quarters in his first chapter of *The Wretched of the Earth* [1968]. It's getting that bad. One speaks English or French, but the other doesn't. One wears Western clothes, and the other doesn't. One does engage in international travels, but the other doesn't. One sends his children to European and American schools, but the other doesn't. And so it goes. One drinks wine, and the other doesn't. So in general matters of culture also we are now getting dual, triple societies, even more than in the colonial times.

We have talked a lot about foundations and other supporting agencies.

They all have agendas, and their agendas shape us. As the process of decolonization began, there was an element of uncertainty about what these nationalist crazies might do. And you remember how much that uncertainty produced an effort of two kinds, particularly from the United States, but Britain and France followed very closely. That created two institutions to control that situation. One was the U.S. Agency of International Development, and the other was the Military Assistance Plan [MAP].

One addressed the civilian bureaucratic class; the other addressed the soldier class. That still left the gray area of the political elite, and the social scientists went to work. While I am not completely certain about my count, I believe that I have read at least twenty-five modernization studies that are only on elites of the Third World. All of them were published in two decades, between 1950 and 1970. Elites in Latin America, elites in Africa, elites in West Africa, elites of North Africa, elites of South Asia, but now elite studies is gone. Nobody is studying elites anymore. There is a certainty about who these elites are. They are known. There's no need for studies. Fashion has changed. We move onto something else.

What I'm saying is that foundations have agendas. Amrita Basu mentioned just a while ago that the Ford Foundation and the SSRC [Social Science Research Council] do not appear to have an agenda right now. She may be right, but it is not because interests have changed. It is because it is a time of big confusion. It is a time of such confusion after the collapse of the Soviet Union and other changes that nobody knows how to deal with this new world. It is such a time of confusion that for nearly eight months Fukuyama's "End of History" essay [reprinted in Fukuyama 1992] became a celebrated piece of writing in America. Everybody reprinted it. An absolute absurdity, a total intellectual absurdity. Now who would take that essay seriously unless you were confused? Uncertain. Not knowing what might happen. And as soon as Fukuyama's thesis receded into the background, which it had to do, in comes our friend Samuel Huntington with his thesis about [the] "clash of civilization" [1993], and it lasted almost two years before it started its recession. See, it is so confusing a time. They don't know what to do.

They are groping a little bit in the dark. And they are in the process of defining and redefining because interests do not change, and, yes, you might perhaps take advantage of it by targeting matters strategically. But we shouldn't have too many illusions about how far one can push these people with deep interests.

I do not want to leave the impression that nothing has changed or that new intellectual challenges do not exist. They do. For example, global and local boundaries are merging today constantly, so much that sometimes it's very hard to demarcate them. Demarcation of the boundaries between what Arturo [Escobar] called the *place* and the *metropolis* has become much harder to draw. I'll take a few examples. Studies in the contemporary Islamic movement abound. We have so far got something like thirty, forty volumes that have appeared in the last six years because they all have the compulsion to draw the boundary; they have seen the rise of Islamic fundamentalism as an Islamic problem. None of them, to my knowledge, has pointed out that the parentage of the Islamic fundamentalist movement in our time belongs to the United States of America. They are the parents, the fathers of Jihad International Incorporated. It's a transnational incorporation; it really is. But the father of the Jihad International Incorporated is the United States of America, and its mother is, of course, Mohammad Zia ul-Haq of Pakistan and King Fayed of Saudi Arabia.

Let me explain. An extraordinary event occurred when the Soviet Union intervened in Afghanistan. As the Soviet Union intervened in Afghanistan, Zia ul-Haq, isolated dictator in Pakistan, saw an opportunity in it and contacted the [U.S.] CIA station agent in Pakistan, a man named Price. Zia ul-Haq said, "We want to produce an anti-Soviet revolt here." He received a piddling sum of $3 million. With $3 million, he organized an insurgency in Afghanistan. That insurgency took hold, and it was Islamic. As soon as it took hold in 1979, Jimmy Carter offered Zia ul-Haq $350 million. By now Zia ul-Haq is so sure of himself and his achievement that he called a press conference and said, "Peanuts." Carter was a peanut producer, you remember? So he says, "Peanuts," and Carter took him seriously and developed another aid program, and six weeks later offered him $2.5 billion. And this time Zia ul-Haq did not say "peanuts" because Zia ul-Haq knew another thing, that he would get more. Between 1980 and 1988, the United States sunk $8 billion worth of armaments into the Jihad in Afghanistan.

But by now it was not Afghan Jihad. It's Reagan who jumped on an opportunity to mobilize the whole Muslim world against the Evil Empire and to do so through armed struggle. CIA agents, Pakistani agents, Egyptian agents, Saudi agents traveled all over the world, the Muslim world, recruited C-130 planes, brought people; camps were established; some of them were bombed recently. . . . By the way, in 1986 I interviewed Osama Bin Ladin in exactly the camps where the U.S. missiles hit in August. In exactly the same camps and the same man, who was earlier working for America. Those of you who are Middle East experts know that Jihad in the Muslim world in the previous three centuries, five centuries, had never been an armed transnational, Pan-Islamic phenomenon. It was made into one by the efforts of a superpower and the idiocy of another superpower. Nobody is doing that particular analysis because the boundaries are hard to demarcate, and we have gotten into the habit of demarcating boundaries.

Last, I should say there is a negative side to the transnationalization of talents and movements. I'm not merely talking of the brain drain. The women's movement in the Third World countries, for example, often loses its sharpness as soon as it develops a transnational connection. I'll give you a specific example. The Women's Action Forum in Pakistan [WAFP] was an organization of young women who broke away from APWA, the All Pakistan Women's Association, which was a more traditional organization that promoted handicraft work and opened schools and things like that in poor neighborhoods. "We are not social workers; this is a political problem! It has to be politically fought, and we are going to do it!" Fortunately for males, the influence of the West at that time was in ascendance, supporting Zia ul-Haq, the great dictator. And Zia ul-Haq had beaten the hell out of the opposition movement. He had put 30,000 people in jail; he had slogged about 10,000; he had murdered about 200, and on and on. Our bones were broken, but WAFP was out in the street in protest against the Diat and the Hudood Ordinances. WAFP was out in the street while police forces in that macho society were beating women. During this struggle, when women were courting arrest, being beaten up, going to jail, there was no transnational connection. Sisters in the West didn't hear, didn't care. But after Zia ul-Haq fell, more travel occurred, and WAFP became a major figure, and the West developed all sorts of international connections. Today, I'm very sorry to say, WAFP is divided into five different factions, and all that division has some connection to a foreign group. Second, they are traveling so much, there is so much travel by WAFP leaders, that hardly anything is done at home. One person, a former WAFP leader, left the feminist movement, not because she was protesting; she went out to do something else. She founded the Pakistan Human Rights Commission. And in that situation she has done more than any human rights commission I can think of in the entire Third World. But the rest have broken up into competing factions. So that kind of negative transnationalization is occurring, which we ought to recognize and focus on.

I should now say a word about area studies and our disciplines. Tim Mitchell's presentation I found quite excellent, but I was surprised that perhaps because of the paucity of time, his recommendations were focused on structural reform, and most of the discussion that followed were also focused on changing structures. I would submit that the problem is actually ideological. Change the structure as much as you want. Unless we confront the ideological problem, real change won't occur. The nexus of knowledge and imperialism is old. You all know that, and Tim himself wrote one of the finest works on this subject concerning Egypt. The problem is old, and it is conceptual. Therefore, we must tackle the ideology, tackle the problem that is ideological, and approach the matter conceptually. Changing structures will do very little, if anything. Sandra Greene, during one of the question periods on the first day, said, "I'm hearing from the Middle East people that your entry points are narrower." Do you remember that? "Your entry points seem to be terrorism, religion, oil. What explains the narrowness of your entry points compared to Latin America and compared to Africa?" The answer I was tempted to give, right then and there, is that our entry points are just about as wide as the interests of the Great Powers have wished them to be. They're interested in terrorism. This is the threat; therefore, this is what people have paid attention to. They have become interested, especially after Afghanistan, in somehow putting back into the box the monster that they raised with so much money and so much arms.

Therefore, the concentration [is] on fundamentalism. Oil is their main thing; that's why they are there. That's why a million Iraqi children and old people have died in the last eight years. Therefore, we write on oil and political economy. Other issues are not of deep interest to them, and, therefore, putting it very crudely, the other issues get left out.

The second point that I want to make is that the failures of area studies scholarship have been rather more incredible than we portray them to be. And they have been most dramatic. Tim Mitchell and Sandra Greene were totally right, but I would say they could be even more right if they wanted to be as brutal and nasty as I'm going to be. Take specific cases: China. U.S. scholarship on China was decimated because it showed signs of independence. Don't forget men like Owen Latimore were kicked out of the country. The State Department experts on China were forced to resign. For the first fifteen years of the Cold War, the entire China studies establishment in this country was clobbered. John K. Fairbanks survived at Harvard University because he had lots of former students from Harvard who were important in government. And, incidentally, apart from United States-China relations, he refused to write for a very, very long time. So that was the fate of China studies. The revolt against this finally occurred when graduate students, among them Jim Peck and Mark Seldon, got together to found a contrary magazine and a contrary organization called the Committee of Concerned Asian Scholars and the *Bulletin of Concerned Asian Scholars*. This was not the work of professors; this was the work of students. This was also true of the *Middle East Report* in the case of Middle East studies.

The worst case, of course, is Southeast Asia. The bloody Indochina War developed from 1950—actually 1945, when the United States, Britain, and France broke all promises and reestablished colonial rule over Vietnam, which had thrown the fascists out. And from 1945 to 1975, all the Southeast Asia experts, I think without an exception, all the Vietnam experts collaborated with the U.S. government. And some collaborated to the point where they couldn't imagine that it was possible to be a professional without such a collaboration. I'm tempted to tell another story.

Daniel Ellsberg made the Pentagon Papers public. Do you remember that? At that time, Daniel Ellsberg was a research fellow at MIT. In the MIT faculty room, Ithiel de Sola Pool, then chairman of the Department of Political Science at MIT, said to the effect, "He blew it. He will never be able to do more research now. He will never be able to get his security clearance back." Can you imagine? Their whole notion of being able to do research was based on security clearances. It's a true story. It's not a joke. It actually happened. Real life. The one exception I would think of was George Cohen, who was not a Vietnam scholar, but was a Southeast Asia scholar who wrote a book about Vietnam, exposing the U.S. policy. Otherwise, not one, not one expert emerged. Who did emerge? Noam Chomsky emerged. George Ward emerged. Scientists, linguists, all kinds of people who had never known about Vietnam wrote about it and produced a literature on Vietnam, but not the experts. Not the area experts.

Or take my own part of the Third World, the Middle East. What a horror. For fifty years, what has happened in the Middle East was something extraordinary and totally ahistorical. In the age of decolonization, which begins with the independence of India and Pakistan in 1947, Palestine is colonized. And the colonization that the Palestinians suffer is that of the pioneering variety, the sixteenth- and seventeenth-century variety, the settler variety. And by God, very few wrote about it. Very few said anything about it. And when they did, they were lying. It took revisionist Israeli historians to write for the West and say, "No, you have been hearing lies because nobody wanted to hear the Arabs."

That's the significance of Israeli revisionism. Israeli revisionism is really a slap on the face of the entire establishment of Middle East area studies, especially to those who were writing history, politics, or sociology. I can give more examples: the shah of Iran. This bloody dynasty was isolated, illegitimate, idiotic, and stupid to boot. And we all knew that. And the truth is not a single area expert to my knowledge, not one in the United States, wrote even the truth, even a realistic analysis of Iran, until the Iranian Revolution had broken out and succeeded. This includes Mr. Marvin Zoniz of Chicago. In 1977, this Middle East area expert at the University of Chicago writes a whole book on Iran, on the elites in Iran, and he dedicates it to the king of kings, the light of the Ilium, blah, blah, blah. You can't believe that these people are serious scholars. So area studies has been a disaster area in many ways.

It's not just area studies; it has been equally true of the political scientists and other types, anybody who got hooked into the Cold War syndrome and became some sort of an academic functionary; their work was rotten. Rotten to the core, that's for sure. I will cite two very living examples of them from Harvard at the top of the rotten pile. Henry Kissinger and Samuel Huntington. There did come a point where I stopped identifying myself as a political scientist lest people conjure up Henry Kissinger or Sam Huntington. This gentleman [Huntington] produced such extraordinary things. Do you remember Huntington's urbanization paper on Vietnam? Extraordinary. Or Kissinger? This one wrote a whole book arguing that nuclear weapons in our time are the equivalent to the battle ship. To quote him directly, I'll close my eyes and remember, "Nuclear weapons are the twentieth century equivalent of showing the flag. So occasionally show it off." This has been the quality of this phenomenon. So where to do we go from here?

If area studies is to be revisioned, I would suggest that you look critically, before you make suggestions to the Ford Foundation, at how to frame your proposals in such a way that they look sexy but don't compromise. Two of the courses that were announced here, both fortunately or unfortunately from Hampshire College, I found very appealing. They talk about globalization in the right way, in a perfect Islamic fashion.

I would suggest that we should focus on certain issues. Three issues seem to me to be primary. My own list is much longer, but I'll mention these.

The first would be to try to take a deep look at histories and cultures of various areas and include a serious search for patterns of congruence between tradition and modernity. Unless modern forms, especially secular forms in our time, are not congruent with some important aspects of inherited political culture of these peoples, any peoples, they will not take root. So find, please, that which is hospitable to the modern, to the progressive in the older soil. If you can identify the hospitable in the old soil, they may very well profit greatly from your research.

Second, if the real focus of the [area studies program] is on the mechanics of the emergence of the world system, of imperialism, and of resistance to it, it will be very useful. I'll give you one example. About three years ago, I gave a talk in Karachi; this was in relation to the university that I'm trying to found. I didn't talk about my university, but I talked about why Islamic civilization, civilizations, or cultures were defeated by the West. My argument, rightly or wrongly, was that they were defeated because the empires, in their historic compromise, handed over education and justice to the religious class. And the religious class, of course, from the beginning was opposed to the philosophical school, to the social school, and to the aesthetic schools of Islam. The bloody argument so appealed to my listeners that, believe it or not, that day I got pledges of $3 million. I am telling you, if I had not used that example, I would not have made sense to them.

Third, we need a strong emphasis throughout on the relationship between knowledge and power. A continuous emphasis on this relationship—which has now become so much better understood after the works of

Gandhi, Said, Foucault, Chomsky, and so on—is imperative. With that, I would say foundations, other supporting agencies, may very well, in these times of confusion, be a little bit more open and a bit more clean than they were forty years ago.

I've taken too much of your time. I'm very grateful.

Works Cited

Index

Works Cited

Abu-Lughod, Lila. 1993. "Editorial Comment: On Screening Politics in a World of Nations." *Public Culture* 5: 465–67.

———. 1995. "The Objects of Soap Opera." In *Worlds Apart: Modernity Through the Prism of the Local,* edited by D. Miller, 190–210. London and New York: Routledge, 1995.

———. 1997a. "Dramatic Reversals: Political Islam and Egyptian Television." In *Political Islam,* edited by Joel Beinin and Joe Stork, 269–82. Berkeley and Los Angeles: Univ. of California Press.

———. 1997b. "Seeing Through the Suds." *Al-Ahram Weekly,* 4–10 Sept., 15.

Achebe, Chinua. 1987. *Anthills of the Savannah.* New York: Doubleday.

Adelson, Roger. 1994. *London and the Invention of the Middle East.* New Haven, Conn.: Yale Univ. Press.

Agrawal, Arun. 1995. "Dismantling the Divide Between Indigenous and Scientific Knowledge." *Development and Change* 26: 413–39.

———. 1996. "Poststructuralist Approaches to Development: Some Critical Reflections." *Peace and Change* 21, no. 4: 464–77.

Agrawal, Arun, and Clark C. Gibson. Forthcoming. "Enchantment and Disenchantment: The Role of Community in Natural Resource Conservation." *World Development.*

Ahmed, Akbar S. 1992. *Postmodernism and Islam: Predicament and Promise.* London: Routledge.

Alvarez, Sonia E. 1997. " 'Even Fidel Can't Change That': Trans/national Feminist Advocacy Strategies and Cultural Politics in Latin America." Paper presented at the Department of Cultural Anthropology, Duke Univ., Durham, N.C., Oct.

———. 1998. "Latin American Feminisms 'Go Global': Trends of the 1990s and Challenges for the New Millennium." In *Cultures of Politics/Politics of Cultures: Revisioning Latin American Social Movements,* edited by Sonia E. Alvarez, Evelina Dagnino, and Arturo Escobar, 293–324. Boulder, Colo.: Westview.

Alvarez, Sonia E., Evelina Dagnino, and Arturo Escobar, eds. 1998. *Cultures of Politics/Politics of Cultures: Revisioning Latin American Social Movements.* Boulder, Colo.: Westview.

Amin, Samir. 1989. *Eurocentrism.* New York: Monthly Review.

Ang, Ien. 1998. "Eurocentric Reluctance: Notes for a Cultural Studies of 'the New Europe.' " In *Trajectories: Inter-Asia Cultural Studies,* edited by Chen Kuan-hsing, 87–108. New York: Routledge.

Antonius, George. 1946. *The Arab Awakening: The Story of the Arab National Movement.* New York: G. P. Putnam's Sons.

Apffel-Marglin, Frédérique, and Julio Valladolid. 1995. "Regeneration in the Andes." *Interculture* 28, no. 1: 18–31.

Appadurai, Arjun. 1990. "Disjuncture and Differences in the Global Cultural Economy." *Public Culture* 2, no. 2: 1–24.

———. 1991. "Global Ethnoscapes: Notes and Queries for a Transnational Anthropology." In *Recapturing Anthropology: Working in Present,* edited by R. Fox, 191–210. Santa Fe, N.M.: School of American Research.

———. 1996. *Modernity at Large: Cultural Dimensions of Globalization.* Minneapolis and London: Univ. of Minnesota Press.

Appadurai, Arjun, and Carol A. Breckenridge, eds. 1995a. *Consuming Modernity: Public Culture in a South Asian World.* Minneapolis and London: Univ. of Minnesota Press.

———. 1995b. "Public Modernity in India." In *Consuming Modernity: Public Culture in a South Asian World,* edited by Arjun Appadurai and Carol A. Breckenridge, 4–20. Minneapolis and London: Univ. of Minnesota Press.

Arce, Alberto, and Norman Long, eds. 2000. *Anthropology, Development, and Modernity.* London: Routledge.

Arendt, Hannah. 1963. *On Revolution.* New York: Viking.

Armbrust, Walter. 1996. *Mass Culture and Modernism in Egypt.* Cambridge: Cambridge Univ. Press.

———. 1999. "Bourgeois Leisure and Egyptian Media Fantasies." In *New Media in the Muslim World,* edited by Dale Eickelman and Jon Anderson, 106–32. Bloomington: Indiana Univ. Press.

Asad, Talal. 1973. *Anthropology and the Colonial Encounter.* London: Ithaca.

———. 1993. *Genealogies of Religion: Discipline and Reasons of Power in Christianity and Islam.* Baltimore: Johns Hopkins Univ. Press.

Ashcroft, Bill, Gerreth Griffins, and Helen Tiffin, eds. 1995. *The Post-Colonial Studies Reader.* New York: Routledge.

Ayrout, Henry. 1938. *Fellahs d'Egypte.* Cairo: Editions Horus.

Baik, Young-seo. 1999. "Conceptualizing 'Asia' in the Modern Chinese Mind: A

Korean Perspective." Paper presented at the conference "Searching for East Asian Identity: A Modern Myth or Post-modern Reflection," Seoul, 30 Sept.–1 Oct.

Bakhtin, M. M. 1990. *Art and Answerability: Early Philosophical Essays.* Edited by Michael Holquist and Vadim Liapunov. Austin: Univ. of Texas Press.

Bakir, Amal. 1994. "Hiwar ma' Salah al-Sa'dani al-shahir bi 'Hasan al-Na'mani'." *Al-Ahram* (Friday supplement), 25 Mar., 2.

Baron, Beth. 1997. "Nationalist Iconography: Egypt as a Woman." In *Rethinking Nationalism in the Arab Middle East,* edited by James Jankowski and Israel Gershoni, 105–24. New York: Columbia Univ. Press.

Basu, Amrita, and C. Elizabeth McGrory, eds. 1995. *The Challenge of Local Feminisms: Women's Movements in Global Perspective.* Boulder, Colo.: Westview.

Bates, Robert H. 1996. "Letter from the President: Area Studies and the Discipline." *American Political Science Association, Comparative Politics* 7, no. 1 (winter): 1–2.

———. 1997a. "Area Studies and the Discipline: A Useful Controversy?" *PS: Political Science and Politics* 30: 106–69.

———. 1997b. "Area Studies and Political Science: Rupture and Possible Synthesis." *Africa Today* 44, no. 2: 123–32.

———. 1997c. "Letter from the President: Theory in Comparative Politics?" *American Political Science Association, Comparative Politics* 8, no. 1: 1–2.

Bates, Robert H., Valentin Mudimbe, and Jean O'Barr, eds. 1993. *Africa and the Disciplines: The Contributions of Research in Africa to the Social Sciences and Humanities.* Chicago: Univ. of Chicago Press.

Bender, Thomas. 1997. "Politics, Intellect, and the American University, 1945–1995." *Daedalus* 126, no. 1: 1–38.

Benhabib, Seyla. 1992. *Situating the Self: Gender, Community, and Postmodernism in Contemporary Ethics.* Cambridge: Polity.

Benhabib, Seyla, Judith Butler, Drucilla Cornell, and Nancy Fraser. 1995. *Feminist Contentions: A Philosophical Exchange.* Introduction by Linda Nicholson. New York: Routledge.

Benjamin, Walter. 1969. *Illuminations.* Edited and with an introduction by Hannah Arendt. Translated by Harry Zohn. New York: Schocken.

Berger, Iris. 1997. "Contested Boundaries: African Studies Approaching the Millennium—Presidential Address to the 1996 African Studies Association Annual Meeting." *African Studies Review* 40, no. 2: 1–14.

Berger, Morroe. 1967. "Middle Eastern and North Africa Studies: Development and Needs." *MESA Bulletin* 1, no. 2 (15 Nov.): 1–18.

Berman, Marshall. 1988. *All That Is Solid Melts into Air.* New York: Penguin.

————. 1992. "Why Modernism Still Matters." In *Modernity and Identity*, edited by Scott Lash and Jonathan Friedman, 33–58. Oxford: Blackwell.

Bhabha, Homi. 1994. *The Location of Culture*. New York: Routledge.

Blackman, Winifred. 1927. *The Fellahin of Upper Egypt: Their Religious, Social, and Industrial Life To-day with Special Reference to Survivals from Ancient Times.* London: George G. Harrap.

Blaut, J. M. 1993. *The Colonizer's Model of the World: Geographical Diffusionism and Eurocentric History.* New York: Guilford.

Bonne, Alfred. 1955. *State and Economics in the Middle East: A Society in Transition.* London: Routledge and Kegan Paul.

Boyd, Douglas. 1999. *Broadcasting in the Arab World.* Ames: Iowa State Univ. Press.

Bromley, Simon. 1994. *Rethinking Middle East Politics.* Austin: Univ. of Texas Press.

Brosius, Peter. 1997. "Endangered Forests, Endangered People: Environmentalist Representations of Indigenous Knowledge." *Human Ecology* 25, no. 1: 47–69.

Bunch, Charlotte, and Susan Fried. 1996. "Beijing '95: Moving Women's Human Rights from Margin to Center." *SIGNS* 22, no. 1: 192–211.

Burke, Edmund. 1979. "La mission scientifique au Maroc." In *Actes de Durham: Recherches recentes sur le Maroc moderne*, 37–56. Rabat: Publication du Bulletin Economique et Social du Maroc.

————. 1980. "The Sociology of Islam: The French Tradition." In *Islamic Studies: A Tradition and Its Problems*, edited by Malcolm H. Kerr, 73–88. Malibu: Undena.

————. 1984. "The First Crisis of Orientalism, 1890–1914." In *Connaissances du Maghreb: Sciences sociales et colonisation*, edited by Jean-Claude Vatin, 213–26. Paris: Editions du CNRS.

Butler, Judith. Forthcoming. "Sovereign Performatives in the Contemporary Scene of Utterance." *Critical Inquiry.*

Callahan, William A. n.d. "Negotiating Cultural Boundaries: Confucianism and Trans/national Identity in Korea." Unpublished paper.

Cammack, Paul. 1990. "Statism, New Institutionalism, and Marxism." In *Socialist Register:* 147–70.

Carpentier, Alejo. 1969. "Problematica de la actual novela latinoamericana." In *Literatura y conciencia politica en America Latina*, 9–46. Madrid: Alberto Corazon.

Casey, Edward. 1993. *Getting Back into Place: Toward a Renewed Understanding of the Place-World.* Bloomington: Indiana Univ. Press.

————. 1997. *The Fate of Place*. Berkeley and Los Angeles: Univ. of California Press.

Cassidy, John. 1996. "The Decline of Economics." *The New Yorker* 72, no. 37: 50–60.

Castells, Manuel. 1996. *The Rise of the Network Society*. Oxford: Blackwell.

Chakrabarty, Dipesh. 1997. "Minority Histories, Subaltern Pasts." *Perspectives* (Nov.): 37–43.

————. 1998. "Reconstructing Liberalism: Notes Towards a Conversation Between Area Studies and Diasporic Studies." *Public Culture* 10, no. 3: 457–82.

Chatterjee, Partha. 1986. *Nationalist Thought and the Colonial World: A Derivative Discourse?* Minneapolis: Univ. of Minnesota Press.

Chaudhry, Kirin Aziz. 1994. "The Middle East and the Political Economy of Development." *Items* 48, nos. 2–3 (June-Sept.): 41–49.

————. 1997. *The Price of Wealth: Economics and Institutions in the Middle East*. Ithaca and London: Cornell Univ. Press.

Chernaik, Laura. 1996. "Spatial Displacements: Transnationalism and the New Social Movements." *Gender, Place, and Culture* 3, no. 3: 251–75.

Chow, Esther Ngan-ling. 1996. "Making Waves, Moving Mountains: Reflections on Beijing '95 and Beyond." *SIGNS* 22, no. 1: 185–91.

Chow, Rey. 1993. *Writing Diaspora: Tactics of Intervention in Contemporary Cultural Studies*. Bloomington: Indiana Univ. Press.

Clowse, Barbara. 1981. *Brainpower for the Cold War: The Sputnik Crisis and National Defense Education Act of 1958*. Westport, Conn.: Greenwood.

Cohn, Bernard. 1996. *Colonialism and Its Forms of Knowledge: The British in India*. Princeton, N.J.: Princeton Univ. Press.

Cook, Michael, ed. 1970. *Studies in the Economic History of the Middle East: From the Rise of Islam to the Present Day*. London and New York: Oxford Univ. Press.

Cooper, Frederick A. 1997. "Modernizing Bureaucrats, Backward Africans, and the Development Concept." In *International Development and the Social Sciences: Essays on the History and Politics of Knowledge,* edited by Frederick Cooper and Randall Packard, 64–92. Berkeley and Los Angeles: Univ. of California Press.

Cooper, Frederick, and Randall Packard. 1997. "Introduction." In *International Development and the Social Sciences: Essays on the History and Politics of Knowledge,* edited by Frederick Cooper and Randall Packard, 1–41. Berkeley and Los Angeles: Univ. of California Press.

Crush, Jonathan. 1995. "Introduction: Imagining Development." In *The Power of Development,* edited by Jonathan Crush, 1–26. New York: Routledge.

Crystal, David. 1998. *The Global Tongue: English*. Video recording. London: BBC, Open University.

Cumings, Bruce. 1997. "Boundary Displacement: Area Studies and International Studies during and after the Cold War." *Bulletin of Concerned Asian Scholars* 29, no. 1 (Jan.-Mar.): 6–26.

Curtin, Philip. 1995. "Ghettoizing African History." *Chronicle of Higher Education,* 3 Mar., A4.

Cverkovich, Ann, and Douglas Kellner. 1997. *Articulating the Global and the Local: Globalization and Cultural Studies.* Boulder, Colo.: Westview.

Dahl, Gudrun, ed. 1993. *Green Arguments for Local Subsistence.* Stockholm: Stockholm Studies in Social Anthropology.

Dahl, Robert. 1982. *Dilemmas of Pluralist Democracy: Autonomy Versus Control.* New Haven, Conn.: Yale Univ. Press.

Davis, R. Hunt, Jr. 1998. "A Comment on Ron Kassimir's Article 'The Internationalization of African Studies: A View from the SSRC.' " *Africa Today* 45, no. 10: 71–74.

Descola, Philippe. 1996. "Constructing Natures: Symbolic Ecology and Social Practice." In *Nature and Society: Anthropological Perspectives,* edited by Philippe Descola and Gísli Pálsson, 82–102. London: Routledge.

Descola, Philippe, and Gísli Pálsson, eds. 1996. *Nature and Society: Anthropological Perspectives.* London: Routledge.

Dirlik, Arif. 1987. "Culturalism as Hegemonic Ideology and Liberating Practice." *Cultural Critique* 6 (spring): 13–50.

———. 1995. "Confucius in the Borderlands: Global Capitalism and the Reinvention of Confucianism." *boundary 2* 22, no. 3 (Nov.): 229–73.

———. 1996. "Chinese History and the Question of Orientalism." *History and Theory* (theme issue) 35 (Dec.): 96–118.

———. 1997a. "Critical Reflections on Chinese Capitalism and the Reinvention of Confucianism." *Identities: Global Studies in Culture and Power* 3, no. 3: 303–30.

———. 1997b. "No Longer Far Away: The Reconfiguration of Global Relations and Its Challenges to Modern Asian Studies." In *Unsettled Frontiers and Transnational Linkages: New Tasks for the Historian of Modern Asia,* edited by Leo Douw, 19–32. Amsterdam: Free Univ. Press.

———. 1997c. *The Postcolonial Aura: Third World Criticism in the Age of Global Capitalism.* Boulder, Colo.: Westview.

———. 2000. "Reading Ashis Nandy: 'The Return of the Past or Modernity with a Vengeance.' " In *Postmodernity's Histories: The Past as Legacy and Project,* 119—41. Lanham, Md.: Rowman and Littlefield.

———. 2001. "Place-Based Imagination: Globalism and the Politics of Place." In

Places and Politics in the Age of Globalization, edited by Roxann Prazniak and Arif Dirlik, 15–52. Lanham, Md.: Rowman and Littlefield.

———. In press. "History Without A Center? Reflections on Eurocentrism." In *Historiographical Traditions and Cultural Identities in the Nineteenth and Twentieth Centuries,* edited by Eckhardt Fuchs and Benedict Stuchtey. Washington, D.C.: German Historical Institute.

Dirlik, Arif, and Zhang Xudong. 1997. "Introduction: Post Moderism and China." *boundary 2* 24, no. 7 (fall): 1–18.

Dongyoun, Hwang. 1999. "Wang Jingwei, the Nanjing Government, and the Problem of Collaboration in World War II China." Ph.D. diss., Department of History, Duke Univ., Durham, N.C.

Doutté, Edmond. 1908. *Magie et religion dans l'Afrique du Nord.* Algiers: Jourdan.

Douwed, Leo. 1997. *Unsettled Frontiers and Transnational Linkages: New Tasks for the Historian of Modern Asia.* Amsterdam: Free Univ. Press.

Du Bois, W. E. B. 1965. *The Souls of Black Folk.* 1903. In *Three Negro Classics,* 213–390. Reprint. New York: Avon.

Early, Evelyn. 1993. *Baladi Women of Cairo.* Boulder, Colo.: Lynne Rienner.

Edelman, Marc. 1998. "Transnational Peasant Politics in Central America." *Latin American Research Review* 33, no. 3: 49–86.

Eickelmen, Dale. 1998. *The Middle East and Central Asia: An Anthropological Approach.* 3rd ed. Upper Saddle River, N.J.: Prentice Hall.

Eley, Goeff, and Ronald Grigor. 1996. *Becoming National: A Reader.* Albany: State Univ. of New York Press.

El-Hamamsy, Laila. 1982. "The Assertion of Egyptian Identity." In *Ethnic Identity: Cultural Continuities and Change,* 2d ed., edited by George DeVos and Lola Romanucci-Ross, 276–306. Chicago: Univ. of Chicago Press.

El-Messiri, Sawsan. 1978. *Ibn al-Balad: A Concept of Egyptian Identity.* Leiden: Brill.

Emerson, Ralph Waldo. 1860. "Fate." In *The Conduct of Life,* 1–42. Boston: Ticknor and Fields. Reprinted in *The Norton Anthology of American Literature,* compiled by Ronald Gottsman, 794–816. New York: Norton, 1979.

Erlmann, Veit. 1997. "Africa Civilized, Africa Uncivilized: Local Culture, World System, and South African Music." In *Readings in African Popular Culture,* edited by Karin Barber, 170–77. Bloomington: Indiana Univ. Press.

Escobar, Arturo. 1995. *Encountering Development: The Making and Unmaking of the Third World.* Princeton, N.J.: Princeton Univ. Press.

———. 1997. "Cultural Politics and Biological Diversity: State, Capital, and Social Movements in the Pacific Coast of Colombia." In *Between Resistance and Rev-*

olution, edited by R. Fox and O. Starn, 40–64. New Brunswick, N.J.: Rutgers Univ. Press.

———. 1998. "Whose Knowledge, Whose Nature? Biodiversity Conservation and the Political Ecology of Social Movements." *Journal of Political Ecology* 5: 58–82.

———. 1999. "Gender, Place, and Networks: A Political Ecology of Cyberculture." In *Women@Internet: Creating New Cultures in Cyberspace,* edited by Wendy Harcourt, 31–54. London: Zed.

Escobar, Arturo, and Wendy Harcourt. 1998. "Editorial Note." In *Globalism and the Politics of Place,* edited by Arturo Escobar. Special issue of *Development* 41, no. 2: 1–5.

Escobar, Arturo, and Alvaro Pedrosa, eds. 1996. *Pacífico: Desarrollo o diversidad? Estado, capital, y movimientos sociales en el Pacifico Colombiano.* Bogotá: CEREC/Ecofondo.

Esteva, Gustavo. 1992. "Development." In *The Development Dictionary: A Guide to Knowledge as Power,* edited by Wolfgang Sachs, 6–25. London: Zed.

Evans-Pritchard, E. E. 1937. *Witchcraft, Oracles, and Magic among the Azande.* Oxford: Clarendon.

———. 1940. *The Nuer: A Description of the Modes of Livelihood and Political Institutions of a Nilotic People.* Oxford: Clarendon.

Fadil, Mohammad. 1993. Interviewed by Lila Abu-Lughod. 17 June, Cairo.

Fanon, Frantz. 1968. *The Wretched of the Earth.* New York: Grove.

Ferguson, James. 1990. *The Anti-Politics Machine: Development, Depoliticization, and Bureaucratic Power in Lesotho.* Cambridge: Cambridge Univ. Press.

Fernández, G. Roberto. 1997. *Raining Backwards.* Houston: Arte Público.

Fisher, Sidney, ed. 1955. *Social Forces in the Middle East.* Ithaca, N.Y.: Cornell Univ. Press.

Fisher, William. 1996. Review of *Encountering Development: The Making and Unmaking of the Third World,* by Arturo Escobar. *American Ethnologist* 23. no. 1: 137–39.

Fishman, Ted C., Jeffrey E. Garten, and William Greider. 1996. "Defining the Local in the Arun Controversy: Villagers, NGOs, and the World Bank in the Arun Valley, Nepal." In *Who's Local Here? The Politics of Participation in Development.* Special issue of *Cultural Survival Quarterly* 20, no. 3: 31–34.

———. 1998. "Global Roulette: In a Volatile World Economy, Can Everyone Lose?" *Harper's Magazine* 296, no. 1777: 39–50.

Fisk, Milton. 1993. "Introduction: The Problem of Justice." In *Key Concepts in*

Critical Theory: Justice, edited by Milton Fisk, 1–8. Atlantic Highlands, N.J.: Humanities.

Forbes, Anne Armbrecht. 1996. "Defining the 'Local' in the Arun Controversy: Villagers, NGOs, and the World Bank in the Arun Valley, Nepal." *Cultural Survival Quarterly* 20, no. 3: 31–34.

Frank, Gundar Andre. 1998. *ReOrient: Global Economy in the Asian Age.* Berkeley and Los Angeles: Univ. of California Press.

Friedman, Elizabeth. n.d. "The Effects of 'Transnationalism Reversed' in Venezuela: Assessing the Impact of UN Global Conferences on the Women's Movement." Unpublished manuscript.

Friedman, Jonathan. 1994. *Cultural Identity and Global Process.* London: Sage.

Friedman, Thomas L. 2000. *The Lexus and the Olive Tree.* New York: Anchor, Random House.

Fuchs Eckhardt, and Benedict Stuchtey, eds. Forthcoming. *Historiographical Traditions and Cultural Identities in the Nineteenth and Twentieth Centuries.* Washington, D.C.: German Historical Institute.

Fukuyama, Francis. 1992. *The End of History and the Last Man.* New York: Free Press.

Fusco, Coco. 1996. *English Is Broken Here.* New York: New Press.

Geertz, Clifford. 1973. *The Interpretation of Cultures.* New York: Basic.

———. 1995. *After the Fact: Two Countries, Four Decades, One Anthropologist.* Cambridge, Mass.: Harvard Univ. Press.

Gibb, H. A. R. 1932. *Whither Islam?* London: V. Gollancz.

Gibb, Hamilton, and Harold Bowen. 1950. *Islamic Society and the West: A Study of the Impact of Western Civilization on Moslem Culture in the Near East.* Vol. 1., part 1. London: Oxford Univ. Press.

———. 1957. *Islamic Society and the West: A Study of the Impact of Western Civilization on Moslem Culture in the Near East.* Vol. 1, part 2. London: Oxford Univ. Press.

Gibson-Graham, J. K. 1996. *The End of Capitalism (As We Knew It).* Oxford: Basil Blackwell.

Giddens, Anthony. 1990. *The Consequences of Modernity.* Stanford, Calif.: Stanford Univ. Press.

Gilroy, Paul. 1993. *The Black Atlantic: Modernity and Double Consciousness.* Cambridge, Mass.: Harvard Univ. Press.

Globalization Project. *Area Studies, Regional Worlds: A White Paper for the Ford Foundation.* Chicago: Univ. of Chicago.

Glyn, Andrew, and Bob Sutcliffe. 1992. "Global but Leaderless? The New Capitalist Order." *Socialist Register:* 76–95.

Gordon, Joel. 2000. "Nasser 56/Cairo 96: Reimaging Egypt's Lost Community." In *Mass Mediations,* edited by Walter Armbrust, 161–81. Berkeley and Los Angeles: Univ. of California Press.

Gotanda, Neil. 1991. "A Critique of 'Our Constitution Is Color-Blind.' " *Stanford Law Review* 44, no. 1 (Nov.): 1–58.

Green, Donald P., and Ian Shapiro. 1994. *Pathologies of Rational Choice Theory: A Critique of Applications in Political Science.* New Haven, Conn.: Yale Univ. Press.

Grillo, Eduardo. 1991. *Cultura andina agrocéntrica.* Lima: PRATEC.

Grillo, R. D. 1997. "Discourses of Development: The View from Anthropology." In *Discourses of Development: Anthropological Perspectives,* edited by R. D. Grillo and R. L. Stirrat, 1–33. New York and Oxford: Berg.

Grosz-Ngaté, Maria. 1997. "Introduction." In *Gendered Encounters: Challenging Cultural Boundaries and Social Hierarchies in Africa,* edited by Maria Grosz-Ngaté and Omari H. Kokole, 1–21. New York: Routledge.

Grueso, Libia, Carlos Rosero, and Arturo Escobar. 1998. "The Process of Black Community Organizing in the Southern Pacific Coast of Colombia." In *Cultures of Politics/Politics of Culture: Revisioning Latin America Social Movements,* edited by Sonia E. Alvarez, Evelina Dagnino, and Arturo Escobar, 196–219. Boulder, Colo.: Westview.

Guattari, Félix. 1995. *Chaosophy.* New York: Semiotext(e).

Gudeman, Stephen. 1996. "Sketches, Qualms, and Other Thoughts on Intellectual Property Rights." In *Valuing Local Knowledge,* edited by S. Brush, 102–21. Washington, D.C.: Island.

Gudeman, Stephen, and Alberto Rivera. 1990. *Conversations in Colombia: The Domestic Economy in Life and Text.* Cambridge: Cambridge Univ. Press.

Gulbenkian Commission on the Restructuring of the Social Sciences. 1995. *Open the Social Sciences.* Lisbon: Gulbenkian Foundation.

Gupta, Akhil, and James Ferguson. 1992. "Beyond 'Culture': Space, Identity, and the Politics of Difference." *Cultural Anthropology* 7, no. 1: 6–23.

———. 1997a. "Culture, Power, Place: Ethnography at the End of an Era." In *Culture, Power, Place: Explorations in Critical Anthropology,* edited by Akhil Gupta and James Ferguson, 1–29. Durham, N.C., and London: Duke Univ. Press.

———, eds. 1997b. *Culture, Power, Place: Explorations in Critical Anthropology.* Durham, N.C.: Duke Univ. Press.

———. 1997. "Distant Beacons and Immediate Steps: Area Studies, International Studies, and the Disciplines in 1996." *Africa Today* 44, no. 2: 179–84.

Guyer, Jane I. 1996. *African Studies in the United States: A Perspective.* New Brunswick, N.J.: African Studies Association Press. Also available at: www.africanstudies.org.

Habermas, Jürgen. 1987. *The Philosophical Discourse of Modernity.* Translated by Frederick Lawrence. Cambridge, Mass.: MIT Press.

Hahm, Chaibong. 1997. "The Clash of Civilizations Revisited: A Confucian Per-spective." In *"The Clash of Civilizations?" Asian Responses,* edited by Salim Rashid, 75–97. Karachi: Oxford Univ. Press.

Hall, Peter, and Sidney Tarrow. 1998. "Globalization and Area Studies: When Is Too Broad Too Narrow?" *Chronicle of Higher Education,* 23 Jan., B4-B5.

Hall, Robert, 1947. *Area Studies, with Special Reference to Their Implications for Re-search in the Social Sciences.* New York: Social Science Research Council.

Hamdi, Ismat. 1997. "Awlad al-balad madhalim 'ala al-shasha." *Majallat al-idha'a w al-tilivizyun,* 15 Mar., 46–47.

Hannerz, Ulf. 1989. "Notes on the Global Ecumene." *Public Culture* 1, no. 2: 66–75.

———. 1996. *Transnational Connections.* New York and London: Routledge.

———. 1997. "Sophiatown: The View from Afar." In *Readings in African Popular Culture,* edited by Karin Barber, 164–70. Bloomington: International African Institute in association with Indiana Univ. Press.

Harbeson, John. 1997. "Area Studies and the Disciplines: A Rejoinder." *Issue: A Journal of Opinion* 25, no. 1: 29–31.

Harootunian, Harry. 1970. *Toward Restoration.* Berkeley and Los Angeles: Univ. of California Press.

Haugerud, Angelique. 1995. *The Culture of Politics in Modern Kenya.* Cambridge: Cambridge Univ. Press.

———. 1997. "Editor's Introduction." In *The Future of Regional Studies.* Special issue of *Africa Today* 44, no. 2: 111–22.

———. In press. "Rethinking Boundaries." In *Regional Modernities: The Cultural Politics of Development in India,* edited by K. Sivaramakrishnan and Arun Agrawal. Stanford, Calif.: Stanford Univ. Press.

Haugerud, Angelique, and Wendy Cadge. 2000. *The Social Sciences and Area Stud-ies: An Evaluation of the Social Science Research Council's International Predis-sertation Fellowship Program, 1991–2000. A Report to the Ford Foundation.* New York: Ford Foundation.

Hay, Stephen. 1970. *Asian Ideas of East and West: Tagore and His Critics in Japan, China, and India.* Cambridge, Mass.: Harvard Univ. Press.

Heginbotham, J. Stanley. 1994. "Rethinking International Scholarship: The Challenge of the Transition from the Cold War Era." *Items: The Social Science Research Council Newsletter* 48, nos. 2–3 (June-Sept.): 33–40.

Heilbrunn, Jacob. 1996. "The News from Everywhere: Does Global Thinking Threaten Local Knowledge? The Social Science Research Council Debates the Future of Area Studies." *Lingua Franca* 6, no. 4: 49–56.

Heredia, Blanca. 1997. "Prosper or Perish? Development in the Age of Global Capital." *Current History* 96, no. 613: 383–88.

Hershberg, Eric. 2000. "From Cold War Origins to a Model for Academic Internationalization: Latin American Studies at a Crossroads." *Disposition* 23, no. 50: 117–31.

Herskovits, Melville. 1958a. *Dahomey: An Ancient West African Kingdom.* 2 vols. New York: J. J. August.

———. 1958b. *The Myth of the Negro Past.* Boston: Beacon.

Heyworth-Dunne, G. 1968. *An Introduction to the History of Education in Modern Egypt.* 1939. Reprint. London: Cass.

Hijazi, Ahmad 'Abd al-Mu'ati. 1994. "Al-'A'ila wa Arabisk." *Al-Ahram*, 13 Apr., 18.

Hobart, Mark, ed. 1993. *An Anthropological Critique of Development.* London: Routledge.

Hodgson, Marshall G. S. 1974. *The Classical Age of Islam.* Vol. 1 of *The Venture of Islam: Conscience and History in a World Civilization.* Vol. 1, *The Classical Age of Islam.* Chicago: Univ. of Chicago Press.

Hoodfar, Homa. 1997. *Between Marriage and the Market.* Berkeley and Los Angeles: Univ. of California Press.

Hourani, A. H. 1946. *Syria and Lebanon.* London: n.p.

Huntington, Samuel. 1993. "The Clash of Civilizations?" *Foreign Affairs* 72, no. 3 (summer): 22–49.

———. 1996. *The Clash of Civilizations and the Remaking of World Order.* New York: Simon and Schuster.

Inden, Ronald. 1990. *Imagining India.* Oxford: Blackwell.

Ingold, Tim. 1992. "Culture and the Perception of the Environment." In *Bush Base: Forest Farm,* edited by E. Croll and D. Parkin, 39–56. London: Routledge.

———. 1993. "The Temporality of the Landscape." *World Archaeology* 25, no. 2: 152–73.

———. 1995. "Building, Dwelling, Living: How Animals and People Make Themselves at Home in the World." In *Shifting Contexts: Transformations in Anthropological Knowledge,* edited by M. Strathern, 57–80. London: Routledge.

———. 1996. "The Optimal Forager and Economic Man." In *Nature and Society,* edited by Philippe Descola and Gísli Pálsson, 25–44. London: Routledge.

Issawi, Charles. 1947. *Egypt: An Economic and Social Analysis.* London: Oxford Univ. Press.

Johnson, Chalmers. 1997. "Preconception Versus Observation: The Contributions of Rational Choice Theory and Area Studies to Contemporary Political Science." *PS: Political Science and Politics* 30: 170–74.

Johnson, Peter, and Judith Tucker. 1975. "Middle East Studies Network in the United States." *MERIP Reports* 38: 3–20.

al-Kardusy, Mahmud. 1994. "Al-'Ashiq Hasan was al-Ishq Arabisk." *Nusf al-Dunya* 214 (20 Mar.): 57–60.

Karl, Rebecca. 1995. "Secret Sharers: Chinese Nationalism and the Non-Western World at the Turn of the Twentieth Century." Ph.D. diss., Department of History, Duke Univ., Durham, N.C.

Karp, Ivan. 1997. "Does Theory Travel? Area Studies and Cultural Studies." *Africa Today* 44, no. 3 (July-Sept.): 281–96.

Kassimir, Ron. 1997. "The Internationalization of African Studies: A View from the SSRC." *Africa Today* 44, no. 2: 155–62.

———. 1998. "A Reply to R. Hunt Davis Jr.'s Article." *Africa Today* 45, no. 1: 75–77.

Kearney, Michael. 1995. "The Local and the Global: The Anthropology of Globalization and Transnationalism." *Annual Review of Anthropology* 24: 547–65.

Keck, Margaret E., and Kathryn Sikkink. 1998. *Activists Beyond Borders: Advocacy Networks in International Politics.* Ithaca, N.Y.: Cornell Univ. Press.

Keen, Bernard Augustus. 1946. *The Agricultural Development of the Middle East.* London: H.M. Stationary Office.

Keller, William W., and Louis W. Pauly. 1997. "Globalization at Bay." *Current History* 96, no. 613: 370–76.

Khadduri, Majid. 1951. *Independent Iraq: A Study in Iraqi Politics Since 1932.* London: Oxford Univ. Press.

Khalidi, Rashid. 1995. "Presidential Address: Is There a Future for Middle East Studies?" *Middle East Studies Association Bulletin* 29, no. 1 (July): 1–6.

Khilnani, Sunil. 1997. *The Idea of India.* New York: Farrar, Strauss, Giroux.

Khoury, Philip. 1998. "Letter from the President: Global and Local Perspectives." *Middle East Studies Association Newsletter* 20, no. 2 (May): 1–3.

Kiernan, V. G. 1969. *The Lords of Human Kind: Black Man, Yellow Man, and White Man in an Age of Empire*. Boston: Little Brown.

Kinzer, Stephen. 1997. "A Brussels Meeting Dims Turks' Hopes." *New York Times*, 11 Mar., A7.

Kohn, Hans. 1929. *A History of Nationalism in the East*. New York: Harcourt, Brace.

———. 1932. *Nationalism and Imperialism in the Hither East*. New York: Harcourt, Brace.

Kritzeck, James, and R. Bayly Winder. 1960. "Philip K. Hitti." In *The World of Islam: Studies in Honor of Philip K. Hitti*, edited by James Kritzeck and R. Bayly Winder, 1–37. London: Macmillan.

Krugman, Paul. 1997. "In Praise of Cheap Labor: Bad Jobs at Bad Wages Are Better Than No Jobs at All." *Slate* (20 Mar.): 1–3.

Kuan-hsing, Chen, ed. 1998. *Trajectories: Inter-Asia Cultural Studies*. New York: Routledge.

Kumar, Radha. 1995. "From Chipko to Sati: The Contemporary Indian Women's Movement." In *The Challenge of Local Feminisms: Women's Movements in Global Perspective*, 58–86. Boulder, Colo.: Westview.

Kuttner, Robert. 1985. "The Poverty of Economics." *Atlantic Monthly* (Feb.): 74–84.

Laclau, Ernesto. 1990. *New Reflections on the Revolution of Our Time*. New York: Verso.

———. 1995. "Universalism, Particularism, and the Question of Identity." In *The Identity in Question*, edited by John Rajchman, 93–108. New York: Routledge.

Laitin, David. 1993. "Letter from the Incoming President." *American Political Science Association, Comparative Politics* 4, no. 3: 1–3.

Lapidus, Ira, ed. 1969. *Middle Eastern Cities: A Symposium on Ancient, Islamic, and Contemporary Middle Eastern Urbanism*. Berkeley and Los Angeles: Univ. of California Press.

Laroui, Abdullah. 1976. *The Crisis of the Arab Intellectual: Traditionalism or Historicism?* Berkeley and Los Angeles: Univ. of California Press.

Lawuyi, Olatunde Bayo. 1997. "The World of the Yoruba Taxi Driver: An Interpretive Approach to Vehicle Slogans." In *Readings in African Popular Culture*, edited by Karin Barber, 146–51. Bloomington: International African Institute in association with Indiana Univ. Press.

Levenson, Joseph. 1968. *The Problem of Historical Significance*. Vol. 3 of *Confucian China and Its Modern Fate, a Trilogy*. Berkeley and Los Angeles: Univ. of California Press.

Levinas, Emmanuel. 1969. *Totality and Infinity*. Pittsburgh: Duquesne Univ. Press.

———. 1981. *Otherwise Than Being*. Boston: Kluwer Academic.

Lewis, Bernard. 1992. "The Roots of Muslim Rage." *Atlantic Monthly* (Sept.): 57–69.

Lewis, W. Martin, and Karen E. Wigen. 1997. *The Myth of Continents: A Critique of Metageography*. Berkeley and Los Angeles: Univ. of California Press.

Leys, Colin. 1996. *The Rise and Fall of Development Theory*. Bloomington: Indiana Univ. Press; London: James Currey; Nairobi: EAP.

Lipschutz, Ronnie. 1992. "Reconstructing World Politics: The Emergence of Global Civil Society." *Millennium* 21, no. 3: 389–420.

Lowe, Christopher C. 1997. "Unexamined Consequences of Academic Globalism in African Studies." *Africa Today* 44, no. 2: 297–307.

Lynch, Cecelia. 1998. "Social Movements and the Problem of Globalization." *Alternatives* 23: 149–73.

MacCormack, Carol, and Marilyn Strathern, eds. 1980. *Nature, Culture, and Gender*. Cambridge: Cambridge Univ. Press.

Mahfouz, Naguib. 1989. *Palace Walk*. New York: Doubleday.

Malkki, Liisa. 1997. "National Geographic: The Rooting of Peoples and the Territorialization of National Identity among Scholars and Refugees." In *Culture, Power, Place: Explorations in Critical Anthropology,* edited by Akhil Gupta and James Ferguson, 52–74. Durham, N.C., and London: Duke Univ. Press.

Martin, William. 1996. "After Area Studies: A Return to a Transnational Africa?" *Comparative Studies in South Asia, Africa, and the Middle East* 16, no. 2: 53–61.

Massey, Doreen. 1994. *Space, Place, and Gender*. Minneapolis: Univ. of Minnesota Press.

———. 1997. "A Global Sense of Place." In *Studying Culture,* edited by A. Gray and J. McGuigan, 232–40. London: Edward Arnold.

Matsuda, Mari. 1991. "Voices of America: Accent, Antidiscrimination Law, and a Jurisprudence for the Last Reconstruction." *Yale Law Journal* 100, no. 5 (Mar.).

McCaughey, Robert. 1984. *International Studies and Academic Enterprise*. New York: Columbia Univ. Press.

McCloskey, Donald N. 1985. *The Rhetoric of Economics*. Madison: Univ. of Wisconsin Press.

McMichael, Philip. 1996. "Globalization: Myths and Realities." *Rural Sociology* 61, no. 1: 25–55.

Milton, Kay, ed. 1993. *Environmentalism: The View from Anthropology.* London: Routledge.

———. 1996. *Environmentalism and Cultural Theory.* London: Routledge.

Mitchell, Timothy P. 1991a. "America's Egypt: Discourse of the Development Industry." *Middle East Report* 21, no. 2 (Mar.-Apr.): 18–34.

———. 1991b. "The Limits of the State: Beyond Statist Approaches and Their Critics." *American Political Science Review* 85: 77–96.

———. 1998. "Fixing the Economy." *Cultural Studies* 12, no. 1: 82–101.

———. 1999. "Society, Economy, and State Effect." In *State/Culture: State-Formation after the Cultural Turn,* edited by George Steinmetz, 76–97. Ithaca, N.Y.: Cornell Univ. Press.

———, ed. 2000. *Questions of Modernity.* Minneapolis: Univ. of Minnesota Press.

———. 2002. *Rule of Experts: Egypt, Techno-Politics, Modernity.* Berkeley and Los Angeles: Univ. of California Press.

Mkandawire, Thandika. 1997. "The Social Sciences in Africa: Breaking Local Barriers and Negotiating International Presence." *African Studies Review* 40, no. 2: 15–36.

Moghadam, Valentine M. 1996a. "Feminist Networks North and South: DAWN, WIDE, and WLULM." *Journal of International Communication* 3, no. 1: 111–25.

———. 1996b. "The Fourth World Conference on Women: Dissension and Consensus." *Indian Journal of Gender Studies* 3, no. 1: 93–102.

Montagne, Robert. 1986. *La vie sociale et la vie politique du Berbères.* 1931. Reprint. Paris: CHEAM.

Muhanna, Magdi. 1998. "Fi al-mamnu'." *Al-Wat,* 5 Feb., 9.

Muharram, Mustafa. 1997. Telephone interview by Lila Abu-Lughod, May.

Nandy, Ashis. 1998. "A New Cosmopolitanism: Toward a Dialogue of Asian Civilizations." In *Trajectories: Inter-Asia Cultural Studies,* edited by Chen Kuan-hsing, 142–49. New York: Routledge.

———. Forthcoming. "The Return of the Past or Modernity with a Vengeance." In *Dissenting Knowledges, Open Futures: The Multiple Selves and Strange Destinations of Ashis Nandy,* edited by Vinal Laled. Delhi: Oxford Univ. Press.

Narayan, Uma. 1997. *Dislocating Cultures: Identities, Traditions, and Third World Feminism.* New York: Routledge.

Nicholson, Linda. 1995. *Feminist Contentions: A Philosophical Exchange.* New York: Routledge.

Panitch, Leo. 1994. "Globalisation and the State." *Socialist Register:* 60–93.

Parajuli, Pramod. n.d. "Governance at the Grassroots: From Global Civil Society to Ecosystem Communities." Unpublished manuscript.

Parkin, David. 1990. "Eastern Africa: The View from the Office and the Voice from the Field." In *Localizing Strategies: Regional Traditions of Ethnographic Writing*, edited by Richard Fardon, 182–203. Washington, D.C.: Smithsonian Institution Press.

Peck, Jamie. 2000. "Political-Economies of Scale." Paper presented at the research symposium "Producing Place(s)," Miami Univ., Oxford, Ohio, May 12–13.

Pérez Firmat, Gustavo. 1994. *Life on the Hyphen: The Cuban-American Way.* Austin: University of Texas Press.

Pipes, Daniel. 1981. *Slave Soldiers and Islam: The Genesis of a Military System.* New Haven, Conn.: Yale Univ. Press.

———1990. *Greater Syria: The History of an Ambition.* New York: Oxford University Press.

Piterburg, Gabriel. 1997. "The Tropes of Stagnation and Awakening in Nationalist Historical Consciousness: The Egyptian Case." In *Rethinking Nationalism in the Arab Middle East*, edited by James Jankowski and Israel Gershoni, 42–62. New York: Columbia Univ. Press.

Pocock, J. G. A. 1994. "Deconstructing Europe." *History of European Ideas* 18, no. 3: 329–45.

Polanyi, Karl. 1944. *The Great Transformation: The Political and Economic Origins of Our Time.* Boston: Beacon.

Prewitt, Kenneth. 1996. "Presidential Items." *Items: The Social Science Research Council Newsletter* 50, no. 1: 15–18; nos. 2–3: 31–40.

Rafael, Vicente. 1994. "The Culture of Area Studies in the United States." *Social Text* 41 (winter): 91–111.

———. 1999. "Regionalism, Area Studies, and the Accidents of Agency." *American Historical Review* (Oct.): 1208–20.

Rahnema, Majid. 1992. "Poverty." In *The Development Dictionary: A Guide to Knowledge as Power*, edited by Wolfgang Sachs, 158–76. London: Zed.

Rahnema, Majid, and Victoria Bawtree. 1997. *The Postdevelopment Reader.* London: Routledge.

Rapley, John. 1996. *Understanding Development: Theory and Practice in the Third World.* Boulder, Colo.: Lynne Rienner.

Rawls, John. 1985. "Justice as Fairness: Political Not Metaphysical." *Philosophy and Public Affairs* 14: 223–51.

"Remapping Area Studies: An Interview with Toby Volkman, Program Officer, Office of Education, Media, Arts, and Culture, the Ford Foundation, Winter 1999." 1999. In *The Ford Foundation Report, Winter 1999,* 10–11. New York: Ford Foundation.

Resnick, Stephen, and Rick Wolff. 1987. *Knowledge and Class: A Marxian Critique of Political Economy.* Chicago: Univ. of Chicago Press.

Restrepo, Eduardo, and Jorge I. del Valle, eds. 1996. *Renacientes del Guandal.* Bogotá: Proyecto Biopacífico, Universidad Nacional.

Richards, Alan, and John Waterbury, eds. 1996. *A Political Economy of the Middle East.* 2d ed. Boulder, Colo.: Westview.

Richards, Paul. 1993. "Cultivation, Knowledge, or Performance?" In *An Anthropological Critique of Development,* edited by Mark Hobart, 61–78. London: Routledge.

Robinson, Pearl T. 1997. "Local/Global Linkages in the Future of African Studies." *Africa Today* 44, no. 2: 169–79.

Roe, Emery M. 1991. "Development Narratives, or Making the Best of Blueprint Development." *World Development* 19, no. 4: 287–300.

Rosenau, James. 1997. "The Complexities and Contradictions of Globalization." *Current History* 96, no. 613: 360–64.

Ross, Dorothy. 1991. *The Origins of American Social Science.* Cambridge: Cambridge Univ. Press.

Sachs, Wolfgang, ed. 1992. *The Development Dictionary: A Guide to Knowledge as Power.* London: Zed.

al-Sa'dani, Akram. 1994. "Hasan Arabisk: Sura 'a'iliya 'ab qurb." *Sabah al-Khayr* (10 Mar.): 44–45.

Said, Edward. 1978. *Orientalism.* New York: Vintage.

———. 1997. *Covering Islam: How the Media and the Experts Determine How We See the Rest of the World.* New York: Vintage.

Sakai, Naoki. 1997. *Translation and Subjectivity: On "Japan" and Cultural Nationalism.* Minneapolis: Univ. of Minnesota Press.

Salmon, Claudine, ed. 1987. *Literary Migrations: Traditional Chinese Fiction in Asia (17–20th Centuries).* Beijing: International Culture.

Sanger, David E. 1998. "As Economies Fail, the IMF Is Rife with Recriminations." *New York Times,* 2 Oct., A1 and A10.

Sassen, Saskia. 2000. "Cracked Casings: Notes Toward an Analytics for Studying Transnational Processes." In *Sociology for the Twenty-first Century,* edited by Janet Abu-Lughod, 117–28. Chicago: Univ. of Chicago Press.

al-Sayyid, 'Ali. 1994. "Dunyat al-arabisk." *Nusf al-Dunya* 214 (20 Mar.): 74–77.

Scott, James. 1995. "The Role of Theory in Comparative Politics: A Symposium." *World Development* 48: 1–49.

———. 1998. *Seeing Like a State: How Certain Schemes to Improve the Human Condition Have Failed.* New Haven, Conn.: Yale Univ. Press.

Shafiq, Viola. 1998. *Arab Cinema.* Cairo: American Univ. in Cairo Press.

"Shuttle Between Worlds, A." 1998. *New York Times,* 21 July.

Sibley, Elbridge. 1974. *Social Science Research Council: The First Fifty Years.* New York: Social Science Research Council.

Singerman, Diane. 1995. *Avenues of Participation.* Princeton, N.J.: Princeton Univ. Press.

Sivaramakrishnan, K., and Arun Agrawal. In press. "Regional Modernities: An Introduction." In *Regional Modernities: The Cultural Politics of Development in India,* edited by K. Sivaramakrishnan and Arun Agrawal. Stanford, Calif.: Stanford Univ. Press.

Skursi, Julie. 1996. "The Ambiguities of Authenticity in Latin America: *Dona Barbara* and the Construction of National Identity." In *Becoming National: A Reader,* edited by Goeff Eley and Ronald Grigor Suny, 371–402. New York and Oxford: Oxford Univ. Press.

Slaughter, Sheila, and Larry I. Leslie. 1997. *Academic Capitalism: Politics, Policies, and the Entrepreneurial University.* Baltimore: Johns Hopkins Univ. Press.

Smith, Rogers M. 1997. "Still Blowing in the Wind: The American Quest for a Democratic, Scientific Political Science." In *American Academic Culture in Transformation: Fifty Years, Four Disciplines.* Special issue of *Daedalus* 126, no. 1: 253–87.

Sollors, Werner. 1997. *Neither Black Nor White Yet Both.* New York: Oxford Univ. Press.

Sreberny-Mohammadi, Annabelle, ed. 1996. *Globalization, Communication, and Transnational Civil Society.* Cresskill, N.J.: Hampton.

Strange, Susan. 1997. "The Erosion of the State." *Current History* 96, no. 613: 365–76.

Strathern, Marilyn. 1980. "No Nature, No Culture: The Hagen Case." In *Nature, Culture, and Gender,* edited by C. MacCormack and M. Strathern, 174–22. Cambridge: Cambridge Univ. Press.

Swyngedouw, Erik. 1998. "Homing In and Spacing Out: Re-configuring Scale." In *Europa im Globalisierungsporzess von Wirtschaft und Gesellschaft,* edited by H. Gebhart, 81–100. Stuttgart: Franz Steiner.

Tannous, Afif. 1944. *The Arab Village Community in the Middle East.* Washington, D.C.: Government Printing Office.

"Telemundo." 1998. *New York Times,* 19 Sept.

Tomlinson, John. 1999. *Globalization and Culture.* Chicago: Univ. of Chicago Press.

Tonelson, Alan. 1997. "Globalization: The Great American Non-Debate." *Current History* 96, no. 613: 353–59.

'Ukasha, Usama Anwar. 1992. Interview. *Akhar sa'a,* 8 Apr., 27–29.

———. 1993. "Al-tilifizyun yarfa' al masahif." *Ruz-al-Yusuf,* 27 Dec., 68.

———. 1997. Interviews by Lila Abu-Lughod, 10 Mar. and 27 May, Cairo.

Van Gennep, Arnold. 1914. *En Algerie.* Paris: Mercure de France.

Varese, Stefano. 1996. "The New Environmentalist Movement of Latin American Indigenous People." In *Valuing Local Knowledge,* edited by S. Brush, 122–42. Washington, D.C.: Island.

Vasconcelos, José. 1979. *The Cosmic Race/La raza cósmica.* Translated by Didier T. Jaén. 1925. Los Angeles: Centro de Publicaciones, California State Univ.

Vatin, Jean-Claude, ed. 1984. *Connaissances du Maghreb: Sciences sociales et colonisation.* Paris: Editions du CNRS.

Vigil, Evangelina. 1982. *Thirty an' Seen a Lot.* Houston: Arte Püblico.

Virilio, Paul. 1997. *The Open Sky.* New York: Verso.

———. 1999. *Politics of the Very Worst.* New York: Semiotext(e).

Vitalis, Robert. 1999. Review of *The Price of Wealth: Economics and Institutions in the Middle East* by Kirin Aziz Chaudhry. *International Journal of Middle East Studies* 31: 659–61.

Volkman, Toby Alice. 1998. "Crossing Borders: The Case for Area Studies." *Ford Foundation Report* 29, no. 2: 28–29.

Wagley, Charles. 1948. *Area Research and Training: A Conference Report on the Study of World Areas.* New York: Social Science Research Council.

Wallerstein, Immanuel. 1974. *The Modern World System.* Vols. 1 and 2. New York: Academic.

———. 1996. "Open the Social Sciences." *Items: The Social Science Research Council Newsletter* 50, no. 1 (Mar.): 1–7.

———. 1997. "The Unintended Consequences of Cold War Area Studies." In *The Cold War and the University: Toward an Intellectual History of the Postwar Years,* 195–231. New York: New Press.

Wapner, Paul. 1995. "Politics Beyond the State: Environmental Activism and World Civic Politics." *World Politics* 47 (Apr.): 311–40.

Watts, Michael. 1992. "Capitalisms, Crises, and Cultures I: Notes Toward a Totality of Fragments." In *Reworking Modernity: Capitalisms and Symbolic Discontent,* edited by Allan Pred and Michael J. Watts, 1–19. New Brunswick, N.J.: Rutgers Univ. Press.

———. 1998. "Geographical Imaginaries and the Crisis of Development: Collective Wish Images." In *Human Geography Today,* edited by Doreen Massey and John Allen. Cambridge: Polity Press. [Page numbers cited in chapter 4 refer to manuscript version.]

Wee, C. J. W-L. 1997. "Framing the 'New' East Asia: Anti-Imperialist Discourse and Global Capitalism." In *"The Clash of Civilizations?" Asian Responses,* edited by Salim Rashid, 75–97. Karachi: Oxford Univ. Press.

West, Michael, and William G. Martin. 1997. "A Future with a Past: Resurrecting the Study of Africa in the Post-Africanist Era." *Africa Today* 44, no. 3: 309–26.

Westermark, Edward. 1968. *Ritual and Belief in Morocco.* 1926. Reprint. New Hyde Park, N.Y.: University Books.

Williams, Daniel, and Michael Patterson. 1996. "Environmental Psychology: Mapping Landscape Meanings for Ecosystem Management." In *Integrating Social Science and Ecosystem Management,* edited by H. K. Cordell and J. C. Bergstrom, 141–60. Champaign, Ill.: Sagamore.

Winder, Bayly. 1987. "Four Decades of Middle Eastern Study." *Middle East Journal* 41, no. 1 (winter): 40–63.

Wolff, Robert Paul, Barrington Moore Jr., and Herbert Marcuse, eds. 1969. *A Critique of Pure Tolerance.* Boston: Beacon.

Woods, John. 1996. "Imagining and Stereotyping Islam." In *Muslims in America: Opportunities and Challenges,* position Paper no. 2, by A. Husain, J. Woods, and J. Akhtar, 45–77. Chicago: International Strategy and Policy Institute.

Yergin, Daniel. 1977. *Shattered Peace: The Origins of the Cold War and the National Security State.* Boston : Houghton Mifflin.

Zeleza, Paul Tiyambe. 1997. "The Perpetual Solitudes and Crises of African Studies." *Africa Today* 44, no. 2: 193–210.

———. 2000. *Manufacturing African Studies and Crises.* Dakar, Senegal: CODESRIA.

Index

Abu-Lughod, Lila, 16, 17, 18

Achebe, Chinua, 60n

African American studies, 2

African studies, 19, 20, 138, 143

African Studies Association (ASA), 138, 139, 141, 144, 146

African Studies in the United States: A Perspective (Guyer), 138

Africa Today, 138, 73n. 23

Agrawal, Arun, 64n. 7, 69n. 18, 71n

Aguilar, Yellen, 37, 53n

Ahmad, Eqbal, 21

Ahmed, Akbar S., 199n. 3

Al-Ahram, 118

Allison, Anne, 101

All Pakistan Women's Association (APWA), 224

Almond, Gabriel, 157

Alvarez, Sonia, 84, 91

American Council of Learned Societies (ACLS), 2, 5, 137, 138–39

American Historical Association, 139

American Israel Public Affairs Committee (AIPAC), 186n

American Political Science Association, 181–82

American Research Center (Egypt), 101

American studies, 15, 27, 28

American University (Cairo, Egypt), 101

American University of Beirut (AUB), 150, 150n

Annan, Kofi, 219

Anthills of the Savannah (Achebe), 60n

anthropology, 37, 39–40

anticommunism, 3

Antonius, George, 153

apartheid, 221

Appadurai, Arjun, 5, 9, 39n, 64, 65n, 104

Arabesque, 105–6, 115–17, 119–20, 120–22, 126, 127

Aramco, 166

area studies: and academic disciplines, 5, 6–7, 19–20, 82; and capitalism, 141; during Cold War, 3; as contextual knowledge, 18; criticism of, 9; and cultural areas, 134, 135; and cultural studies, 9, 14; decline of, 100; and Defense Information Act of 1958, 3–4, 149; definition, 1, 19; and diasporic studies, 9–10; evolution of, 131–32, 133–34, 148; foundation support, 2, 4–5, 82–83, 137–38; and geopolitics, 3, 4; and globalization, 2, 3, 5, 10, 13–14, 20–21; and globalization studies, 14–15; government support of, 3–4; importance of, 12–13; and language, 136; and modernity, 136; political origins of, 3, 5; and political science, 7; and Royal Institute of International Affairs, 151–52; and social science theory, 61; and women's studies, 82–83

Area Studies, with Special Reference to Their Implications for Research in the Social Sciences (Hall), 149n
Arendt, Hannah, 32n. 4
Armbrust, Walter, 104n, 107n, 114
Asia: Asia Pacific, 201; East Asia, 200–201, 202; Southeast Asia, 200, 201, 202
Asian studies, 193
assimilationism, 34
Ataturk, Kemal, 205
Atlantic Monthly, 184
autonomous women's movement, 92
'Awdat al-ruh (al-Hakim), 117n. 10
'Awdat al-wa'i (al-Hakim), 117n. 10

Bakir, Amal, 116
Basu, Amrita, 16–17, 18, 101, 222
Basyouni, Iman Farid, 101
Bates, Robert H., 7–8, 79, 138, 163
Beijing Plan of Action, 86, 98
Beijing Plus Five, 98
Benedict, Ruth, 155
Benhabib, Seyla, 31n. 2
Benjamin, Walter, 32n. 4
Berger, Iris, 138
Berger, John, 202
Berman, Marshall, 11–12
Bharatiya Janata Party (BJP), 93, 95
Bhutto, Benazir, 218, 221
bilingualism, 28
Bin Laden, Osama, 224
Black Atlantic, The (Gilroy), 13
Boas, Franz, 155
Bolívar, Simón, 33
Bowen, Harold, 151–52, 153
Braschi, Giannina, 27
Breasted, James Henry, 149–50, 179
British Library, 136
Bromley, Simon, 165

Brown v. Board of Education, 149
Buddhism, 198
Bulletin of Concerned Asian Scholars, 4, 226
Bunch, Charlotte, 86
Butler, Judith, 31n. 2

Callahan, William A., 201n
Camdessus, Michael, 79
capital, global, 38, 39
capitalism, 217
Captan, Elwi, 101
Carnegie Corporation, 157
Carpentier, Alejo, 25–26
Carter, Jimmy, 223
Casey, Edward, 38
Castells, Manuel, 38n, 48n
Centers for International Business Education and Research, 183
Central Intelligence Agency (CIA), 177–78, 223; funding of area studies, 4
Chakrabarty, Dipesh, 9–10, 167
Challenge of Local Feminisms: Women's Movements in Global Perspective, The (Basu and McGrory), 83
Chaudhry, Kirin, 165–66, 167
Chiapas rebellion, 70–71
China, 2, 203; and area studies, 226; and Defense Information Act of 1958, 4
Chipko, 93
Chomsky, Noam, 226, 229
Chow, Esther Ngan-ling, 86
Chronicle of Higher Education, 144
class, in Egyptian soap operas, 109–15
Clowse, Barbara, 149
code switching, 28, 35
Cohen, George, 226
Cold War, 3, 4, 5
Columbia University, 4

Committee of Concerned Asian Scholars, 226

Committee on Asian Studies, 4

Confucian China and Its Modern Fate (Levenson), 197

Confucianism, 197–98, 200–201, 201n, 202, 205

Confucius, 197

Congress Party, 93

convergence, 12

Cooper, Frederick, 71–72

Council for the Development of Economic and Social Research in Africa (CODESRIA), 141, 146

Crisis of the Arab Intellectual, The (Laroui), 193–94

Critical Asian Studies, 4

Crossing Boundaries, 219

"Cuban-American Way, The" (Pérez Firmat), 35

cultural studies, 6, 8; and area studies, 9, 14; and place, 39; and postcolonial studies, 9

Cultural Survival Quarterly, 69–70

culture: and globalization, 37, 134, 221; local, 39; and place, 39–40; transnationalism of, 60

Cumings, Bruce, 4, 5–6

Curtin, Philip, 144, 145

Dahl, Gudrun, 44n. 7

Dahl, Robert, 32n. 4

Davis, R. Hunt, Jr., 73n. 23

de Andrade, Oswald, 34

decolonialization, 195–96, 217, 218, 222, 227

Defense Information Act of 1958, 3–4, 149

delineation, 2, 4

de Sola Pool, Ithiel, 226

Development Alternatives with Women for a New Era (DAWN), 88, 90

development and environment, 38

Development Dictionary, The (Sachs), 68

diaspora studies, 5, 9–10

Dirlik, Arif, 20–21, 37, 38, 38n, 48–49, 56

disciplines, academic: and area studies, 5, 6–7, 19–20, 82, 133; and globalization, 10–11, 15–16; and modernization, 11–12; as universal knowledge, 18

diversification, 132

diversity, 26–27, 31n. 1

double-consciousness, 27, 28–30, 32, 34, 35, 36

Du Bois, W. E. B., 30; assimilation, 32; and double-consciousness, 28–29, 33–34; *Encyclopedia Africana,* 144; *Souls of Black Folk* (Du Bois), 27

Duke University, 101

Early, Evelyn, 107n

East Asia, 2

economics, 7, 14

economy and globalization, 38

Edelman, Marc, 75n. 30

El-Hamamsy, Laila, 123

elites, 203, 220, 221, 222, 227

Ellsberg, Daniel, 226

El-Messiri, Sawsan, 107n, 119

Emerson, Ralph Waldo, 29–30, 32

Emerson, Steve, 185n. 18

Encyclopedia Africana, 144

English Is Broken Here (Fusco), 35

Enlightenment, The (European), 16, 18, 31, 131, 133, 135, 203

environment and development, 38

Escobar, Arturo, 15–16, 52n, 61, 66, 67n. 11, 69n. 17, 223

ethnic pluralism, 5
Euro-America, 199, 202, 203
Eurocentrism, 9, 20, 196, 211n
Europe, 2
European Union, 185

Fadil, Mohammad, 124
Fahmy, Khaled, 101
Fairbanks, John K., 226
Fanon, Frantz, 195, 221
Far East, 171
Fayed, King of Saudi Arabia, 223
feminism, 83
Feminist Majority, 89, 92
Ferguson, James, 39n, 61
Fernández, Roberto, 35
Fisher, William, 71, 69n. 17
Fisk, Milton, 32n. 3
Ford Foundation, 2, 4, 83, 137–38, 212,
    222; and area studies, 228; "Crossing
    Borders: Revitalizing Area Studies," 5,
    60; globalization studies, 6; women's
    rights, 89
Foreign Affairs, 184
Foucault, Michel, 31n. 2, 229
Frank, Gundar, 211n
Fried, Susan, 86
Friedman, Elizabeth, 97
Fukuyama, Francis, 183, 217, 222
Fusco, Coco, 35

Gandhi, Indira, 93
Gandhi, Mohandas, 205, 229
Garcia Canclini, Nestor, 34
Garten, Jeffrey E., 76
gender apartheid in Afghanistan, 90, 99
gender relations, 5
General Agreement on Tariffs and Trade
    (GATT), 71

General Education Board, 149
geopolitics, 3, 4
Gibb, H. A. R., 151–52, 153, 154n
Gibson, Catherine, 46–48, 69n. 18
Giddens, Anthony, 11, 50, 67n. 10, 73n.
    22
Gilroy, Paul, 13
global agency, 38
global capitalism, 2
global history, 38
globalization, 199, 216; and academic
    disciplines, 10–11, 15–16; and area
    studies, 2, 3, 5, 10, 13–14, 20–21; and
    class, 220; and culture, 134, 196, 200,
    221; and economic theory, 134; and
    economy, 38; as imperialism, 199,
    216–18; of knowledge, 219; and labor,
    218–19; and local, 61; and mass
    media, 102; and place, 39; and
    placelessness, 37; as universality,
    132
globalization studies, 6; and area studies,
    14–15; and modernization, 11
global-local, 15–16, 20; feminism, 83; and
    women's movements, 16–17
"Global-Local: Revisioning the Area
    Studies Debate," 14
global space, 38, 39
Global Tongue: English, The, 29
Globo Television, 17, 102
glocal, 49
Gomez de Avellaneda, Gertrudis, 34
Gordon, Joel, 127
Gotanda, Neil, 31n. 1
Graham, Julie, 37, 46–48
Greater Syria: The History of an Ambition
    (Pipes), 185n. 17
Greene, Sandra, 18–19, 225–26
Grueso, Libia, 37, 52n, 53n
Guangzhou (Canton) Uprising of 1927,
    205

Gudeman, Stephen, 46

Guevara, Ernesto Che, 195–96

Gulbenkian Commission on the Restructuring of the Social Sciences, 3

Gupta, Akhil, 39n

Guyer, Jane, 138

Habermas, Jürgen, 11, 31n. 2

Hahm, Chaibong, 201n

al-Hakim, Tawfiq, 117n. 10

Hall, Peter, 6

Hall, Robert, 149n

Hamdan, Jamal, 120

Hampshire College, 14, 60, 101, 219, 228

Hannerz, Ulf, 39n, 126

Harootunian, Harry, 200n

Harvard University, 4, 139n, 154n, 184, 226, 227

Haugerud, Angelique, 15, 16, 63n

Hegel, Georg, 133

Heisel, Don, 101

Heredia, Blanca, 74n. 25

Herring, Pendleton, 157

Herskovits, Melville, 144

Higher Institute of Cinema (Cairo, Egypt), 101

Hilmiyya Nights, 105, 119, 127

Hinduism, 198

Hitti, Philip, 150

Holmquist, Frank, 60, 68n. 15, 70n

Hoodfar, Homa, 107n

Hourani, Albert, 153

Human Life International, 87

Human Rights Watch, 89

Huntington, Samuel P., 184–85, 202, 227

Hunwick, John, 139n

Hutcheson, Linda, 33n. 6

ibn al-balad, 107n, 119, 121; and *Arabesque,* 115, 116–17, 118; and *I Won't Live in My Father's Shadow (Lan a'ish fi gilbab abi),* 106, 107, 109

Ibn al-Balad: A Concept of Egyptian Identity (El-Messiri), 107n

identity and transnationalization, 102

imperialism, 228

India, 92–96

Indochina, 4

Indo-China War, 5, 226

Indyk, Martin, 186n

Ingold, Tim, 45, 50

International Monetary Fund (IMF), 74, 79–80, 219, 221

International Right to Life Committee, 87

Iran, 227

Iran, Islamic Republic of, 87

Islam, 175, 198, 223

Islamization, 103

Issawi, Charles, 153

I Won't Live in My Father's Shadow (Lan a'ish fi gilbab abi), 106–9, 114–15, 116, 117n. 9, 121, 127,

Japan, 200, 200n, 203

John Simon Guggenheim Foundation, 101

Johnson, Chalmers, 8

Kahn, Herman, 202

Kamil, 'Abla, 106, 110

Kanwar, Roop, 95

al-Kardusy, Majmud, 120

Kassimir, Ron, 60, 73n. 23, 78n. 36

Kearney, Michael, 64nn. 6, 7

Keck, Margaret E., 94

Keller, Susan, 31n. 1, 35n,

Keller, William W., 73n. 24

Khalidi, Rashid, 20

Kissinger, Henry, 227–28

Kluckhohn, Clyde, 155

knowledge: contextual, 131–32; local, 135; and power, 228–29; universal, 131–32

Korea, 200, 203

Kroeber, A. L., 155

Krugman, Paul, 73n. 23

Kuttner, Robert, 78, 78n. 34, 79

Kuwait, 173

Laclau, Ernesto, 31, 35, 169

Lahore University of Management Scientists, 221

Laitin, David, 162, 164

Lan a'ish fi gilbab abi (I Won't Live in My Father's Shadow), 106–9, 114–15, 116, 117n. 9, 121, 127

La reza cosmica (Vasconcelo), 33

Laroui, Abdallah, 193–95, 194n, 196–97, 197n, 212

Latimore, Owen, 226

Latin America, 2

Lawuyi, Olatunde Bayo, 60n

Leff, Enrique, 37

Lenczowski, George, 154n

Lesotho, 61–62

Levenson, Joseph, 196–97

Lewis, Bernard, 184, 185

Lewis, Martin W., 172n. 2

Leys, Colin, 61n. 3, 73n. 22, 74n. 27, 75n. 29, 81n

local: concepts of, 61; culture, 39; as historical process, 63–65; labor, 38; noncapitalism, 39; place, 38, 39; and postwar development theory, 61–63, 61n. 3; tradition, 38

local-global, 15–16, 20; feminism, 83; and women's movements, 16–17

Location of Culture, The (Bhabba), 31n. 2

Lowe, Christopher C., 75

Ludden, David, 18, 19, 20

MacArthur Foundation, 6

Mahan, Alfred Thayer, 171n

Maharashtra, 93

Mahfouz, Naguib, 108, 112, 119, 119n

Al-Majdub, Ahmad, 119

"Manifesto antropofago" (de Andrade), 34

Mankekar, Purnima, 101

Mao Zedong, 195

Marcos, Ferdinand, 221

marginalization, 220

Maria Esteves, Sandra, 27

Marx, Karl, 11, 132, 133

Masekela, Hugh, 65

Massachusetts Institute of Technology (MIT), 226

Mass Culture and Modernism in Egypt (Armbrust), 107n

Massey, Doreen, 48n

mass media, 17, 102

Matsuda, Mari, 32n. 3, 35n, 35–36,

McMichael, Philip, 67n. 12, 67n. 13, 70n, 73n. 24

Mellon Foundation, 5, 6, 138

Melodrama of Nationhood, 101

mestizaje, 32–33

Metro Broadcasting v. FCC, 31n. 1

Middle East, 2

Middle East Report, 226

Middle East studies, 20, 227

Military Assistance Plan (MAP), 222

Mill, John Stuart, 133

Miller, Judith, 185n. 18

Ministry of Higher Education (Egypt), 101

Mirsepassi, Ali, 216

miscegenation, 32–33

Mitchell, Timothy, 19–20, 101, 225–26

Mkandawire, Thandika, 141–42, 142n

mobility, 38

modernity, 11–12, 31n. 2, 195, 228; definition, 11; Euro-American, 202; global, 39

modernization, 34, 196; and academic disciplines, 11–12; and community, 66; economic, 5, 12; and globalization studies, 11; and Royal Institute of International Affairs, 151–52

Moghadam, Valentine, 84, 91

monoculturalism, 27, 35

Morgan, Robin, 83

Movement for the Survival of the Ogoni People (MOSOP), 69

Muharram, Mustafa, 101, 106n, 107, 118n

multiculturalism, 25–27, 199–200

multitemporal heterogeneity, 34

Myth of Continents: A Critique of Metageography, The (Lewis and Wigen), 172n. 2

Myth of the Negro Past, The (Herskovits), 144

Nandy, Ashis, 208, 210

Narayan, Uma, 94

Naser '56 (film), 124

Nasser, Gamal, 103

"National by Subtraction" (Schwarz), 34

National Center for Sociological and Criminological Research, 119

National Defense Education Act of 1957, 178n. 10

National Endowment for the Humanities, 101

nationalism, 194n, 194–95; collapse of, 217; economic, 217

National Organization for Women (NOW), 89

National Political Congress of Black Women, 89

National Resource Centers, 187

National Summit on Africa, 139, 145

nature and place, 38

Near East, 172

Near East Report, 186n

Neo-York, 15, 26

networks: global, 132; and place, 38n; transnational, 83, 84, 87

New Cultural History of Latin America, 33n. 6

New York (N.Y.), 15

New York Times, 79–80, 185, 220

New York University, 101

noncapitalism, 39

North American Free Trade Agreement (NAFTA), 70–71

Northwestern University, 139n, 144

Nusf al-Dunya, 120

Observing Islam (Said), 185

Office of Strategic Services (OSS), 4, 178

Omohundro Institute of Early American History and Culture, 139n, 140n. 4

Oriental Institute, 149, 179

Orientalism, 194, 202, 206

Orientalism (Said), 179, 185, 194, 177n. 8

Ortiz, Fernando, 33

Packard, Randall, 71–72

Pahwa, Sonali, 101

Paik Nak-chung, 203n. 9

Pakistan, 224

Pakistan Human Rights Commission, 225

Palace Walk (Mahfouz), 108
Palestine, 227
Palmer, Colin, 140n. 4
Panitch, Leo, 73n. 24
Parkin, David, 65
Parsons, Talcott, 156
Pauly, Louis W., 73n. 24
Peck, Jim, 226
Pedrosa, Alvaro, 52n
Pérez Firmat, Gustavo, 35
Pipes, Daniel, 185, 185n. 17
Piterburg, Gabriel, 117n. 10
place: in anthropology, 37, 39–40; and
    cultural studies, 38–39; and culture,
    39–40; definition, 37; in disciplines,
    academic, 38; and economy, 38; and
    globalization, 39; and information
    technology, 38n; local, 39; and nature,
    38; and networks, 38n
placelessness, 37
Polanyi, Karl, 165
Political Economy of the Middle East, A
    (Richards and Waterbury), 164
political science, 7–8
popular cultural practices, 5
Postcolonial Aura, The (Dirlik), 194n
postcolonial studies, 6, 8–9, 134
postdevelopment, 46
postmodernism, 8, 134
poststructuralism, 134
power and knowledge, 228–29
Prewitt, Kenneth, 61n. 2, 137
Princeton University, 150, 152, 152n. 3
Process of Black Communities (PCN), 37,
    53
Program in Near Eastern Studies, 150
Proyecto Andino de Tecnología
    Campesina (PRATEC), 44n. 6

al-Quddus, 'Abd, 106n

Radical History Review, 139n
Radio and Television Magazine, 119
Rafael, Vicente, 76, 149n
Rahnema, Majid, 72n
Rapley, John, 61n. 3
al-Rashidi, Faruq, 101
rational choice, 7, 8, 14
Rawls, John, 32n. 3
Reagan, Ronald, 223
Redfield, Jamie, 180
Regents of University of California v.
    Bakke, 31n. 1
Regional Modernities: The Cultural
    Politics of Development in India, 71n
Resnick, Stephen, 47n
Richards, Alan, 164
Richards, Paul, 45
Rise of the Network Society, The (Castells),
    38n
Rivera, Alberto, 46
Robinson, Pearl, 138
Rockefeller, John D., 149
Rodriguez, Richard, 34, 35
Roe, Emery M., 62
Rorty, Richard, 35n
Rosenau, James, 61n. 2
Rosenthal, Franz, 154n
Rosero, Carlos, 37, 52n, 53n
Royal Institute of International Affairs,
    151–52
Rutgers Center for Historical Analysis,
    139n

Sachs, Wolfgang, 61, 67–68
Sa'dani, Salah, 105
Said, Edward W., 134, 149, 182, 229;
    Observing Islam, 185; Orientalism,
    177n. 8, 179, 185, 194,
    Saro-Wiwa, Ken, 69
Sassen, Saskia, 102

sati, 95

Saudi Arabia, 173

Schwarz, Roberto, 34

Scott, James, 62n, 62–63, 79

Seldon, Mark, 226

Self-Employed Women's Association, 93

September 11, 2001, 14

Shafiq, Viola, 104n

Shakry, Omnia, 101

Shalala, Donna, 99

Sharif, Nawaz, 217–18

al-Sharif, Nur, 106, 106n, 110

Shiv Sena, 95

Shramik Sangathana, 93

Shroud of Silence, A (video), 90

Sikkink, Kathryn, 94

Simon, Paul, 65

Singer, Milton, 180

Singerman, Diane, 115

Sivaramakrishnan, K., 64n. 7, 71n

Skursi, Julie, 115n

Slave Soldiers and Islam: The Genesis of a Military System (Pipes), 185n. 17

Smith, Elizabeth, 101

soap operas: 17, 101–2; class, 109–15; and cultural identity, 107

Social Science Research Council (SSRC), 2, 77n. 33, 152n. 4 222; and area studies, 137, 138–39; and CIA, 4; and deterritorialization, 160; funding support, 5; globalization studies, 6; and Middle East studies, 152

social science theory, 6, 14, 61

Sommer, Doris, 15

Souls of Black Folk (Du Bois), 27, 29

South Asia, 2, 4

South Asian studies, 20

Southeast Asia, 2; and area studies, 226; and Defense Information Act of 1958, 4; funding support, 4–5

Soviet-Afghan War, 223–24

Soviet Union, 2; and area studies, 5; collapse of, 222; and Defense Information Act of 1958, 4

Sreberny-Mohammadi, Annabelle, 102n. 2

Stanford University, 137

state formation, 5

Strathern, Marilyn, 42

subaltern resistance, 5

Suharto, 79, 221

Sultan, Huda, 122

Tabishart, Mohammad, 101

Tagore, Rabindranath, 206

Taliban, 89, 90, 92

Tarrow, Sidney, 6

Tawila, Sahar, 101

terrorism, 225

Tomlinson, John, 102n. 2

tradition, 195, 228

Trajectories: Inter-Asian Cultural Studies, 210

transculturation, 33

transnationalization: and identity, 102, 199; and women's movements, 224–25

UBUNTU 2000, 146

'Ukasha, Usama Anwar, 101, 123, 126–27; *Arabesque,* 105, 116–17, 118, 119, 122; *Hilmiyya Nights,* 127; *Zizinya,* 120–21, 124, 125, 127

Uniform Civil Code, 95

United Nations, 85, 88; and area studies, 133; Beijing Plus Five, 98

United Nations Declaration on the Elimination of Violence Against Women, 89

United Nations Educational, Scientific, and Cultural Organization (UNESCO), 139n

United States: and area studies scholarship, 2, 3; Defense Information Act of 1958, 3–4; influence of, 7; and Islam, 223; in Southeast Asia, 4; and Soviet-Afghan War, 223–24

universalism, 31, 31n. 2

University of California at Los Angeles, 101

University of Chicago, 149, 179, 180, 181, 227

University of Ghana at Legon, 143

University of Karlsruhe, 101

Unocal, 89

U.S. Agency of International Development (USAID), 62, 219, 222

U.S. PL480 collections, 136

U.S. Women Connect (USWC), 98–99

Valdés, Mario, 33n. 6

Vasconcelo, José, 33

Vatican, 87

Vienna Human Rights Declaration and Program of Action, 89

Vietnam, 4, 200, 203, 226–27

Virilio, Paul, 50

Vitalis, Robert, 166

von Grunebaum, Gustav, 154n

Wahdan, Dalia Essam, 101

Wallerstein, Immanuel, 3, 73n. 23, 180

Ward, George, 226

Washington Institute for Near East Policy, 186n

Waterbury, John, 164

Watts, Michael, 66n, 68–69

Weber, Max, 11, 132, 133

Wee, C. J. W-L., 201n

Westernization, 193–94

Wigen, Karen E., 172n. 2

Winegar, Jessica, 101

Wittgenstein, Ludwig, 28

Wolff, Robert Paul, 31n. 1

Women Living Under Muslim Law (WLUML), 99–100

Women's Action Forum in Pakistan (WAFP), 224–25

Women's Alliance for Peace and Human Rights, 89

women's movements: in India, 92–96; transnationalism of, 83–85

women's rights, 89

women's studies, 2; and area studies, 82–83; and feminism, 82

Woods, John, 185

World Bank, 62, 70, 74, 137, 219, 221

World History Association, 139

World Trade Organization (WTO), 74

World Wide Web, 132

Wretched of the Earth, The (Fanon), 221

Zia ul-Haq, Mohammed, 223, 224

Zizinya, 120, 124, 125, 127

Zoniz, Marvin, 227